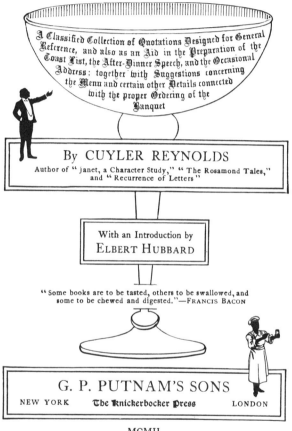

The Banquet Book

A Classified Collection of Quotations Designed for General Reference, and also as an Aid in the Preparation of the Toast List, the After-Dinner Speech, and the Occasional Address; together with Suggestions concerning the Menu and certain other Details connected with the proper Ordering of the Banquet

By CUYLER REYNOLDS

Author of "Janet, a Character Study," "The Rosamond Tales," and "Recurrence of Letters"

With an Introduction by
ELBERT HUBBARD

"Some books are to be tasted, others to be swallowed, and some to be chewed and digested."—FRANCIS BACON

G. P. PUTNAM'S SONS

NEW YORK   The Knickerbocker Press   LONDON

MCMII

Republished by Omnigraphics • Penobscot Building • Detroit • 1999

A man will turn over half a library
to make one book.—SAMUEL JOHNSON.

Library of Congress Cataloging-in-Publication Data

Reynolds, Cuyler, 1866–1934.
    The banquet book : a classified collection of quotations designed
for general reference, and also as a aid in the preparation of the
toast list, the after-dinner speech, and the occasional address;
together with suggestions concerning the menu and certain other
details connected with the proper ordering of the banquet / by
Cuyler Reynolds ; with an introduction by Elbert Hubbard.
        p.   cm.
    Reprint. Originally published: New York : G.P. Putnam's Sons,
1902.
    ISBN 0-7808-0301-9 (lib. bdg. : alk. paper)
    I. Title.
IN PROCESS
851'.914—dc21   99-28920
                                                         CIP

TO

HON. ANDREW HAMILTON

A friend whose qualities of mind combine
　Those graces which enchantment lend :
The power to think, to wish, to act,—in fine
　In him all generous virtues blend.

INTRODUCTION

IT has been said that "a good wine needs no bush," and it may be as truly asserted that a good book requires no introduction. But it is recorded that the Bard of Avon did make fair Rosalind say, after her scene with fond friends in the Forest of Arden, "Yet to good wine they do use good bushes," which would seem that an introduction be proper if it be but good. To pen the foreword places one in the position of the bashful Rosalind, for "what a case am I in then," being neither a good introducer, "nor cannot insinuate with you in the behalf of" a good book.

Undoubtedly, in the days of Shakespeare, as now, it was known widely that a taste of certain liquors concocted with perspicuity prepares one's inner man the better for things to come than had the cork been allowed to remain cobwebbed to the bottle ; so for an equally long time it has been thought mete that a good book, like the good dinner, receive encouragement afore it.

Some persons compose their meal of a staple course, one that is substantial for the body's need, yet at times, dining with their friends, enjoy with relish the dinner whose chief ambition is of numerous courses. They remind one of those who for a season find staple reading in a novel ; but turn at times to those works wherein appear the mixture of many talents, and in the change find relish and enjoyment.

Everyone knows that some dinners but prove to be time elaborately thrown away, but this cannot be said of that book which permits a feast in which many authors furnish parts. The feasting which the mind partakes of in this case is such as to strengthen one for better personal endeavour. It takes him away from self so completely, by reason of the brilliancy, that the mind assumes a status in a degree like that of the one who wrote ; as one lady at a feast will imbibe ideas to serve her in good stead when she next time becomes the hostess.

Note the meal of the busy man of professional trade in the great cities, and it would seem that he hopes for the day when he may wash down his pellet of substantial meal, to be the sooner again about his business. To such a man the restaurant that can furnish him with a meal for endurance in the smallest form is the one that he likes, while the writer or compiler does the most who puts before his reader the most wisdom and demands of him the least time.

As one sagaciously spurns poorly or half-cooked food, so we should lay aside those writings of weak minds whose ill-conceived thoughts have found too hasty expression. If we demand that the food which we place within our bodies be wholesome, how much more so should we desire that what we allow to enter the mind be whole-souled. Even the babe makes choice of food that pleases ; so should the mind of the youth make early discernment of that sort of literature that it considers better than some other, only let it be a fancy born of sound reason.

Who has not found it so, that the cookie abstracted from the pantry by the youth is far sweeter than any bought by affluence, and a compiler must stand in the same position towards his production, for Alexander Pope recognised and remarked : " O'er his books his eyes began to roll in pleasing memory of all he stole."

He who cannot relish the best sayings of the greatest writers, is like the dyspeptic at the banquet-hall : he has all that is good set before him, yet is unable to appreciate. A clever compiler is a good chef : he not only knows what to select, but in what order to present it.

The literary reader should greet with as much delight a book of cleverly chosen quotations as the tired and hungry man feels, who finds a good hostelry, whose menu is of such length and merit that he knows he may there find what he desires.

If we are capable of appreciating a well-served dinner, how much more should a person of thought appreciate a book of wise sayings when one thinks how much greater was the effort and how much more of thought was given to their preparation than to the most elaborate menu of choicest viands. Here are the things we would all have said, if we 'd had the mind.

Next in importance to the man who first voices a great thought is the man who quotes it. Knowledge consists in having a clerk who can find the thing—and here it is for you, all pigeonholed and labelled. Give thanks, and partake.

Elbert Hubbard

Roycroft

CONTENTS

ix

x   **Contents**

Actor—Singer—Musician

The play 's the thing.—*Hamlet.*

The Banquet Book

Actor—Singer—Musician

Play a set.

Henry V. i, 2.

Play me no plays.

FOOTE, The Knight. ii.

We burn daylight.

Merry Wives of Windsor. ii, 1.

Play out the play.

Henry IV. Pt. I, ii, 4.

As good as a play.

MACAULAY, Charles II.

I cannot play alone.

HEMANS, Child's First Grief.

Be the players ready?

Hamlet. iii, 2.

He makes sweet music.

Two Gentlemen of Verona. ii, 7.

Music's golden tongue.

KEATS, Eve of St. Agnes. St. 3.

The play 's the thing.

Hamlet. ii, 2.

Music tells no truths.

BAILEY, Festus. Sc., a village street.

There are the players.

Hamlet.   ii, 2.

Sea of upturned faces.

SCOTT, *Rob Roy.*   Ch. 20.

Wouldst not play false.

Macbeth.   i, 5.

Now then for soft music.

SHERIDAN, *The Critic.*   ii, 2.

Go on, obliging creatures.

POPE, *Prologue to Satires.*

Play, and make good cheer.

TUSSER, *Farmer's Daily Diet.*

Your play needs no excuse.

Midsummer Night's Dream.   v, 1.

What a voice was here now!

BEAUMONT AND FLETCHER, *Beggar's Bush.*

A hit, a very palpable hit.

Hamlet.   v, 2, l. 294.

Lap me in soft Lydian airs.

MILTON, *L'Allegro.* l. 131.

But the whelp has no voice.

COLLEY CIBBER, *The Refusal.*   iv.

Bid the players make haste.

Hamlet.   iii, 2.

In hollow murmurs died away.

COLLINS, *The Passions.*   l. 68.

I do but sing because I must.

TENNYSON, *In Memoriam.*   Pt. XXI.

Music, the mosaic of the air.

MARVELL, *Music's Empire.*   l. 17.

But who can count the stars?

JAMES THOMSON, *Seasons.*   Winter, l. 528.

I sit, and play with similes.

WORDSWORTH, To the Daisy.

He sings psalms to hornpipes.

Winter's Tale. iv, 3, 1. 46.

Our whole life is like a play.

BEN JONSON, Discoveries de Vita Humana.

Thy voice is a celestial melody.

LONGFELLOW, Masque of Pandora. Pt. V.

The lively Shadow-World of Song.

SCHILLER, The Artists.

" Come, and I will play with thee ! "

DE VERE, Song—When I Was Young.

Players that offer service.

Taming of the Shrew. Induction.

I thank you for your voices.

Coriolanus. ii, 3.

What a falling off was there !

Hamlet. i, 5.

Musical as is Apollo's lute.

MILTON, Comus. 1. 474.

I will play a part no longer.

WHITMAN, Children of Adam.

He the sweetest of all singers.

LONGFELLOW, Hiawatha. Pt. VI, 1. 21.

It was love who invented music.

VIREY.

Shall we have a play extempore ?

King Henry IV. Pt. I, ii, 4, 1. 305.

Scared out of his seven senses.

SCOTT, Rob Roy. Ch. 34.

For his acts so much applauded.

King Henry VI. Pt. I, ii, 2.

A character dead at every word.
SHERIDAN, *School for Scandal.* ii, 2.

The still, sad music of humanity.
WORDSWORTH, *Poems of Imagination.* xxvi.

I know a trick worth two of that.
King Henry IV. Pt. I, ii, 1.

Listen to that song, and learn it !
LONGFELLOW, *Tales of Wayside Inn.*
Musician's Tale, Pt. V.

Good for a seat and a nearer view.
STEDMAN, *Diamond Wedding.*

A beggarly account of empty boxes.
Romeo and Juliet. v, 1, l. 45.

Such a choice collection of songs.
FOOTE, *The Cozeners.*

Is this the play of fond illusion ?
HORACE, *Odes.* iii, 4.

Music 's the medicine of the mind.
JOHN LOGAN (attributed to), *Danish Ode.*

Almost the whole world are players.
PETRONIUS ARBITER, *Satyricon.*

A thousand melodies unheard before.
ROGERS, *Human Life.*

For discords make the sweetest airs.
BUTLER, *Hudibras.* Pt. III, canto i, l. 919.

Merely to come in, sir, they go out !
POPE, *Epilogue to Satires.* ii.

Not a better pipe at the play-house.
FOOTE, *The Cozeners.*

Surely the stars are images of love.
BAILEY, *Festus.* Garden scene.

A fellow of no mark, or livelihood.
King Henry IV. Pt. I, iii, 2.

He coude songes make, and wel endite.
> CHAUCER, *Canterbury Tales.* **Pro.**

All that we ask is but a patient ear.
> POPE, *Satires.* iii.

It will discourse most eloquent music.
> *Hamlet.* iii, 2, l. 374.

Come, give us a taste of your quality.
> *Hamlet.* ii, 2.

Good at a fight, but better at a play.
> *On a cast of Sheridan's hand.*

Songs consecrate to truth and liberty.
> SHELLEY, *To Wordsworth.* l. 12.

A cursed critic as e'er damned a play.
> DRYDEN, *Epilogue to Secret Love.*

In notes by distance made more sweet.
> COLLINS, *The Passions.* l. 60.

If music be the food of love, play on.
> *Twelfth Night.* i, 1.

Song forbids victorious deeds to die.
> SCHILLER, *The Artists.*

Play on, play on ; I am with you there.
> NATH'L P. WILLIS, *Saturday Afternoon.*

Women and music should never be dated.
> GOLDSMITH, *She Stoops to Conquer.* iii, 1.

Now airs antique and medieval fill me !
> WHITMAN, *Music of the Storm.*

And hears thy stormy music in the drum !
> CAMPBELL, *Pleasures of Hope.* Pt. I.

I can call spirits from the vasty deep.
> *King Henry IV.* Pt. I, iii, 5.

Sing,—though I shall never hear thee.
> CHARLES WOLFE, *Song.*

By magic numbers and persuasive sound.
CONGREVE, *The Mournful Bride.*

We did keep time, sir, in our catches.
Twelfth Night. ii, 3.

And heaven had wanted one immortal song.
DRYDEN, *Absalom and Achitophel.* Pt. I, 1. 197.

The eagle suffers little birds to sing.
Titus Andronicus. iv, 4.

Thou pendulum betwixt a smile and tear.
BYRON, *Childe Harold.* Canto iv, st. 109.

Gayly the troubadour touched his guitar.
BAYLY, *Welcome Me Home.*

Music her soft, assuasive voice applies.
POPE, *S. Cecilia's Day.*

And short retirement urges sweet return.
MILTON, *Paradise Lost.* Bk. IX, 1. 249.

There is in souls a sympathy with sounds.
COWPER, *The Task.* Bk. VI, 1, 1.

The stars above us govern our conditions.
King Lear. iv, 3, 1. 35.

The sound is honey, but the sense is gall.
UNKNOWN, *Soliman and Perseda.* Act IV.

Condemn the fault, and not the actor of it.
Measure for Measure. ii, 2, 1. 37.

Deep meaning often lies in childish plays.
SCHILLER, *Theklo.* St. 6.

Disburthen his full soul of all its music!
COLERIDGE, *The Nightingale.* 1. 43.

He play'd an ancient ditty long since mute.
KEATS, *Eve of St. Agnes.* St. 33.

The great theatre for virtue is conscience.
CICERO.

The tenor's voice is spoilt by affectation.
> BYRON, *Don Juan*. Canto iv, st. 87.

Music is the universal language of mankind.
> LONGFELLOW, *Outre-Mer*. *Ancient Spanish Ballads*.

Such sweet compulsion doth in music lie.
> MILTON, *Arcades*. 1. 68.

That strain again! It had a dying fall.
> *Twelfth Night*. i, 1.

Filled the air with barbarous dissonance.
> MILTON, *Comus*. 1. 550.

I am never merry when I hear sweet music.
> *Merchant of Venice*. v, 1.

And waste their music on the savage race.
> YOUNG, *Love of Fame*. Satire V, 1. 228.

My lungs began to crow like chanticleer.
> *As You Like It*. ii, 7.

These troublesome disguises which we wear.
> MILTON, *Paradise Lost*. Bk. IV, 1. 739.

Superfluous lags the veteran on the stage.
> SAMUEL JOHNSON, *Vanity of Human Wishes*.

He mouths a sentence, as curs mouth a bone.
> CHURCHILL, *The Rosciad*.

Good savage gentlemen, your own kind spare.
> DRYDEN, *Epilogue to Secret Love*.

The vile squeaking of the wry-necked fife.
> *Merchant of Venice*. ii, 5.

Bid me discourse, I will enchant thine ear.
> *Venus and Adonis*. 1. 145.

May my melody not be wanting to the season.
> THOREAU, *Early Spring*.

Soft is the music that would charm forever.
> WORDSWORTH, *Sonnets*.

So may the fates preserve the ear you lend.
ALEXANDER POPE, *Dunciad*.   iii.

I awoke one morning and found myself famous.
BYRON, From his *Life* by Moore.

Bright gem instinct with music, vocal spark.
WORDSWORTH, *A Morning Exercise*.

As stars to thee appear seen in the galaxy.
MILTON, *Paradise Lost*. Bk. VII, l. 575.

Two stars keep not their motion in one sphere.
King Henry IV.   Pt. I, v, 4.

Ye little stars! hide your diminished rays.
POPE, *Moral Essays*. Ep. III, l. 282.

Fairest of stars, last in the train of night.
MILTON, *Paradise Lost*. Bk. V, l. 165.

The pealing anthem swells the note of praise.
GRAY, *Elegy in a Country Churchyard*. St. 10.

How sweetly sounds the voice of a good woman!
MIDDLETON, *The Old Law*.   iv, 2.

Life's a long tragedy ; this globe the stage.
WATTS, *Epistle to Mitis*. Pt. I, l. 1.

Why should the devil have all the good tunes?
ROWLAND HILL, *Sermons*.

Every night he comes with music of all sorts.
All's Well that Ends Well.   iii, 7, l. 39.

Music is well said to be the speech of angels.
CARLYLE, *Essays*.   The Opera.

Soft words, with nothing in them, make a song.
WALLER, *To Mr. Creech*. l. 10.

But would you sing, and rival Orpheus' strain.
POPE, *Summer*. l. 81.

O! she will sing the savageness out of a bear.
Othello.   iv, l. 200.

So dischord ofte in musick makes the sweeter lay.
SPENSER, *Faerie Queene.* Bk. III, canto ii, st. 15.

Odds life! must one swear to the truth of a song?
MATTHEW PRIOR. *A Better Answer.*

Above the pitch, out of tune, and off the hinges.
RABELAIS, *Works.* Bk. IV, ch. 19.

Music revives the recollections it would appease.
DE STAEL, *Corinne.* Bk. IX, ch. 2.

As sweet and musical as bright Apollo's lute.
Love's Labour's Lost. iv. 3.

Act well your part, there all the honour lies.
POPE, *Essay on Man.* Ep. IV, l. 185.

Breasts the keen air, and carols as he goes.
GOLDSMITH, *The Traveller.* l. 185.

She feels no biting pang the while she sings.
GIFFORD, *Contemplation.*

Eft-soones they heard a most melodious sound.
SPENSER, *Faerie Queene.* Bk. II., canto xii, st. 70.

What harmony is this? My good friends, hark.
The Tempest. iii, 3.

All who, like him, have writ ill plays before.
DRYDEN, *Prologue to Rival Ladies.*

Now the plays are begun I shall have no peace.
SHERIDAN, *The Critic.* i.

And witch sweet ladies with my words and looks.
King Henry VI. Pt. III, iii, 2.

Then go we near her, that her ear lose nothing.
Much Ado about Nothing. iii, 1.

Friends, Romans, countrymen, lend me your ears.
Julius Cæsar. iii, 2.

My voice is ragged; I know I cannot please you.
As You Like It. ii, 5.

Straining harsh discords and unpleasant sharps.
Romeo and Juliet.   iii. 5.

Chromatic tortures soon shall drive them hence.
POPE, *The Dunciad.*   iv.

But, gentle heavens, cut short all intermission.
Macbeth.   iv, 3.

For we that live to please must please to live.
SAMUEL JOHNSON.
Opening Drury Lane Theatre.   1747.

Whilst scenes, machines, and empty operas reign.
DRYDEN, *Opening the New House.*   1674.

Whilst I sit meditating on that celestial harmony.
King Henry VIII.   iv, 2.

In what key shall a man take you to go in the song?
Much Ado About Nothing.   i, 1.

While awaiting the tragedy, let us enjoy the farce.
VOLTAIRE.

In earnest, does this puppy really pretend to sing?
COLLEY CIBBER, *The Refusal.*   iv.

Who hears music, feels his solitude peopled at once.
BROWNING, *Balaustion's Adventure.*

True ; my power with the managers is pretty notorious.
SHERIDAN, *The Critic.*   i.

The silent organ loudest chants the master's requiem,
EMERSON, *Dirge.*

May bring his plain-song and have an hour of hearing.
King Henry VIII.   i, 3.

He does it with a better grace, but I do it more natural.
Twelfth Night.   ii, 3.

I do not desire you to please me, I do desire you to sing.
As You Like It.   ii, 5.

I have a little studied physic ; but now, I 'm all for music.
BEN JONSON, *Volpone.*   iii, 2.

Come, sit down, every mother's son, and rehearse your parts.
Midsummer Night's Dream. iii, 1, 1. 74.

Music that brings sweet sleep down from the blissful skies.
TENNYSON, *Lotos Eaters.* Choric Song. St. 1.

God has given you one face, and you make yourselves another.
Hamlet. iii, 1.

You are not like Cerberus, three gentlemen at once, are you?
SHERIDAN, *The Rivals.* iv, 2.

Resolv'd to sing no songs to-day but those of many attachments.
WHITMAN, *Calamus.*

Many an irksome noise, go a long way off, is heard as music.
THOREAU, *Walden.*

Much as he pretends to wit, Sir, he can make a noise at least.
COLLEY CIBBER, *The Refusal.*

Where they do agree on the stage, their unanimity is wonderful!
SHERIDAN, *The Critic.* ii, 2.

Save thee, friend, and thy music ; dost thou live by thy tabour?
Twelfth Night. iii, 1.

To amuse the public : what a sad vocation for a man who thinks!
From the French.

They will not let my play run, and yet they steal my thunder.
JOHN DENNIS, In *Biog. Britannica.*

The musician who always plays on the same string is laughed at.
HORACE.

The players are my pictures, and their scenes my territories.

> STEELE, *The Tatler*.

Let's hear. It is a madrigal ; I affect that kind of poem much.

> BEN JONSON, *Staple of News.* iv, 1.

For my voice, I have lost it with halloing and singing of anthems.

> *King Henry IV.* Pt. II, i, 2.

Untwisting all the chains that tie the hidden soul of harmony.

> MILTON, *L'Allegro.* 1. 143.

That music in itself, whose sounds are song, the poetry of speech.

> BYRON, *Childe Harold.* Canto iv, st. 58.

Speak a huffing part ; I warrant you the gentleman will accept of it.

> BEAUMONT AND FLETCHER,
> *Kt. of Burning Pestle.* Pro.

When she had passed, it seemed like the ceasing of exquisite music.

> LONGFELLOW, *Evangeline.* Pt. I, 1.

Men's muscles move better when their souls are making merry music.

> ELIOT, *Adam Bede.* Bk. II, ch. 19.

Her voice was ever soft, gentle and low, an excellent thing in woman.

> *King Lear.* v, 3, l. 272

I am advised to give her music o' mornings ; they say it will penetrate.

> *Cymbeline.* ii, 3, l. 12.

An excellent musician, and her hair shall be of what colour it please God.

> *Much Ado About Nothing.* ii, 3.

I had rather than forty shillings I had my Book of Songs
and Sonnets here.

Merry Wives of Windsor. i, 1.

Who shall silence all the airs and madrigals that whisper
softness in chambers.

MILTON, *Areopagitica.*

Give me permission to regale the Company with a small
Crash of Instrumental.

COLLEY CIBBER, *The Refusal.* iv.

As Plato holds your music and so does wise Pythagoras,
I take it is your true rapture.

BEN JONSON, *Volpone.*

And since they will not admit of my Playes, they shall
know what a Satyrist I am.

BUCKINGHAM, *The Rehearsal.*

So she poured out the liquid music of her voice to quench
the thirst of his spirit.

HAWTHORNE, *Mosses from an Old Manse.*

Call me what instrument you will, though you can fret
me, yet you cannot play upon me.

Hamlet. iii, 2, 1. 378.

But that which did please me beyond anything in the
whole world was the wind-musick.

PEPYS, *Diary.* February 27, 1668.

Shall we rouse the night-owl in a catch that will draw
three souls out of one weaver?

Twelfth Night. ii, 3.

Sentimentally I am disposed to harmony. But organi-
cally I am incapable of a tune.

LAMB, *Chapter on Ears.*

There is no new music in Nature, neither melody or
harmony. Music is the creation of man.

HAWEIS, *Music and Morals.* Bk. I, 1. 1.

If it be true that good wine needs no bush, 't is true that
a good play needs no epilogue.
As You Like It.   Epilogue, 1. 3.

This wide and universal theatre presents more woful
pageants than the scene wherein we play.
As You Like It.   ii, 7, 1. 137.

A careless song, with a little nonsense in it now and then,
does not mis-become a monarch.
WALPOLE, 1770.

The trained ear has music in it, even when the deft
fingers forget in part to touch the keys.
DOANE, *St. Agnes Addresses*, 1885.

Great men do not play stage tricks with the doctrines of
life and death : only little men do that.
RUSKIN, *Sesame and Lilies.*   Lecture I, 20.

The world was very guilty of such a ballad some three
ages since ; but I think now 't is not to be found.
Love's Labour's Lost.   i, 2.

A look, a gesture, an attitude, a tone of voice, all bear
their parts in the great work of pleasing.
Chesterfield's Letters.   May 15, 1749.

They do no more adhere and keep place together than
the Hundreth Psalm to the tune Greensleeves.
Merry Wives of Windsor.   ii, 1.

Who that has heard a strain of music feared then lest
he should speak extravagantly any more for ever ?
THOREAU, *Walden.*

There are three things that I have always loved and have
never understood : Painting, Music, and Women,
FONTENELLE.

'T is the common disease of all your musicians, that they
know no mean, to be entreated either to begin or end.
BEN JONSON, *The Poetaster.*   ii, 1.

They held opinion that the sweetness of music did re-
create the spirits, and the heart did undertake to love.

  SIR ANTONIE OF GUEVARA, *Familiar Epistles.*

These two hated with a hate
Found only on the stage.

  BYRON, *Don Juan.* Canto iv, st. 93.

Music, when soft voices die,
Vibrates in the memory.

  SHELLEY, *Poems in 1821.*

His voice was propertied
As all the tunéd spheres.

  Antony and Cleopatra. v, 2, l. 28.

Nothing introduces you a
Heroine like soft music.

  SHERIDAN, *The Critic.* ii, 2.

At whose sight all the stars
Hide their diminish'd heads.

  MILTON, *Paradise Lost.* Bk. IV, l. 34.

In a sadly pleasing strain
Let the warbling lute complain.

  POPE, *Ode on St. Cecilia's Day.*

His very foot has music in 't
As he comes up the stairs.

  MICKLE, *Mariner's Wife.*

Though this may be play to you,
'T is death to us.

  ROGER L'ESTRANGE, *Fables.* No. 398.

Makes a swan-like end,
Fading in music.

  Merchant of Venice. iii, 2.

A little nonsense now and then
Is relished by the wisest men.

  ANON.

Many a time and oft
In the Rialto you have rated me.
Merchant of Venice. i, 3.

The music in my heart I bore,
Long after it was heard no more.
WORDSWORTH, *The Solitary Reaper.*

O Music! sphere-descended maid,
Friend of pleasure, wisdom's aid.
COLLINS, *The Passions.*

Do not put me to 't,
For I am nothing if not critical.
Othello. ii, 1.

You 'd scarce expect one of my age
To speak in public on the stage.
EVERETT, *School Declamation.*

You hear her? Or is this the play
Of fond illusion? Hark!
HORACE, *Odes.* iii.

Sometime let gorgeous Tragedy
In sceptred pall come sweeping by.
MILTON, *Il Penseroso.* 1. 94.

Sang in tones of deep emotion,
Songs of love and songs of longing.
LONGFELLOW, *Hiawatha.* Pt. XI, 1. 136.

Untwisting all the chains that tie
The hidden soul of harmony.
MILTON, *L'Allegro.* 1. 143.

In whose heart there is no song,
To him the miles are many and long.
ANON.

I 'll charm the air to give a sound,
While you perform your antic round.
Macbeth. iv, 1.

There still remains to mortify a wit
The many-headed monster of the pit.
POPE, Horace.   Ep. I. Bk. ii, 1. 304.

Cry out upon the stars for doing
Ill offices, to cross their wooing.
BUTLER, Hudibras.   Pt. III., canto i, 1. 17.

How light the touches are that kiss
The music from the chords of life !
COVENTRY PATMORE, By the Sea.

Sweetest the strain when in the song
The singer has been lost.
PHELPS, The Poet and the Poem.

By music minds an equal temper know,
Nor swell too high, nor sink too low.
POPE, Ode on St. Cecilia's Day.

Give me some music ; music, moody food
Of us that trade in love.
Antony and Cleopatra.   ii, 5, l. 1.

Hold ! would you admit
For judges all you see within the pit ?
DRYDEN, Prologue to Rival Ladies.

Her voice was like the voice the stars
Had when they sang together.
ROSSETTI, Blessed Damozel.   St. 10.

Music sweeps by me as a messenger
Carrying a message that is not for me.
ELIOT, Spanish Gypsy.   Bk. III.

Music that gentlier on the spirit lies
Than tir'd eyelids upon tir'd eyes.
TENNYSON, Lotos Eater.   Choric Song, st. 1.

The stars are golden fruit upon a tree
All out of reach.
ELIOT, Spanish Gypsy.   Bk. II.

And cheats the eyes
Of gallery critics by a thousand arts.
COWPER, *The Timepiece.*

Short swallow-flights of song, that dip
Their wings in tears, and skim away.
TENNYSON, *In Memoriam.* Pt. XLVIII., st. 4.

Soprano, basso, even the contra-alto
Wished him five fathom under the Rialto.
BYRON, *Beppo.* St. 32.

Is there no play,
To ease the anguish of a torturing hour?
Midsummer Night's Dream. v, 1, l. 36.

Is there a heart that music cannot melt?
Alas! how is that rugged heart forlorn!
BEATTIE, *The Minstrel.* Bk. I, st. 56.

A sound so fine, there 's nothing lives
'Twixt it and silence.
KNOWLES, *Virginius.*

He worked and sung from morn till night :
No lark more blithe than he.
ISAAC BICKERSTAFF, *Love in a Village.*

Light quirks of music, broken and uneven,
Make the soul dance upon a jig to Heav'n.
POPE, *Moral Essays.* Ep. iv, l. 143.

The world 's a theatre, the earth a stage,
Which God and Nature do with actors fill.
THOMAS HEYWOOD, *An Apology for Actors.*

Thespis, the first professor of our art,
At country wakes, sung ballads in a cart.
DRYDEN, *Pro. to University of Oxford.*

Take but degree away, untune that string,
And, hark, what discord follows!
Troilus and Cressida. i, 3, l. 109.

Music's golden tongue
Flattered to tears this aged man and poor.

KEATS, *Eve of St. Agnes.*

Two voices are there, one is of the sea,
One of the mountains : each a mighty Voice.

WORDSWORTH, *Thoughts of a Briton.*

Music, the greatest good that mortals know,
And all of heaven we have below.

ADDISON, *Song for St. Cecilia's Day.* iii.

Music's force can tame the furious beast ;
Can make the wolf or foaming boar restrain.

PRIOR, *Solomon.* Bk. II, 1. 67.

Sing again, with your dear voice revealing
A tone of some world far from ours.

SHELLEY, *To Jane.*

Plays such fantastic tricks before high heaven
As make the angels weep.

Measure for Measure. ii, 2.

Athlete—Collegian—Youth

Feats of sanguinary hue.—*William Cowper*, 1789.

Athlete—Collegian—Youth

Give him the cup.

Hamlet. v, 2.

Win and wear me.

Much Ado About Nothing. v, 1.

Keep then the path.

Troilus and Cressida. iii, 3.

Let the world slide.

Taming of the Shrew. Induct. Sc. 1.

Stiff bats and clubs.

Coriolanus. i, 1.

I am the best of them.

The Tempest, i, 2.

No gains without pains.

FRANKLIN.

You have hit the mark.

King Henry VIII. ii, 1.

There studious let me sit.

JAMES THOMSON, *Seasons.* Winter. 1, 431.

Read and earn our prize.

TENNYSON, *The Princess.* iii.

There's goodly catching.

Much Ado About Nothing. iii, 4.

Feats of sanguinary hue.

COWPER, 1789.

Shall we give the signal?

King John. ii, 1.

Right noble is thy merit.

King Richard II. v, 6.

Myself did win them both.
> *King Henry VI.* Pt. II, i, 1.

A hit, a very palpable hit.
> *Hamlet.* v, 2.

The champions are prepared.
> *King Richard II.* i, 3.

Economy is a great revenue.
> CICERO.

Out of debt, out of danger.
> ANON.

As chaste as unsunned snow.
> *Cymbeline.* ii, 5.

To be young was very heaven.
> WORDSWORTH, *The Prelude.* Bk. XI.

How green you are and fresh.
> *King John.* iii, 4.

Gashed with honourable scars.
> MONTGOMERY, *Battle of Alexandria.*

You must run to win the race.
> ANON.

Victory sits on our helms.
> *King Richard III.* v, 3.

'T is deeds must win the prize.
> *Taming of the Shrew.* ii, 1.

You won it, wore it, kept it.
> *King Henry IV.* Pt. II, iv, 5.

Even our sports are dangerous.
> BEN JONSON, *Underwoods.*

Show it a fair pair of heels.
> *King Henry IV.* Pt. I, ii, 4.

Some of us will smart for it.
> *Much Ado About Nothing.* v, 1.

Children are poor men's riches.
> ANON.

Youth should be a savings-bank.

MADAME SWETCHINE.

Work in youth is repose in age.

From the German.

Punched full of deadly holes.

King Richard III. v, 3.

I must a dozen mile to-night.

King Henry IV. Pt. II, iii, 2.

Oh, how the wheel becomes it.

Hamlet. iv, 5.

Come, wilt thou see me ride?

King Henry IV. Pt. I, ii, 3.

Could I but catch it for them.

Timon of Athens. v, 1.

Despise school and remain a fool.

From the German.

Tush! tush! fear boys with bugs.

Taming of the Shrew. i, 2.

Honour, high honour and renown!

As You Like It. v, 4.

He doeth well who doeth his best.

ANON.

Youth holds no society with grief.

Euripides. l. 73.

Youth comes but once in a lifetime.

LONGFELLOW, *Hyperion.* Bk. II, ch. x.

Ah, youth! forever dear, forever kind.

HOMER, *Iliad.* Bk. XIX, l. 303. Pope's Trans.

The child is father of the man.

WORDSWORTH, *My Heart Leaps Up.*

He prov'd best man i' the field.

Coriolanus. ii, 2, l. 99.

A college joke to cure the dumps.

SWIFT, *Cassinus and Peter.*

Bend the willow while it is young.
ANON.

There be some sports are painful.
The Tempest. iii, 1.

Childhood is the sleep of reason.
ROUSSEAU.

Take this reward ; make merry, man.
King Henry VI. Pt. II, i, 2.

Tall oaks from little acorns grow.
EVERETT, *School Declamation.*

I wear it for a memorable honour.
King Henry V. iv, 7.

There is no royal road to learning.
ANON.

The sounding jargon of the schools.
COWPER, *Truth.*

With the swiftest wing of speed !
All 's Well that Ends Well. iii, 2.

'T is now the summer of your youth.
MOORE, *The Gamester.*

Ignorance is the mother of Impudence.
ANON.

When you whirl round the circle.
SHELLEY, *Faust.* ii.

Young fellows will be young fellows.
ISAAC BICKERSTAFF, *Love in a Village.*

Here 's a parchment with the seal.
Julius Cæsar. iii, 2.

O well done ! I commend your pains.
Macbeth. iv, 1.

Brave conquerors,—for so you are.
Love's Labour 's Lost. i, 1.

That unlettered small-knowing soul.
Love's Labour 's Lost. i, 1.

Children and fools have merry lives.
                                        ANON.

He that runs fastest gets the ring.
                    Taming of the Shrew.   i, i.

To be swift is less than to be wise.
                    POPE, *Iliad.*   xxiii, l. 385.

He wears the rose of youth upon him.
                    Antony and Cleopatra.   iii, 2.

He that is full of himself is empty.
                                        ANON.

A mother's pride, a father's joy.
                            SCOTT, *Rokeby.*

There is not a moment without some duty.
                                        CICERO.

Grasp no more than thy hand will hold.
                                        ANON.

Has never heard the sanguinary yell?
                    COWPER, *The Task.*   iii, 335

Certain issue strokes must arbitrate.
                            Macbeth.   v, 4.

Towering in confidence of twenty-one.
    SAMUEL JOHNSON, *Letter to Bennet Langton.*
                            Jan., 1758.

In books, or work, or healthful play.
                    WATTS, *Divine Songs.*

He who begins many things finishes few.
                                        ANON.

Then may I set the world on wheels.
                    Two Gentlemen of Verona.   iii, i.

Diligence is the mother of Good Luck.
                                    FRANKLIN.

Being nimble footed he hath outrun us.
                    Two Gentlemen of Verona.   v, 3.

As the twig is bent, the twig will grow.

ANON.

Good fighting was before good writing.

MARSTON, *Mountebank's Masque.*

An idle brain is the devil's workshop.

From the German.

A good man dies when a boy goes wrong.

ANON.

A health to all that shot and miss'd.

Taming of the Shrew. v, 2.

Experience is the best of schoolmasters.

Old Proverb.

He sleeps by day more than the wild-cat.

Merchant of Venice. ii, 5, 1. 47.

When the brisk minor pants for twenty-one.

POPE, *Epistle I.* Bk. I, 1. 38.

To whom this wreath of victory I give.

Pericles. ii, 3.

An idle man is the devil's playfellow.

ANON.

In single opposition, hand to hand.

King Henry IV. Pt. I, i, 3.

The rich advantage of good exercise.

King John. iv, 2.

The wise for cure on exercise depend.

DRYDEN, *Epistle to John Dryden.*

Is not parchment made of sheepskins?

Hamlet. v, 1.

Lucky men are as rare as white crows.

JUVENAL.

Some are born to lift and some to lean.

ANON.

Self conceit is harder to cure than cancer.

ANON.

We are the Jasons, we have won the fleece.
Merchant of Venice.   iii, 2.

And both were young, and one was beautiful.
Byron, *The Dream.*   St. 2.

The force of his own merit makes his way.
King Henry VIII.   i, 1.

A lazy boy and a warm bed are hard to part.
Anon.

This monument of victory will I bear.
King Henry VI.   Pt. II, iv, 3.

A pound of pluck is worth a ton of luck.
Garfield.

Match to match I have encounter'd him.
King Henry VI.   Pt. II, v, 2.

A boy untaught will be taught by the devil.
Anon.

We will our youth lead on to higher fields.
King Henry IV.   Pt. II, iv, 4.

His studie was but litel on the Bible.
Chaucer, *Canterbury Tales.*

The hour is fixed ; the match is made.
Merry Wives of Windsor.   ii, 2.

Every man thinks his own geese swans.
Anon.

With surety stronger than Achilles' arm.
Troilus and Cressida.   i, 3.

Their flight must be swifter than fire.
Shelley, *Prometheus Unbound.*

A healthy size for a man is exercise.
Anon.

You imagine me too unhurtful an opposite.
Measure for Measure.   iii, 2.

Diamond me no diamonds ! prize me no prizes.
Tennyson, *Idylls of the King.*   Canto ii, st. 2.

A schoolboy's tale, the wonder of an hour !
BYRON, *Childe Harold.* Canto ii, st. 2.
As you make your bed so must you lie on it.
ANON.
It is a wise father that knows his own child.
Merchant of Venice. ii, 2.
Her hardy face repels the tanning wind.
THOMAS PARNELL, *Health.*
So doth the greater victory dim the less.
Merchant of Venice. v, 1.
The energetic man and his bed are soon parted.
ANON.
The wheel has come full circle, I am here.
King Lear. v, 3.
With just enough of learning to misquote.
BYRON, *English Bards*, 1. 66.
Ambition should be made of sterner stuff.
Julius Cæsar. iii, 2.
If youth only knew ; if old age only could.
ANON.
I 'll catch it ere it come to the ground.
Macbeth. iii, 5.
It is a conquest for a prince to boast of.
King Henry IV. Pt. I, i, 1.
He that can work is a born king of something.
CARLYLE.
Let me be umpire in this doubtful strife.
King Henry VI. Pt. I, iv, 1.
Advance in learning as you advance in life.
ANON.
If thou love learning thou shalt be learned.
ISOCRATES.
A young twig is easier to twist than an old one.
ANON.

The harder match'd, the greater victory.
King Henry VI. Pt. III, v, 1.

Of all studies, study your present condition.
ANON.

Experience is good if not bought too dear.
ANON.

Every man is the architect of his own fortune.
From the Latin.

Arrows fled not swifter toward their aim.
King Henry IV. Pt. II, i, 1.

Genius is a capacity for evading hard work.
ELBERT HUBBARD, *Philistine.*

Studious of ease, and fond of humble things.
AMBROSE PHILIPS, *Epistles from Holland.* 1. 21.

A little more sleep and a little more slumber.
ISAAC WATTS, Moral Songs, *The Sluggard.*

Diogenes struck the father when the son swore.
BURTON, *Anatomy of Melancholy.*
Pt. III, Sec. ii, Memb. 6.

The atrocious crime of being a young man.
SAMUEL JOHNSON, *On Pitt's Reply to Walpole.* 1741.

Live to learn and you will learn to live.
Portuguese Saying.

So wise so young, they say, do never live long.
King Richard III. iii, 1.

It is hard to put old heads on young shoulders.
ANON.

Better a good head than a hundred strong hands.
ANON.

The mother's heart is the child's schoolroom.
BEECHER.

He capers, he dances, he has eyes of youth.
Merry Wives of Windsor. iii, 2.

When the brisk minor pants for twenty-one.
POPE, *Epilogue to Satires.* Ep. I, Bk. i, l. 73.

Use your legs, take the start, run away.
Merchant of Venice. ii, 2.

The warnings of age are the weapons of youth.
ANON.

I never knew so young a body with so old a head.
Merchant of Venice. iv, 1.

The spirit of the time shall teach me speed.
King John. iv, 2.

An honest countenance is the best passport.
ANON.

The time to bend the willow bow is in the spring.
ANON.

Youth should watch joys and shoot them as they fly.
DRYDEN, *Aureng-Zebe.* iii, 1.

Draw, archers, draw your arrows to the head!
King Richard III. v, 3.

Don't sow your wild oats; they 're bad reaping.
ANON.

We find in life exactly what we put in it.
EMERSON.

What strong hand can hold his swift foot back?
Sonnets. lxv.

In life's morning march, when my bosom was young.
CAMPBELL, *Soldier's Dream.*

Rise from the ground like feather'd Mercury.
King Henry IV. Pt. I, iv, 1.

When we have matched our rackets to these balls.
King Henry V. i, 2.

Better sense in the head than cents in the pocket.
ANON.

Many wearing rapiers are afraid of goose-quills.
Hamlet. ii, 2

The secret of success is constantly to purpose.
DISRAELI, *Speech at Crystal Palace.* 1870.

Now are our brows bound with victorious wreaths.
King Richard III. i, 1.

In leading a child you may be commanding an army.
ANON.

Let the foils be brought, the gentleman willing.
Hamlet. v, 2.

Whatever is worth doing at all is worth doing well.
CHESTERFIELD, *Letters.* March 10, 1746.

The little mite thinks itself the whole cheese.
ANON.

Marry go before to field, he 'll be your follower.
Romeo and Juliet. iii, 1.

The man who is lazy never has time to do anything.
ANON.

It is as easy to be a lead horse as a wheel horse.
ANON.

In this world a man must be either anvil or hammer.
LONGFELLOW, *Hyperion.* Bk. IV, ch. vi.

To be proud of learning is the greatest ignorance.
ANON.

Allow me such exercises as may become a gentleman.
As You Like It. i, 1.

Arise with the lark, but avoid larks in the evening.
ANON.

'T is no sin for a man to labour in his vocation.
King Henry IV. Pt. I, i, 2.

Be the first to the field and the last to the couch.
Chinese Saying.

Home-keeping youth have ever homely wits.
Two Gentlemen of Verona. i, 1.

If you would go to the top, first go to the bottom.
ANON.

Youth on the prow, and Pleasure at the helm.
GRAY, *The Bard.*

Sloth maketh all things difficult ; industry, easy.
FRANKLIN.

Acquire not only learning but the habit of learning.
ANON.

Ah! happy years! once more who would not be a boy?
BYRON, *Childe Harold.* Canto ii, st. 23.

Children are certain cares, but uncertain comforts.
ANON.

Young saint, old devil ; young devil, old saint.
Old Saying.

Your strong hand shall help to give him strength.
King John. ii, 1.

The faith they have in tennis and tall stockings.
King Henry VIII. i, 3.

If you do not hear Reason she will rap your knuckles.
FRANKLIN.

Ignorance has no light, but error follows a false one.
COLTON, *Lacon.*

The more we study, we the more discover our ignorance.
SHELLEY, *Prodigioso of Calderon.* Sc. 1.

One's character will never rise higher than his aims.
ANON.

No man ever followed his genius till it misled him.
THOREAU, *Walden.*

The ass is not learned though he be loaded with books.
ANON.

Innocence, like an icicle, once melted is gone forever.
ANON.

Rashness is the error of youth, timid caution of age.
COLTON, *Lacon.*

If you would have things come your way, go after them.
ANON.

He hath in this action outdone his former deeds doubly.
Coriolanus. ii, 1.

If the devil catch a fellow idle, he will set him to work.
ANON.

If you would earn fame, let not the sun find you in bed.
ANON.

This scholar, rake, Christian, dupe, gamester, and poet.
GARRICK, *Jupiter and Mercury.*

Let the great book of the world be your principal study.
CHESTERFIELD.

Youth is a continual intoxication, the fever of reason.
ROCHEFOUCAULD.

Each thinks the world a moon and himself the man in it.
ANON.

To the most wholesome physic of thy health-giving air.
Love's Labour 's Lost. i, 1.

There is no other royal path which leads to geometry.
PROCLUS, *Commentary on Euclid.*

"What a dust have I raised," quoth the fly on the coach.
ANON.

He that falls in love with himself will have no rival.
FRANKLIN.

He that spares when he is young may spend when he is
old.
ANON.

Youth is a blunder ; Manhood a struggle ; Old Age a regret.
> DISRAELI, *Coningsby.*

You must scale the mountain if you would view the plain.
> Chinese Saying.

Company, villainous company, hath been the spoil of me.
> *King Henry IV.* Pt. I, iii, 3.

The childhood shews the man, as morning shews the day.
> MILTON, *Paradise Regained.* Bk. IV, l. 220.

If punishment reaches not the mind it hardens the offender.
> LOCKE.

The disappointment of manhood succeeds to the delusion of youth.
> DISRAELI, *Vivian Grey.*

He that looks too much at himself looks too little to himself.
> ANON.

One thorn of experience is worth a whole wilderness of warning.
> LOWELL, *Among my Books.*

He is not only dull himself, but the cause of dulness in others.
> BOSWELL, *Life of Johnson.*

He (Steele) was a rake among scholars, and a scholar among rakes.
> MACAULAY, *Review of Aikin's Life of Addison.*

He who is never guilty of follies is not so wise as he imagines.
> ROCHEFOUCAULD.

And when he caught it he let it go again ; and after it
again.

Coriolanus.   i, 3.

The man who does a little and does it well, does a great
deal.

ANON.

Who does not beat his own child will later beat his own
breast.

Persian Saying.

Every ass thinks itself worthy to stand with the king's
horses.

ANON.

Be not ashamed to own thy follies, but ashamed not to
end them.

HORACE.

When industry goes out of the door, poverty comes in at
the window.

Dutch Saying.

Youth is the period of happiness, but only Age is aware
of the fact.

ANON.

A youth without fire is followed by an old age without
experience.

COLTON, *Lacon.*

Experience keeps a dear school, but fools will learn in
no other, and scarce in that.

FRANKLIN, *Poor Richard's Almanac.*   1758.

Better to be driven out from among men than to be dis-
liked by the children.

R. H. DANA, *The Idle Man.*   Domestic Life

Lose an hour in the morning and you will be all day
hunting for it.

WHATELY.

Discipline is a medicine to be used sparingly lest its
virtue be lost.

ANON.

You are not, I hope, of a lazy, inactive turn, in either body or mind.

     CHESTERFIELD, *Letters*. Dec. 26, 1749.

When young we trust ourselves too much, and others too little when old.

     COLTON, *Lacon*.

It is useless to have youth without beauty, or beauty without youth.

     ROCHEFOUCAULD.

Know your own bone; gnaw at it, bury it, unearth it, and gnaw it still.

     THOREAU, *Letters*.

The scholar who cherishes the love of comfort, is not fit to be deemed a scholar.

     CONFUCIUS, *Analects*. Bk. XIV, ch. 3.

A man soon learns how little he knows when a child begins to ask questions.

     ANON.

They who would be young when they are old must be old when they are young.

     ANON.

The world's great men have not commonly been great scholars, nor its great scholars great men.

     HOLMES, *Autocrat of Breakfast-Table*. vi.

Our life is frittered away by detail. Simplicity, simplicity, simplicity!

     THOREAU, *Walden*.

O youth! thou often tearest thy wings against the thorns of voluptuousness!

     VICTOR HUGO.

Do not consume your energy resisting temptation, else you will go to hell sure.

     ELBERT HUBBARD, *Philistine*.

Want of attention, which is really want of thought, is
either folly or madness.

CHESTERFIELD, *Letters.* Spa, July 25, 1741.

All the goodness of a good egg can not make up for the
badness of a bad one.

CHAS. A. DANA, *Art of Newspaper Making.*

To blame a young man for being in love is like chiding
one for being ill.

DUCLOS.

He that has but one hog, makes him fat ; and but one
son, makes him a fool.

ANON.

Learning without thought is labour lost ; thought without
learning is perilous.

CONFUCIUS.

A man of little learning is like the frog who thinks its
well a great sea.

ANON.

Shun idleness : it is the rust that attaches itself to the
most brilliant metals.

VOLTAIRE.

Author—Writer—Poet

The monument of vanished minds.—SIR WM. DAVE-
NANT, *Gondibert.* Book II, canto v.

Author—Writer—Poet

He reads much.
                    Julius Cæsar. i, 2.

O, my rapt verse !
                    WHITMAN, *As I Sat Alone.*

Plot me no plots.
    BEAUMONT AND FLETCHER, *Knight of the
                        Burning Pestle.*

Few words suffice.
                    Taming of the Shrew. i, 2.

The poet's darling.
                    WORDSWORTH, *To the Daisy.*

I will be your poet.
                    WHITMAN, *Children of Adam.*

Laws die, Books never.
                    BULWER-LYTTON, *Richelieu.* i. 2.

You two are book-men.
                    Love's Labour 's Lost. iv, 2.

Medicine for the soul.
    Inscribed over Thebes library. DIODORUS SICULUS.

I can set down a story.
                    SHAKESPEARE, *Sonnets.* lxxxviii.

My unpremeditated verse.
                    MILTON, *Paradise Lost.* Bk. IX, l. 24.

Books which are no books.
                    LAMB, *Detached Thoughts on Books.*

The spectacles of books.
                    DRYDEN, *Essay on Dramatic Poetry.*

45

Neither rhyme nor reason.
As You Like It. iii, 2.

Beware of the Bibliomanie.
Chesterfield, *Letters.* March 19, 1750.

Married to immortal verse.
Milton, *L'Allegro.* 1. 132.

Syllables govern the world.
Selden, *Power.*

Beware of a man of one book.
Thomas Aquinas, *Reply.*

Here comes one with a paper.
Love's Labour 's Lost. iv, 3.

Look in thy heart and write.
Sidney, *Astrophel and Stella.*

This story will not go down.
Fielding, *Tumble Down Dick.*

Read a page and think an age.
Anon.

The pencil's mute omnipotence.
Moore, *Lalla Rookh.* ii.

Read these instructive leaves.
Pope, *Epistle to Jervas.*

I have immortal longings in me.
Antony and Cleopatra. v, 2.

Books are sepulchres of thought.
Longfellow, *Wind over Chimney.* St. 8.

The monument of vanished minds.
Wm. Davenant, *Gondibert.* Bk. II, canto v.

They had no poet, and they died.
Pope, *Odes.* Bk. IV.

A deal of skimble-skamble stuff.
King Henry IV. Pt. I, iii, 1.

No author ever spared a brother.
Gay, *Elephant and Bookseller.*

Was ever poet so trusted before?
> BOSWELL, *Life of Johnson.*

It was neither rhyme nor reason.
> MORE, *Letter to Author.*

Poetry is the music of the soul.
> VOLTAIRE.

Literature is an avenue to glory.
> DISRAELI, *Literary Character.*

Men of few words are the best men.
> *King Henry V.* iii, 2.

Poetic fields encompass me around.
> ADDISON, *Letter from Italy.*

We turn'd o'er many books together.
> *Merchant of Venice.* iv, 1, l. 156.

Some books are lies frae end to end.
> BURNS, *Death and Dr. Hornbook.*

This dull product of a scoffer's pen.
> WORDSWORTH, *The Excursion.* Bk. II.

The lover of letters loves power too.
> EMERSON, *Society and Solitude.* Clubs.

I 'll make thee glorious by my pen.
> MONTROSE, *My Dear and Only Love.*

The life of poets—love and tears.
> MME. DESBORDES-VALMORE.

The gentleman is not in your books.
> *Much Ado About Nothing.* i, 1.

A poem, round and perfect as a star.
> ALEXANDER SMITH, *A Life Drama.*

A poet is a world enclosed in a man.
> HUGO.

It is not poetry, but prose run mad.
> POPE, *Prologue to Satires.* l. 186.

My library was dukedom large enough.
The Tempest. i, 2.

He was one of a lean body and visage.
FULLER, *Life of Duke of Alva.*

And gentle Dulness ever loves a joke.
POPE, *The Dunciad.* Bk. II, 1. 34.

Let these describe the undescribable.
BYRON, *Childe Harold.* Canto iv, st. 53.

And muse on Nature with a poet's eye.
CAMPBELL, *Pleasures of Hope.*

I am a printer, and a printer of news.
BEN JONSON, *News from New World.*

Nor is thy fame on lesser ruins built.
JOHN DENHAM, *On Fletcher's Works.*

And mighty poets in their misery dead.
WORDSWORTH, *Resolution and Independence.*

I was not born under a rhyming planet.
Much Ado About Nothing. v, 2.

Go, litel boke ! go litel myn tregedie !
CHAUCER, *Troilus and Creseide.* Bk. V, 1. 1800.

Few are better than the books they read.
ANON.

For who can write so fast as men run mad.
YOUNG, *Love of Fame.* Satire I, 1. 286.

Ne'er was flattery lost on poet's ear.
SCOTT, *Lay of Last Minstrel.* Canto iv, st. 35.

For a good poet 's made as well as born.
BEN JONSON, *Memory of Shakespeare.*

I would the gods had made thee poetical.
As You Like It. iii, 3.

Choose an author as you choose a friend.
DILLON, *Essay on Translated Verse.* 1. 96.

Look, then, into thine heart and write !
> LONGFELLOW, *Voices of the Night*. Prelude, st. 19.

'T is the good reader that makes the good book.
> EMERSON, *Success*.

But now nothing is good that is natural.
> BEN JONSON, *Discoveries*.

At every interview their route the same.
> COWPER, *Conversation*.

Old-fashioned poetry, but choicely good.
> WALTON, *Complete Angler*.

He cares not what he puts into the press.
> *Merry Wives of Windsor*. ii, 1.

Who shall dispute what the reviewers say ?
> CHURCHILL, *Apology*.

The mob of gentlemen who wrote with ease.
> POPE, *Epistle I*. Bk. II, 1. 108.

I have ta'en a due and wary note upon 't.
> *Measure for Measure*. iv, 1.

Incessant scribbling is death to thought.
> CARLYLE.

Not to know me argues yourselves unknown.
> MILTON, *Paradise Lost*. Bk. IV, 1. 829.

O grant an honest fame, or grant me none !
> POPE, *Temple of Fame*. Last line.

There is no worse robber than a bad book.
> Italian Saying.

Things unattempted yet in prose or rhyme.
> MILTON, *Paradise Lost*. Bk. I, 1. 16.

And all that poets feign of bliss and joy.
> *King Henry VI*. Pt. III, i, 2.

I do not find that God has made you a poet.
> CHESTERFIELD, *Letters*. Nov. 24, 1749.

That hath a mint of phrases in his brain.
                    Love's Labour 's Lost. i, 1.

Fame is no plant that grows on mortal soil.
                    MILTON, *Lycidas.* 1. 78.

Who says in verse what others say in prose.
                    POPE, *Epistles I.* Bk. II, 1. 202.

Fine words. I wonder where you stole 'em.
                    SWIFT, *Verses occasioned by*
                                Whitshed's Coach.

The sound must seem an echo to the sense.
                    POPE, *Essay on Criticism.* Pt. II, 1. 162.

The lion is not so fierce as they paint him.
                    HERBERT, *Jacula Prudentum.*

We cultivate literature on a little oatmeal.
                    SYDNEY SMITH, *Lady Holland's Memoir.* 1. 23.

Life is the preface to the book of eternity.
                    LOISELEUR.

And torture one poor word ten thousand ways.
                    DRYDEN, *Mac Flecknoe.*

All my skill shall beg but honest laughter.
                    RANDOLPH, *Aristippus.*

A delicate thought is a flower of the mind.
                    ROLLIN.

The varying verse, the full resounding line.
                    POPE, *Odes of Horace.* Ep. I, Bk. ii, 1. 266.

Verse sweetens toil, however rude the sound.
                    GIFFORD, *Contemplation.*

Don't stir, gentlemen ; 't is but an author.
                    LE SAGE, *Gil Blas.* iii, 2.

'T is penning bows and making legs in rhyme.
                    GARRICK, *Prologue to Tragedy of Virginia.*

Deep vers'd in books, and shallow in himself.
                    MILTON, *Paradise Regained.* Bk. IV, 1. 327.

As though I lived to write, and wrote to live.
> ROGERS, *Italy.* A Character. 1. 16.

A small number of choice books are sufficient.
> VOLTAIRE, *Philosophical Dictionary.*

There is no Past, so long as Books shall live !
> BULWER-LYTTON, *Souls of Books.* St. 4, 1. 9.

Romances are not in books, they are in life.
> From the French.

One that excels the quirks of blazoning pens.
> *Othello.* ii, 1.

Critics are brushers of other men's clothes.
> ANON.

Thought and pictures please most well framed.
> ANON.

Who often reads, will sometimes wish to write.
> CRABBE, *Edward Shore.*

Mark now, how a plain tale shall put you down.
> *King Henry IV.* Pt. I, ii, 4.

There is no friend so faithful as a good book.
> ANON.

As good almost kill a man as kill a good book.
> MILTON, *Areopagitica.*

Celebrity sells dearly what we think she gives.
> E. SOUVESTRE.

If you have writ your annals true, 't is there.
> *Coriolanus.* v, 6.

Authors, like coins, grow dear as they grow old.
> POPE, *Satires.* Ep. I, Bk. ii, 1. 35.

Some Books are onely cursorily to be tasted of.
> FULLER, *Holy and Profane State.* Of Books.

Truth is always strange,—stranger than fiction.
> BYRON, *Don Juan.* Canto xiv, st. 101.

Which art our writers used to obscure their art.
BEN JONSON, *The Alchemist.* ii.

The soul of the poet is the mirror of the world.
ANON.

You 're certain to be pleased where errors are !
COLLEY CIBBER, *Prologue to Love Makes a Man.*

Words were given us to communicate our ideas by.
CHESTERFIELD, *Letters.* June 21, 1748.

True ease in writing comes from art, not chance.
POPE, *Essay on Criticism.* Pt. II, l. 160.

He who destroys a good book kills reason itself.
MILTON, *Areopagitica.*

Literature has her quacks no less than medicine.
COLTON, *Lacon.*

Virginity is poetry : it does not exist for fools.
LIMAYRAC.

Books follow manners ; manners do not follow books.
THEO. GAUTIER.

A poet soaring in the high reason of his fancies.
MILTON, *Reason of Church Government.*

No man but a blockhead ever wrote except for money.
BOSWELL, *Life of Johnson.* 1776.

Odds life ! must one swear to the truth of a song ?
MATTHEW PRIOR, *A Better Answer.*

Fame is the spur that the clear spirit doth raise.
MILTON, *Lycidas.* l. 70.

What stuff will please you next, the Lord can tell.
DRYDEN, *Prologue to Kind Keeper.*

Books must follow sciences, and not sciences books.
BACON, *Amendment of Laws.*

No book is worth anything which is not worth much.
RUSKIN, *Queen of the Air.*

But to have the sweet babe of my brain served in pi !
> LOWELL, *Fable for Critics.*

A man will turn over half a library to make one book.
> BOSWELL, *Life of Johnson.*   1775.

It is much easier to be critical than to be correct.
> DISRAELI.

All books are bound to sell, but some are unsalable.
> ANON.

Poets are like birds : the least thing makes them sing.
> CHATEAUBRIAND.

Fit words are fine ; but often fine words are not fit.
> ANON.

The chief glory of every people arises from its authors.
> SAMUEL JOHNSON, *Preface to Dictionary.*

One writes well only of what he has seen or suffered.
> DE GONCOURT.

I am but a gatherer and disposer of other men's stuff.
> WOTTON, *Architecture.*

To make a book is no less a trade than to make a clock.
> LA BRUYÈRE.

Seasoned life of a man preserved and stored up in books.
> MILTON, *Areopagitica.*

Some tell, some hear, some judge of news, some make it.
> DRYDEN, *Spanish Friar.*   iv.

In reading, as in eating, an appetite is half the feast.
> ANON.

Thou wert a beautiful thought, and softly bodied forth.
> BYRON, *Childe Harold.*   Canto iv, st. 115.

He adorned whatever subject he either spoke or wrote upon.
> CHESTERFIELD'S *Characters.*   Bolingbroke.

I never knew a man of letters ashamed of his profession.
> THACKERAY.

A wise scepticism is the first attribute of a good critic.

LOWELL, *Shakespeare Once More.*

In every author let us distinguish the man from his works.

VOLTAIRE, *A Philosophical Dictionary.*

The true University of these days is a collection of Books.

CARLYLE, *Hero as a Man of Letters.*

Our forefathers had no other books but the score and tally.

King Henry VI. Pt. II, iv, 7.

He hath never fed of the dainties that are bred in a book.

Love's Labour's Lost. iv, 2.

Though an angel should write, still 't is devils must print.

MOORE, *Fudges in England.* iii.

Next to being a great poet is the power of understanding one.

LONGFELLOW.

For words are wise men's counters, they do but reckon by them.

HOBBES, *The Leviathan.*

Had in him those brave translunary things that the first poets had.

DRAYTON, *To Henry Reynolds.*

The monarchist boasts more bayonets, the republican more books.

CARNEGIE, *Triumphant Democracy.*

Solitude causes us to write because it causes us to think.

MLLE. DE GUÉRIN.

The press is the foe of rhetoric, but the friend of reason.

COLTON, *Lacon.*

And deeper than did ever plummet sound, I'll drown my book.

The Tempest. v, 1, l. 56.

Books are the best things, well used : abused, among the worst.

> EMERSON, *American Scholar.*

Fool ! said my muse to me, look in the heart, and write.

> PHILIP SIDNEY, *Astrophel and Stella.*

Devise, wit ! write, pen ! for I am for whole volumes in folio.

> *Love's Labour 's Lost.* i, 2.

All men are critics, although very few are connoisseurs.

> COLTON, *Lacon.*

Poetry has been the guardian angel of humanity in all ages.

> LAMARTINE.

Reading maketh a full man, conference a ready man, and writing an exact man.

> BACON, *Essay I.* Of Studies.

A man may write at any time if he will set himself doggedly to it.

> BOSWELL, *Life of Johnson.*

Ignorance makes a fastidious critic ; knowing little, little is liked.

> ALLSTON.

No sooner does he take pen in his hand than it becomes a torpedo to him.

> BOSWELL, *Life of Johnson.*

The true use of speech is not so much to express our wants as to conceal them.

> GOLDSMITH, *The Bee.*

Classical quotation is the parole of literary men all over the world.

> BOSWELL, *Life of Johnson.*

All writing comes by the grace of God, and all doing and having.

> EMERSON, *Essays.* Of Experience.

Sir, he hath never fed of the dainties that are bred in a book.
Love's Labour 's Lost. iv, 2, 1. 24.

Reading a poor book is an opportunity lost of reading a good one.
ANON.

The books which help you most are those which make you think the most.
THEODORE PARKER.

Precisely in proportion as certainty vanishes, verbosity abounds.
COLTON, *Lacon.*

Master! master! news, old news, and such news as you never heard of.
Taming of the Shrew. iii, 2.

I am not only witty in myself, but the cause that wit is in other men.
King Henry IV. Pt. II, i, 2.

Books, like salt fish, should be a good while soaking before served.
ANON.

A great writer does not reveal himself here and there, but everywhere.
LOWELL.

Omit every circumstance that is not material, and beware of digressions.
CHESTERFIELD, *Letters.* Oct. 19, 1748.

To enjoy reading is to transform wearisome hours into delightful ones.
MONTESQUIEU.

Report me and my cause aright
To the unsatisfied.
Hamlet. v, 2.

We prize books, and they prize them most who are themselves wise.
EMERSON, *Letters and Social Aims.*

Write to the mind and heart, and let the ear glean after
what it can.
BAILEY, *Festus.* Sc. Home.

Books must be read as deliberately and reservedly as
they were written.
THOREAU, *Walden.*

It requires a surgical operation to get a joke well into a
Scotch understanding.
SYDNEY SMITH, *Lady Holland's Memoir.*

I begin shrewdly to suspect . . . the young man of
a terrible taint, poetry !
BEN JONSON, *Bartholomew Fair.* iii.

It is a maxim with me that no man was ever written out
of reputation but by himself.
BENTLEY, *Monk's Life of Bentley.*

Fiction lags after truth, invention is unfruitful, and imagination cold and barren.
BURKE, *Thoughts on Discontent.*

Better one line that will survive the author than a hundred books outlived.   ANON.

To be a well-favoured man is the gift of fortune ; but to
write and read comes by nature.
Much Ado About Nothing. iii, 3.

Read the best books first, or you may not have a chance
to read them at all.
THOREAU, *Week.*

What is twice read is commonly better remembered
than what is transcribed.
SAMUEL JOHNSON, *Idler.*

To a woman, the romances she makes are more amusing
than those she reads.
THEO. GAUTIER.

The ink of the scholar is more sacred than the blood of
the martyr.
MOHAMMED, *Tribute to Reason.*

What a sense of security in an old book which Time has
criticised for us !
LOWELL, *My Study Windows.* Lib'y of Old Authors.

Fear of hypocrites and fools is the great plague of thinking and writing.   J. JANIN.

The world is satisfied with words : few care to dive beneath the surface.   PASCAL.

I am sure if he be a good poet he has discovered a good
tavern in his time.
BEN JONSON, *News from New World.*

I 'll give anything for a good copy now, be it true or
false, so it be news.
BEN JONSON, *News from New World.*

'T is a Poet, we call them Bards in our country, sings
ballads and rhymes.
DEKKO, *Satiro-Mastix.*

Behold the whole huge earth sent to me hebdomadally
in a brown-paper wrapper.
LOWELL, *Biglow Papers.*

If this were played upon a stage now, I could condemn
it as an improbable fiction.
Twelfth Night. iii, 4.

It may well wait a century for a reader, as God has
waited six thousand years for an observer.
KEPLER, *Brewster's Martyrs of Science.*

For that fine madness still he did retain,
Which rightly should possess a poet's brain.
DRAYTON, *Of Marlowe.*

A careless song, with a little nonsense in it now and
then, does not misbecome a monarch.
WALPOLE, *Letter to Horace Mann.* 1770.

Learning hath gained most by those books by which the
Printers have lost.
FULLER, *Holy and Profane State.* Of Books.

To judge of poets is only the faculty of poets ; and not
of all poets, but the best.

BEN JONSON, *Discoveries.*

Satire lies about men of letters during their life, and
eulogy after their death.

VOLTAIRE.

The world is a book, the language of which is unintelli-
gible to many persons.

MÉRY.

Let there be gall enough in thy ink, though thou write
with a goose-pen, no matter.

Twelfth Night. iii, 2, 1. 52.

Let your thoughts be well dressed if you would have
them move in good company. ANON.

So full of shapes is fancy
That it alone is high fantastical.

Twelfth Night. i, 1, 1. 14.

Time, in fact, effects that for a fine poem that distance
performs for a fine view.

COLTON, *Lacon.*

A house is no home unless it contains food and fire for
the mind as well as for the body.

OSSOLI.

The whole nation hitherto has been void of wit and
humour, and even incapable of relishing it.

WALPOLE, *Letter to Sir Horace Mann.*

Pray, let me hear you recite some of your Verses, which
to a Wit is a Favour, I 'm sure.

WYCHERLEY, *Love in a Wood.* ii.

In proportion as society refines, new books must ever become more necessary.

GOLDSMITH, *Citizen of the World.* Letter lxxii.

That is a good book which is opened with expectation
and closed with profit.

ALCOTT, *Table Talk.* Learning-Book.

O, Sir, we quarrel in print, by the book ; as you have
books for good manners.
As You Like It. v, 4, 1. 94.

For books are as meats and viands are ; some of good,
some of evil substance.
MILTON, *Areopagitica.*

Let your literary compositions be kept from the public
eye for nine years at least.
HORACE, *An Introduction to the Art of Poetry.*

"There is no book so bad," said the bachelor, " but
something good may be found in it."
CERVANTES, *Don Quixote.* Pt. II, ch. 3.

The love of books is a love which requires neither justifi-
cation, apology, nor defence.
LANGFORD, *The Praise of Books.*

Every author, in some degree, portrays himself in his
· works, even be it against his will.
GOETHE, *The Poet's Year.*

Some books are to be tasted, others to be swallowed, and
some few to be chewed and digested.
BACON, *Essay.* Of Studies.

If you once understand an author's character, the com-
prehension of his writings becomes easy.
LONGFELLOW, *Hyperion.* Bk. I, ch. 5.

If time is precious, no book that will not improve by
repeated readings deserves to be read at all.
CARLYLE, *Essays.* Goethe's Helena.

The great error of our authors is, that they sit down to
make a book rather than to write.
COLTON, *Lacon.*

Oh, poor hearts of poets, eager for the infinite in love,
will you never be understood ?
MME. LOUISE COLET.

Oliver Goldsmith is the only poet who ever considered himself to have been overpaid.

COLTON, *Lacon.*

Reading is useless to some persons ; ideas pass through their heads without remaining.

C. JORDAN.

To judge a country one does not know the language of, is like judging a book from the binding.

ANON.

He knew
Himself to sing, and build the lofty rhyme.

MILTON, *Lycidas.* l. 10.

The spirit of poetry cannot be tamed, even by a marriage with such a shrew as metaphysics.

COLTON, *Lacon.*

Books that you may carry to the fire, and hold readily in your hand, are the most useful after all.

SAMUEL JOHNSON, *Hawkins.*

A little sustenance, a hut and garden, a little money— these, as I rendezvous with my poems.

WHITMAN, *To Rich Givers.*

I 'll make 'em know what it is to injure a Person that does them the honour to write for them !

BUCKINGHAM, *The Rehearsal.*

The true poet is always great ; if compared with others ; not always if compared with himself.

COLTON, *Lacon.*

A poet soaring in the high region of his fancies with his garland and singing robes about him.

MILTON, *Church Government.* Int. II.

You know it 's
A terrible thing to be pestered with poets.

LOWELL, *Fable for Critics.*

Tell stories very seldom, and absolutely never but where they are very apt, and very short.

> CHESTERFIELD, *Letters.* Oct. 12, 1748.

Subtract from many modern poets all that may be found in Shakespeare, and trash will remain.

> COLTON, *Lacon.*

He cometh unto you with a tale which holdeth children from play, and old men from the chimney-corner.

> SIDNEY, *Defence of Poesy.*

Rhyme will undo you, and hinder your growth and reputation in court more than anything beside.

> BEN JONSON, *Love's Welcome at Bolsover.*

Little infants of the time,
Who write new songs and trust in tune and rhyme.

> DRYDEN, *Epilogue to Indian Emperor.*

A dull author just delivered, and a plain woman about to be so, are two very important animals.

> COLTON, *Lacon.*

When one writes of woman, he must reserve the right to laugh at his ideas of the day before.

> A. RICARD.

He who writes prose builds his temple to Fame in rubble ; he who writes verses builds it in granite.

> LYLY, *Euphues.* Anatomy of Wit.

The born writer finds, even in the humblest, some trait that may be of interest to himself or others.

> ANON.

He sometimes affects hard words, by way of ornament, which he always mangles like a learned woman.

> CHESTERFIELD, *Letters.* September 27, 1749.

Those works therefore are the most valuable, that set our thinking faculties in the fullest operation.

> COLTON, *Lacon.*

But these master-poets they will have their own absurd
courses : they will be informed of nothing !
BEN JONSON, Bartholomew Fair.

All truly wise thoughts have already been thought many
times. The best that we can do is to rethink them.
ANON.

A man, who is not born with a poetical genius, can never
be a poet, or, at best, an extreme bad one.
CHESTERFIELD, Letters. December 26, 1749.

I have always felt that whatever the Divine Providence
permitted to occur I was not too proud to report.
DANA, Art of Newspaper Making.

That writer does the most who gives his reader the most
knowledge, and takes from him the least time.
COLTON, Lacon.

Perhaps the greatest lesson which the lives of literary
men teach us is told in a single word : Wait !
LONGFELLOW, Hyperion. Bk. I, ch. 8.

Shall quips and sentences and these paper bullets of the
brain awe a man from the career of his humour ?
Much Ado About Nothing. ii, 3.

A woman who writes commits two sins : she increases
the number of books, and decreases the number of
women.
A. KARR.

Clergy—Religion—Character

To be of no church is dangerous.

SAMUEL JOHNSON, *Life of Milton.*

Clergy—Religion—Character

As firm as faith.

> *Merry Wives of Windsor.* iv, 4.

We lean on faith.

> GILDER, *Love and Death.* St. 2.

Past praying for.

> *King Henry IV.* Pt. I, ii, 4.

Unbelief is blind.

> MILTON, *Comus.* l. 519.

Parish me no parishes.

> PEELE, *Old Wives' Tale.*

A man is a god in ruins.

> EMERSON, *Nature.* Ch. 8, Prospects.

The luxury of doing good.

> HOLMAN, *The Votary of Wealth.* v. 4, l. last.

A holy man is a whole man.

> ANON.

Practise what you preach.

> YOUNG, *Love of Fame.* Satire iii, l. 48.

Servant of God, well done.

> MILTON, *Paradise Lost.* Bk. VI, l. 29.

Heaven's great artillery.

> CRASHAW, *The Flaming Heart.*

Life is what we make of it.

> ANON.

O for a forty-parson power !

> BYRON, *Don Juan.* Canto x. st. 34.

Labor, you know, is Prayer.

> TAYLOR, *Improvisations*. 11.

There is no sex in courage.

> COLTON, *Lacon*.

Faith is a fine invention.

> DICKINSON, *Poems*. Second series, xxx.

Prayer ardent opens heaven.

> YOUNG, *Night Thoughts*. N. viii, 1. 721.

To be, rather than to appear.

> Latin motto.

No rogue like a godly rogue.

> ANON.

Who well lives, long lives.

> DU BARTAS, *Divine Weekes*. Week ii, 4th day.

Like one in prayer I stood.

> LONGFELLOW, *Voices of the Night*. Prelude, st. 11.

Making their lives a prayer.

> WHITTIER, *To A. K. on Receiving Sea-Mosses*.

Evil is only good perverted.

> LONGFELLOW, *The Golden Legend*. ii.

"Amen" stuck in my throat.

> *Macbeth*. ii, 2, l. 32.

Woman is the Sunday of man.

> MICHELET.

Whose very looks are prayers.

> MULOCK, *An Evening Hymn*. A sketch. St. 3.

Pray Heaven for a human heart.

> TENNYSON, *Lady Clara Vere de Vere*.

All their luxury was doing good.

> GARTH, *Claremont*. 1. 149.

God's mills grind slow, but sure.

> HERBERT, *Jacula Prudentum*.

God will estimate success one day.

> BROWNING, *Prince Hohenstiel-Schwangau.*

Trust me not at all or all in all.

> TENNYSON, *Merlin and Vivien.*

Hell is paved with good intentions.

> BOSWELL, *Life of Johnson.* Vol. II, p. 18.

One religion is as true as another.

> BURTON, *Anat. of Melancholy.* Bk. III, sec. iv,
> memb. 2, subsec. i.

Religion, the pious worship of God.

> CICERO.

Prayer, man's rational prerogative.

> WORDSWORTH, *Ecclesiastical Sonnets.* Pt. II, xxiii.

God comes to us without bell.

> Old proverb. Quoted by EMERSON in *Over-Soul.*

The inglorious arts of peace.

> MARVELL, *On Cromwell's Return from Ireland.*

To maken vertue of necessite.

> CHAUCER, *Canterbury Tales.*

Industry is applied religion.

> ANON.

'T was Presbyterian true blue.

> BUTLER, *Hudibras.* Pt. I, canto i, l. 161.

He lives long that lives well.

> FULLER, *Holy and Profane States.* The Good Child.

Indued with sanctity of reason.

> MILTON, *Paradise Lost.* Bk. VII, l. 507.

To be of no church is dangerous.

> SAMUEL JOHNSON, *Life of Milton.*

Above the flight of common souls.

> MURPHY, *Zenobia.*

The gown does not make the friar.

> From the French.

A good example is the best sermon.

ANON.

A very beadle to a humorous sigh.

Love's Labour's Lost. iii, 1.

The soul and the body are enemies.

DE MUSSET.

A holy Sunday brings a happy Monday.

ANON.

Holiness is the best Sabbath dress.

ANON.

And learn the luxury of doing good.

GOLDSMITH, *The Traveller.* 1. 22.

Alms are but the vehicles of prayer.

DRYDEN, *Hind and Panther.* Pt. III.

Religion is not an end, but a means.

GOETHE.

From a pure spring pure water flows.

ANON.

Her eyes are homes of silent prayer.

TENNYSON, *In Memoriam.* xxxii.

A church debt is the devil's salary.

BEECHER.

Past all comforts here, but prayers.

King Henry VIII. iv, 2.

Better rich in God than rich in gold.

ANON.

God helps them that help themselves.

FRANKLIN, *Poor Richard's Almanac.*

Gentle of speech, beneficent of mind.

Odyssey. Bk. IV, 1. 917, Pope's trans.

From seeming evil still educing good.

THOMSON, *Hymn.* 1. 140.

'T is impious in a good man to be sad.
> Young, *Night Thoughts.* N. iv, 1. 676.

My favoured temple is an humble heart.
> Bailey, *Festus.* Sc. Colonnade and Lawn.

A man he was to all the country dear.
> Goldsmith, *Deserted Village.* 1. 141.

A clear conscience is a soft pillow.
> Anon.

Villain and he be many miles asunder.
> *Romeo and Juliet.* iii, 5.

Faith is a higher faculty than reason.
> Bailey, *Festus.* Proem, 1. 84.

I stood among them, but not of them.
> Byron, *Childe Harold.* Canto iii, st. 113.

God looks to pure hands, not full ones.
> Syrus.

Let me be blessed for the peace I make !
> *King Henry VI.* Pt. II, ii, 1.

The tall, the wise, the reverend head.
> Watts, *Spiritual Songs.*

A little, round, fat, oily man of God.
> Thomson, *Castle of Indolence.* Canto i, st. 69.

When a fox preaches, watch your geese.
> From the French.

Prefer to be good rather than seem so.
> Sallust.

What ardently we wish, we soon believe.
> Young, *Night Thoughts.* N. VII, Pt. ii, 1. 1311.

Evil spreads as necessarily as disease.
> Eliot, *Adam Bede.* Bk. V, ch. xli.

He teaches to deny that faintly prayes.
> Quarles, *A Feast for Wormes.* Sec. 7, med. 7.

Stands not within the prospect of belief.

Macbeth. i, 3, 1. 74.

You can never make gross sin look clear.

Timon of Athens. iii, 5.

E'en Sunday shines no Sabbath day to me.

POPE, *Pro. to the Satires.* 1. 12.

I believe there is no devil but fear.

HUBBARD, *Philistine.*

Figure of truth, of faith, of loyalty.

Pericles. v, 3.

The strength of empire is in religion.

BEN JONSON, *Discoveries.*

A faithful preacher is a rare creature.

ANON.

He who lives well is the best preacher.

CERVANTES, *Don Quixote.* vi, 19.

Bound by my charity and my blest order.

Measure for Measure. ii, 3.

When the pirate prays, hide your silver.

ANON.

The good is but the beautiful in action.

ROUSSEAU.

An honest man 's the noblest work of God.

POPE, *Essay on Man.* Ep. iv, 1. 247.

A Christian is the highest style of man.

YOUNG, *Night Thoughts.* N. iv, 1. 788.

The enormous faith of many made for one.

POPE, *Essay on Man.* Ep. iii, 1. 242.

His tribe were God Almighty's gentlemen.

DRYDEN, *Absalom and Achitophel.* Pt. I, 1. 645.

The cause of Freedom is the cause of God.

BOWLES, *To Edmund Burke.*

Sacred religion ! Mother of Form and Fear !
> DANIEL, *Musophilus*. St. 47.

Thou almost makest me waver in my faith.
> *Merchant of Venice*. iv, 1, l. 130.

God's music will not finish with one tune.
> ARNOLD, *With Sadi in the Garden*.

A Christian is God Almighty's gentleman.
> HARE, *Guesses at Truth*.

'T is only God may be had for the asking.
> LOWELL.

Do good to-day, since thou still livest.
> VILLEFRÉ.

Religion lies more in walk than in talk.
> ANON.

I preached as never sure to preach again.
> BAXTER, *Love Breathing Thanks and Praise*.

The noblest mind the best contentment has.
> SPENSER, *Faerie Queene*. Bk. I, canto i, st. 35.

His office sacred, his credentials clear.
> COWPER, *The Task*. ii.

That he is gentil that doth gentil dedis.
> CHAUCER, *The Wif of Bathes Tale*. l. 6695.

He that will not be saved needs no sermon.
> ANON.

You 're welcome, most learned reverend sir.
> *King Henry VIII*. ii, 2.

Sermons in stones and good in every thing.
> *As You Like It*. ii, 1, l. 17.

He taught them how to live and how to die.
> SOMERVILLE, *In Memory of Rev. Mr. Moore*. l. 21.

Hell is full of good meanings and wishings.
> HERBERT, *Jacula Prudentum*.

So upright Quakers please both man and God.
POPE, *The Dunciad.* Bk. IV, 1. 208.

I hold you as a thing enskyed and sainted.
Measure for Measure. i, 4.

A white glove often conceals a dirty hand.
ANON.

Superstition : a foolish fear of the Deity.
LA BRUYÈRE.

A burlesque word is often a mighty sermon.
BOILEAU.

There and there only is the power to save.
COWPER, *Progress of Error.*

One may smile, and smile, and be a villain.
Hamlet. i, 5.

He 's armed without that 's innocent within.
POPE, *Horace.* Ep. i, Bk. I, 1. 94.

He taught these how to live and how to die.
GREEN, *Thomas Tickell.*

They have snared the shepherd of the flock.
King Henry VI. Pt. II, ii, 2.

A pack of cards is the devil's prayer-book.
From the German.

Evil minds change good to their own nature.
SHELLEY, *Prometheus Unbound.* Act i.

Virtue has many preachers, but few martyrs.
HELVETIUS.

Good preachers give fruits and not flowers.
Italian saying.

Distrust him who talks much of his honesty.
DUSSAULX.

Grace is grace, despite of all controversy.
Measure for Measure. i, 2.

Let nothing come between you and the light.
THOREAU, *Letters.*

The Tree of Life, on which redemption hangs.
STEDMAN, *Protest of Faith.*

No faith has triumphed without its martyrs.
DE GIRARDIN.

He serves a raw clergyman up with the toast.
HOLMES, *After Dinner.*

Upon the platform, 'twixt eleven and twelve.
Hamlet. i, 2.

A religion that costs nothing does nothing.
ANON.

The imperfect offices of prayer and praise.
WORDSWORTH, *The Excursion.* Bk. L.

Have faith and thy prayer will be answered.
LONGFELLOW, *Evangeline.* Pt. II, st. 4, l. 139.

Prayer moves the Hand which moves the world.
WALLACE, *There is an Eye.* l. 19.

Example is the lesson that all men can read.
WEST, *Education.* Canto i, lxxxi.

The 'why' is plain as way to parish church.
As You Like It. ii, 7.

Whoever lives true life will love true love.
E. B. BROWNING, *Aurora Leigh.* Bk. I, l. 1096.

Wide was his parish, and houses far asonder.
CHAUCER, *Canterbury Tales.* Pro. l, 493.

Many wish to be pious, but none to be humble.
ROCHEFOUCAULD.

More like a soldier than a man o' the church.
King Henry VI. Pt. II, i, 1.

But looks through nature up to nature's God.
POPE, *Essay on Man.* Ep. iv, l. 331.

Earth, with her thousand voices, praises God.
COLERIDGE, Hymn in Vale.

By the heavens' assistance and your strength.
King Henry IV.

A good conscience makes a joyful countenance.
ANON.

You need but plead your honourable privilege.
All 's Well that Ends Well.   iv, 5.

There 's in you all that we believe of heaven.
OTWAY, Venice Preserved.   i, 1.

Prayer is the spirit speaking truth to Truth.
BAILEY, Festus.   Sc. Elsewhere.

Spires whose "silent finger points to heaven."
WORDSWORTH, The Excursion.   Bk. VI.

The fearful Unbelief is unbelief in yourself.
CARLYLE, Sartor Resartus.   The Everlasting No.
Bk. II, ch. v.

And fools who came to scoff, remain'd to pray.
GOLDSMITH, Deserted Village.   1. 179.

He that will learn to pray, let him go to Sea.
HERBERT, Jacula Prudentum.   No. 89.

The ne' er to the church, the further from God.
HEYWOOD, Proverbs.   Bk. I, ch. ix.

A religious life is a struggle and not a hymn.
DE STAËL, Corinne.   Bk. X, ch. v.

There are no tricks in plain and simple faith.
Julius Cæsar.   iv, 2.

Do good by stealth, and blush to find it fame.
POPE, Epilogue to Satires.   Dia. I, 1. 136.

Does well, acts nobly ; angels could do no more.
YOUNG, Night Thoughts.   N. ii, 1. 90.

Many are skeptical because of their credulity.
ANON.

Take away the motive and you take away the sin.
CERVANTES.

And truths divine came mended from that tongue.
POPE, *Eloisa to Abelard.* 1. 66.

An abridgment of all that was pleasant in man.
GOLDSMITH, *On Garrick.* Retaliation. 1. 94.

He sins against this life, who slights the next.
YOUNG, *Night Thoughts.* N. iii, 1. 399.

I believe that no one can harm you but yourself.
HUBBARD, *Philistine.*

Man punishes the action, but God the intention.
BYRON.

Greatness and goodness are not means, but ends !
COLERIDGE, *Reproof.*

In hope to merit Heaven by making Earth an Hell.
BYRON, *Childe Harold.* Canto i, st. 33.

Our faith comes in moments ; our vice is habitual.
EMERSON, *The Over-Soul.*

There are three sexes—men, women and clerymen.
SYDNEY SMITH, *Memoirs.*

God enters by a private door into every individual.
EMERSON, *Intellect.*

Faith builds a bridge from this world to the next.
YOUNG, *Night Thoughts.* N. viii, 1. 717.

Prayer all his business—all his pleasure praise.
PARNELL, *The Hermit.* 1. 6.

God hath yoked to Guilt her pale tormentor, Misery.
BRYANT, *Inscription for entrance to a wood.*

The gentleman is learned and a most rare speaker.
King Henry VIII. i, 2.

The world is my country ; to do good, my religion.
PAINE.

Goodness is the only investment that never fails.
THOREAU, *Walden.*

I swear I think there is nothing but immortality.
WHITMAN, *To Think of Time.*

How many persons assume bodily the mask of virtue!
MLLE. DE SCUDÉRI.

If you would lift me you must be on higher ground.
EMERSON.

Life is a combat, of which the palm is in heaven.
DELAVIGNE.

A bad man is worse when he pretends to be a saint.
BACON.

A hammer of gold will not open the kingdon of heaven.
ANON.

God made him, and therefore let him pass for a man.
Merchant of Venice. i, 2.

He who has no character is not a man; he is a thing.
CHAMFORT.

Nothing is so firmly believed as what we least know.
MONTAIGNE, *Essays of Divine Ordinances.* Bk. I,
ch. xxxi.

Battering the gates of heaven with storms of prayer.
TENNYSON, *St. Simeon Stylites.* 1. 7.

An itch of disputing will prove the scab of churches.
WOTTON, *A Panegyric to King Charles.*

They never sought in vain that sought the Lord aright!
BURNS, *Cotter's Saturday Night.* St. 6.

God will not love thee less, because men love thee more.
TUPPER, *Proverbial Philosophy.* Of Tolerance.

And (strange to tell!) he practised what he preached.
ARMSTRONG, *Art of Preserving Health.*

People take more pains to be damned than to be saved.
ANON.

The heart that had never loved was the first atheist.
MERCIER.

Where God hath a temple, the Devil will have a chapel.
BURTON, *Anatomy of Melancholy.*   Pt. III, sec. iv.

Twin fools : one doubts nothing ; the other, everything.
ANON.

There is nothing directly moral in our nature but love.
COMTE.

A skeptic is not one who doubts, but one who examines.
SAINTE-BEUVE.

It is a good preacher who follows his own instructions.
ANON.

If God created the world, I would not care to be God.
SCHOPENHAUER.

Fanaticism is to religion what hypocrisy is to virtue.
PALISSOT.

There can be no Christianity where there is no charity.
COLTON, *Lacon.*

An Atheist's laugh 's a poor exchange for Deity offended !
BURNS, *Epistle to a Young Friend.*

A man without religion is like a horse without a bridle.
ANON.

If you would be good, first believe that you are not so.
EPICTETUS.

Nobody is truly unassailable until his character is gone.
BUTLER.

Some of the most deadly serpents have the brightest skin.
ANON.

If there were no God, it would be necessary to invent one.
VOLTAIRE.

Bigotry murders religion, to frighten fools with her ghost.
COLTON, *Lacon.*

Man resolves in himself he will preach ; and he preaches.
DE LA BRUYÈRE, *Characters of Present Age.* Ch. xv.

Persecution is a bad and indirect way to plant religion.
BROWNE, *Religio Medici.* xxv.

Faith is the subtle chain which binds us to the infinite.
ELIZABETH O. SMITH, *Atheism in Three Sonnets.* Faith.

Hide nothing from thy minister, physician, and lawyer.
ANON.

What can be expressed in words can be expressed in life.
THOREAU, *Letters.*

Man is not depraved by true pleasures, but by false ones.
DE LACRETELLE.

I have a good eye, uncle ; I can see a church by daylight.
Much Ado About Nothing, ii, 1.

The healthiest religion is possible only in the healthiest man.
ANON.

Men would be saints if they loved God as they love women.
SAINT THOMAS.

They are never alone that are accompanied with noble thoughts.
SIDNEY, *Arcadia.*

Reputation, reputation, reputation ! O, I have lost my reputation.
Othello. ii, 3.

None preaches better than the ant, and she says nothing.
FRANKLIN.

Dull as an alderman at church, or a fat lap-dog after dinner.
HOLCROFT, *Duplicity*, i, 1.

Christ never wrote a tract, but He went about doing good.
MANN.

Our deeds determine us, as much as we determine our
deeds.

> ELIOT, *Adam Bede*, Bk. IV, ch. xxix.

Good actions are the invisible hinges of the doors of
heaven.

> HUGO.

Beautiful women without religion are flowers without
perfume.

> HEINE.

Many bring their clothes to church rather than themselves.

> ANON.

No man believes his creed who is afraid to hear it at-
tacked.

> PHILLIPS.

A character's like a kettle : once mended always wants
mending.

> ANON.

More things are wrought by prayer than this world
dreams of.

> TENNYSON, *Morte d'Arthur.*

When in God thou believest, near God thou wilt certainly be !

> LELAND, *Return of the Gods.* 1. 150.

I believe that men are inspired to-day as much as men
ever were.

> HUBBARD, *Philistine.*

A bad conscience flies from the light as the devil from
the cross.

> From the German.

Whatever makes men good Christians, makes them good
citizens.

> WEBSTER, *First Settlement of New England.*

6

The shepherd seeks the sheep and not the sheep the shepherd.

Two Gentlemen of Verona. i, 1.

The more honest a man is, the less he affects the air of a saint.

LAVATER.

Religions are many and diverse, but reason and goodness are one.

HUBBARD, *Philistine.*

Never was a hood so holy but the devil could get his head into it.

ANON.

Hell is a separation, and heaven is only a going home to our friends.

HUBBARD, *Philistine.*

Finite knowledge, infinite doubt; infinite knowledge, an end of doubt.

ANON.

Religion is the spice which is meant to keep life from corruption.

FRANCIS BACON.

Trust none ; for oaths are straws, men's faiths are wafer-cakes.

King Henry V. ii, 3.

The practical effect of a belief is the real test of its soundness.

FROUDE, *Short Studies.* Calvinism.

Every vice has a cloak, and creeps in under the name of virtue.

ANON.

Can the man who's on the ground read what's writ upon the housetop?

ANON.

A minister's life should be a sign-board pointing the way to heaven.

ANON.

More goodness in his little finger than you have in your whole body.

RAY, *Proverbs*.

If men are so wicked with religion what would they be without it?

FRANKLIN.

For the breast of a good man is a little heaven commencing on earth.

COLTON, *Lacon*.

It is God himself who speaks to us, when noble thoughts inspire us.

ANON.

Wait till you hear me from the pulpit; there you cannot answer me!

BISHOP GILBERT HAVEN.

We confess small faults in order to insinuate that we have no great ones.

ROCHEFOUCAULD.

He that loses his conscience has nothing left that is worth keeping.

WALTON.

Ejaculations are short prayers darted up to God on emergent occasions.

FULLER, *Good Thoughts in Bad Times*.

We have a Calvinistic creed, a Popish liturgy, and an Arminian clergy.

PITT in Prior's *Life of Burke*. Ch. x. 1790.

He made it a part of his religion never to say grace to his meat.

SWIFT, *Tale of a Tub*. Sec. xi.

The reward in this arena is not to the swift, nor the prize to the strong.

COLTON, *Lacon.*

Most men forget God all day, and ask Him to remember them at night.

ANON.

No sooner is a temple built to God, but the Devil builds a chapel hard by.

HERBERT, *Country Parson.*

Faith always implies the disbelief of a lesser fact in favour of a greater.

HOLMES, *Professor at Breakfast Table.* v.

Well, if my wind were but long enough to say my prayers, I would repent.

Merry Wives of Windsor. iv, 5, 1. 104.

The only way to please God is to follow the good inclinations of our nature.

MERCIER.

An upright minister asks, what recommends a man ; a corrupt minister, who ?

COLTON, *Lacon.*

Virtue is so praiseworthy that wicked people practice it from self-interest.

VAUVENARGUES.

He that has lived without a God, would be very happy to die without one.

COLTON, *Lacon.*

Alas ! how can we always resist ?   The devil tempts us, and the flesh is weak.

VOLTAIRE.

No one perfectly loves God who does not perfectly love some of his creatures.

DE VALOIS.

And what greater calamity can fall upon a nation than the loss of worship ?

EMERSON, *An Address.* July 15, 1838.

Doctor—Medicine—Health

Remedy worse than the disease.

FRANCIS BACON, *Of Seditions.*

Doctor—Medicine—Health

Then the doctors!

> TENNYSON, *The Princess.* ii.

He doth not kill us.

> BROWNE, *Religio Medici.*

When taken to be shaken.

> COLMAN (the Younger), *Broad Grins.*

In poison there is physic.

> *King Henry IV.* Pt. II, i, 1.

A dog may look at a doctor.

> ANON.

The first wealth is health.

> EMERSON.

The accident of an accident.

> THURLOW, *Speech in reply to Lord Grafton.*

Bitter pills cure bitter ills.

> ANON.

Remedy worse than the disease.

> BACON, *Of Seditions and Troubles.*

Fill all thy bones with aches.

> *The Tempest.* i, 2.

Sickness tells us what we are.

> ANON.

Budge doctors of the Stoic fur.

> MILTON, *Comus.* 1. 707.

I was not always a man of woe.

> SCOTT, *Lay of Last Minstrel.* Canto ii, st. 12.

More die by food than by famine.

ANON.

Poverty is the mother of health.

ANON.

Temperance is the best medicine.

ANON.

Music 's the medicine of the mind.

LOGAN (attributed to), *Danish Ode.*

Time is generally the best doctor.

OVID.

He in peace is wounded, not in war.

Rape of Lucrece. 1. 831.

Feasting sows ; the physician reaps.

ANON.

Medicines are not meant to feed on.

ANON.

Come in consumption's ghastly form.

HALLECK, *Marco Bozzaris.*

Health that snuffs the morning air.

GRAINGER, *Solitude, An Ode.* 1. 35.

A silver sofa cannot cure the sick.

ANON.

Fear kills more than the physician.

ANON.

The proper study of mankind is man.

POPE, *Essay on Man.* Ep. ii, l. 1.

I take not on me here as a physician.

King Henry IV. Pt. II, iv, 1.

Health is the first good lent to men.

HERRICK, *Hesperides.* 121.

Seek not a physician for every qualm.

ANON.

Death is the common medicine for woe.

REYNOLDS, *Werter.* iii, 1.

What cannot be cured must be endured.

Old proverb.

Pills should be swallowed, not chewed.

ANON.

What wounds sorer than an evil tongue ?

AMBROSE PHILLIPS, *Pastoral.* ii.

Taking the measure of an unmade grave.

Romeo and Juliet. iii, 3.

Make the plaster as large as the sore.

ANON.

The labour we delight in physics pain.

Macbeth. ii, 1.

Health consists with Temperance alone.

POPE, *Essay on Man.* Ep. iv, 1. 81.

Who shall decide when doctors disagree ?

POPE, *Moral Essays.* Ep. iii, 1. 1.

One man's meat is another man's poison.

ANON.

Better pay a good cook than the doctor.

ANON.

Quiet sleep is the best patent medicine.

ANON.

God never made his work for man to mend.

DRYDEN, *To John Dryden, of Chesterton.*

Quackery has no friend like gullibility.

ANON

What wound did ever heal but by degrees?

Othello. ii, 3, 1. 377.

Charm ache with air and agony with words.

Much Ado About Nothing. v, 1, 1. 20.

To scorn delights, and live laborious days.
MILTON, *Lycidas.* 1. 70.

To the well man every day is a feast.
ANON.

We now prescribe, like Doctors in Despair.
DRYDEN, *Pro. Albion and Albanius.*

When I was sick, you gave me bitter pills.
Two Gentlemen of Verona. ii, 4, 1. 149.

Health without wealth is half a sickness.
ANON.

Throw physic to the dogs ; I 'll none of it.
Macbeth. v, 3.

Canst thou not minister to a mind diseased?
Macbeth. v, 3.

While there is life there 's hope, he cried.
GAY, *Sick Man and Angel.*

Out, loathed medicine ! hated potion, hence !
Midsummer Night's Dream. iii, 2.

Dr. Diet and Dr. Quiet are fine physicians.
ANON.

Pains are the payment for sinful pleasures.
ANON.

If you sit in a draft doctors will cash it.
ANON.

Will toys amuse when med'cines cannot cure?
YOUNG, *Night Thoughts.* N. ii, 1. 67.

It is part of the cure to wish to be cured.
SENECA, *Hippolytus.* ccxlix.

The sick man sleeps when the debtor cannot.
ANON.

My Lord Jupiter knows how to gild the pill.
MOLIÈRE, *Amphitryon.* iii, 11.

Better a healthy peasant than a sickly king.
FERDINAND III.

The patient dies while the physician sleeps.
> *Rape of Lucrece.* 130.

If you mock the lame, you may limp the same.
> ANON.

If you want to die, take a quack's medicine.
> ANON.

To the well-bred doctor all babies are angels.
> ANON.

God healeth and the physician hath the thanks.
> ANON.

I think you 'll force me to become your patient.
> SHACKERLEY, *The Antiquary.*

What deep wounds ever closed without a scar?
> BYRON, *Childe Harold.* Canto iii, st. 84.

Banished the doctor, and expell'd the friend.
> POPE, *Essay on Man.* Ep. iii, 1. 330.

Give no man counsel or physic till he asks it.
> ANON.

Physicians are joked at only when we are well.
> ANON.

Sickness seizes the body from bad ventilation.
> OVID, *Ars Amatoria.* ii, 310.

Diseases of the mind impair the bodily powers.
> OVID, *Tristium.* iii, 8, 25.

Before you doctor others, try your own physic.
> ANON.

Learn from the beasts the physic of the field.
> POPE, *Essay on Man.* Ep. iii, 1. 174,

Wounds cannot be cured unless they are probed.
> LIVY, *Annales.* xxviii, 27.

Better miss a dinner than make work for a doctor.
> ANON.

Health and cheerfulness mutually beget each other.
> ADDISON, *The Spectator.* No. 387.

H' had got a hurt o' th' inside of a deadlier sort.
                    BUTLER, *Hudibras.*   Pt. I, canto iii, 1. 309.

Every man is either a fool or a physician at forty.
                    ANON.

Where there is no woman the sick man groans in vain.
                    RABELAIS.

We will be brave, Puffe, now we have the medicine.
                    BEN JONSON, *The Alchemist.*

We are usually the best men when in the worst health.
                    ANON.

Health without wealth is a mill without corn to grind.
                    ANON.

It 's ill when the physician had need to be the patient.
                    ANON.

When the physician can advise best the patient is dead.
                    ANON.

A doctor and a ploughman know more than a doctor alone.
                    ANON.

Search not the wound too deep lest thou make a new one.
                    ANON.

Hide nothing from thy minister, physician and lawyer.
                    ANON.

Laying his hand on many a heart, had healed it forever.
                    LONGFELLOW, *Evangeline.*

If you make a good profession, make good your profession.
                    ANON.

The two best physicians are Doctor Diet and Doctor
Merryman.
                    ANON.

The sickness of the body may prove the health of the
soul.
                    ANON.

Extreme remedies are very appropriate for extreme diseases.

> HIPPOCRATES, *Aphorisms*. 6.

The chapter of accidents is the longest chapter in the book.

> SOUTHEY, *Attrib'd to John Wilkes*. The Doctor. Ch. 98.

The best surgeon is he that has been well hacked about himself.

> ANON·

A pill that at the present moment is daily bread to thousands.

> JERROLD, *The Catspaw*. i, 1.

When a man loses his health then he begins to take care of it.

> JOSH BILLINGS.

Eating too much fills the churchyard faster than eating too little.

> ANON.

Until the physician has killed one or two, he is not a physician.

> ANON.

Preserving the health by too strict a regimen is a wearisome malady.

> ROCHEFOUCAULD, *Maxims*. No. 285.

Life and health, which are both inestimable, we have of the physician.

> BEN JONSON, *Discoveries*.

Surgeons should have an eagle's eye, a lion's heart, and a lady's hand.

> ANON.

Cheerfulness, Sir, is the principal ingredient in the composition of health.

> MURPHY, *The Apprentice*. ii, 4.

If the rascal have not given me medicines to make me
love him, I 'll be hanged.
King Henry IV. Pt. I, ii, 2.

It is only when the rich are sick, that they fully feel the
importance of wealth.
COLTON, *Lacon.*

They are as sick that surfeit with too much, as they that
starve with nothing.
Merchant of Venice. i, 2.

Health is the second blessing that we mortals are capable
of : a blessing that money cannot buy.
WALTON, *The Complete Angler.* Pt. I, ch. xxi.

When a man has lived with his stomach forty years, he
ought to know how to feed it.
SAMUEL JOHNSON.

Can honour set to a leg? no : or an arm? no : or take
away the grief of a wound? no.
King Henry IV. Pt. I, v, 1, l. 129

It is true that each disorder has a thousand prescriptions,
but not a single remedy.
COLTON, *Lacon.*

Men call physicians only when they suffer ; women,
when they are merely afflicted with ennui.
MME. DE GENLIS.

The wound will perhaps be cured in the process of time,
but it shrinks from the touch while it is fresh.
OVID, *Epistolæ Ex Ponto.* i, 3, 15.

Neglect of health
Is doctor's wealth.
ANON.

Therein the patient
Must minister to himself.
Macbeth. v. 3.

The best physic is fresh air ;
The best pill is plain fare.

ANON.

The direful art
To taint with deadly drugs.

POPE, *Odyssey.* Bk. I.

Fond of doctors, little health ;
Fond of lawyers, little wealth.

ANON.

How the Doctor's brow should smile
Crown'd with wreaths of camomile.

MOORE, *Wreaths for Ministers.*

Apoplexie, and Lethargie,
As forlorn hope, assault the enemy.

DU BARTAS, *Divine Weekes and Workes.*

Week II, Day 1.

You rub the sore,
When you should bring the plaster.

The Tempest.   ii, 1, 1. 138.

Is there no hope ? the sick man said ;
The silent doctor shook his head.

GAY, *Sick Man and Angel.*

The patient must minister to himself.
Throw physic to the dogs.

Macbeth.   v, 3.

For gold in phisike is a cordial ;
Therefore he loved gold in special.

CHAUCER, *Canterbury Tales.*   Pro., 1. 445.

The miserable have no other medicine,
But only hope.

Measure for Measure.   iii, 1.

And he that will his health deny,
Down among the dead men let him lie.

—— DYER.   Published in reign of George I.

I counted two-and-seventy stenches,
All well defined, and several stinks.
COLERIDGE, *Cologne.*

When pain and anguish wring the brow,
A ministering angel thou!
SCOTT, *Marmion.* Canto vi, st. 30.

No greater grief than to remember days
Of joy when misery is at hand.
DANTE, *Hell.* Canto v.

This sickness doth infect
The very life-blood of our enterprise.
King Henry IV. Pt. I, iv, 1, l. 28.

That dire disease, whose ruthless power
Withers the beauty's transient flower.
GOLDSMITH, *Double Transformation.* l. 75.

But just disease to luxury succeeds,
And ev'ry death its own avenger breeds.
POPE, *Essay on Man.* Ep. iii, l. 165.

Diseased nature oftentimes breaks forth
In strange eruptions.
King Henry IV. Pt. I, iii, 1.

O, he 's a limb, that has but a disease ;
Mortal, to cut it off ; to cure it, easy.
Coriolanus. iii, 1, l. 296.

For want of timely care
Millions have died of medicable wounds.
ARMSTRONG, *Art of Preserving Health.*
Bk. III, l. 515.

And took his leave with signs of sorrow,
Despairing of his fee to-morrow.
GAY, *Sick Man and the Angel.*

'Zounds ! how has he the leisure to be sick
In such a justling time ?
King Henry IV. Pt. I, iv, 1.

'T is a maxim with me, that an hale
Cobbler is a better man than a sick king.
BICKERSTAFF, Love in a Village.   i, 3.

A good stout plague amongst 'em
Or half a dozen new fantastical fevers?
BEAUMONT AND FLETCHER, Spanish Curate.

For there was never yet philosopher
That could endure the toothache patiently.
Much Ado About Nothing.   v, 1.

Take physic, pomp ;
Expose thyself to feel what wretches feel.
King Lear.   iii, 4, 1. 33.

Against diseases here the strongest fence,
Is the defective vertue, abstinence.
HERRICK, Abstinence.

Nature, too unkind,
That made no medicine for a troubled mind !
BEAUMONT AND FLETCHER, Philaster.   ii, 1.

What medicine then can such disease remove,
Where love draws hate, and hate engendereth love?
SIDNEY, Arcadia.   Bk. III.

Time hath found
In desp'rate cures a salve for every wound.
FLETCHER, Piscatorie Eclogues.   v, st. 9.

I do remember an apothecary,—
And hereabouts he dwells.
Romeo and Juliet.   v, 1.

Health to the art whose glory is to give
The crowning boon that makes it life to live.
HOLMES, Modest Request.

By medicine life may be prolonged, yet death
Will seize the doctor too.
Cymbeline.   v, 5, 1. 29.

7

Or catches some doctor quite tender and young
And basely insists on a bit of his tongue.
HOLMES.

Gold that buys health can never be ill spent,
Nor hours laid out in harmless merriment.
WEBSTER, *Westward Ho.* v, 3, 1. 345.

Better to hunt in fields for health unbought,
Than fee the doctor for a nauseous draught.
DRYDEN, *Cymon and Iphigenia.* Ep. xiii, 1. 92.

The surest road to health, say what they will,
Is never to suppose we shall be ill.
CHURCHILL, *Night.* 1. 67.

'T is time to give 'em physic, their diseases
Are grown so catching.
King Henry VIII. i, 3, 1. 36.

The first physicians by debauch were made.
Excess began, and sloth sustains the trade.
DRYDEN, *To John Dryden.* Ep. xiv.

And telling me, the sovereign'st thing on earth
Was parmaceti for an inward bruise.
King Henry IV. i, 3.

Take a little rum, the less you take the better,
Pour it in the lakes of Werner or of Wetter.
BISHOP GEO. W. DOANE, *Lines on Homeopathy.*

When health, affrighted, spreads her rosy wing,
And flies with every changing gale of spring.
BYRON, *Childish Recollections.* 1. 3.

A malady
Preys on my heart that medicine cannot reach.
MATURIN, *Bertram.* iv, 2.

Love is the mind's strong physic, and the pill
That leaves the heart sick and o'erturns the will.
MIDDLETON, *Blurt Master Constable.* iii, 1.

O, pardon me, thou bleeding piece of earth,
That I am meek and gentle with these butchers!
Julius Cæsar.   iii, 1.

Not so sick, my lord,
As she is troubled with thick-coming fancies.
Macbeth.   v, 3.

So liv'd our sires, ere doctors learn'd to kill,
And multiplied with theirs the weekly bill.
DRYDEN, *To John Dryden, Esq.*   l. 71.

But when ill indeed,
E'en dismissing the doctor don't always succeed.
COLMAN (the Younger), *Broad Grins.*   Lodgings.

Every other day take a drop of water,
You 'll be better soon, or at least you oughter.
BISHOP GEO. W. DOANE, *Lines on Homeopathy.*

Diseases desperate grown
By desperate appliance are relieved, or not at all.
Hamlet.   iv, 3, l. 9.

The doctors are our friends ; let 's please them well,
For though they kill but slow, they are certain.
BEAUMONT AND FLETCHER, *Spanish Curate.*

Some maladies are rich and precious and only to be ac-
quired by the right of inheritance or purchased with
gold.
HAWTHORNE, *Mosses from an Old Manse.*

A man's own observation, what he finds good of, and
what he finds hurt of, is the best physic to preserve
health.
BACON, *Essays.*   Of Regimen of Health.

So long as people are subject to disease and death, they
will run after physicians, however much they may
deride them.
LA BRUYÈRE.

If we read the history of disorders, we are astonished that men live ; if of cures, we are still more astonished that they die.

COLTON, *Lacon.*

Medicine is to be praised when it is in the hands of a physician that is learned, grave, wise, stayed and of experience.

ANTONIE of Guevara, *Familiar Epistle.*

It is with diseases of the mind, as with those of the body : we are half dead before we understand our disorder, and half cured when we do.

COLTON, *Lacon.*

Polygamy ought to be obligatory on physicians. It would be only just to compel those who depopulate the world to repopulate it a little.

ANON.

I feel not within me those sordid and unchristian desires of my profession ; I do not secretly implore and wish for plagues, rejoice at famines.

BROWNE, *Religio Medici.*

Of the professions, it may be said, that soldiers are becoming too popular, parsons too lazy, physicians too mercenary, and lawyers too powerful.

COLTON, *Lacon.*

Courage, man ; the hurt cannot be much.
No, 't is not so deep as a well, nor so wide as a church-door ; but 't is enough, 't will serve.

Romeo and Juliet. iii, 1, 1. 99.

Physicians, of all men, are most happy ; whatever good success soever they have, the world proclaimeth ; and what faults they commit, the earth covereth.

QUARLES, *Hieroglyphics of the Life of Man.*

Physicians must discover the weaknesses of the human mind, and even condescend to humour them, or they will never be called in to cure the infirmities of the body.

COLTON, *Lacon.*

I firmly believe that if the whole materia medica could be sunk to the bottom of the sea, it would be all the better for mankind and all the worse for the fishes.

HOLMES, *Lecture before Harvard Med. School.*

O health! health! the blessing of the rich! the riches of the poor! who can buy thee at too dear a rate, since there is no enjoying the world without thee.

BEN JONSON, *Volpone.*

As Adrian VI. said, he is very necessary to a populous country, for were it not for the physician, men would live so long and grow so thick, that one could not live for the other.

HOWELL, *Familiar Letters.*

It is better to have recourse to a quack, if he can cure our disorder, although he cannot explain it, than to a physician, if he can explain our disease, but cannot cure it.

COLTON, *Lacon.*

Educator—Philosopher—Scientist

Deep versed in books.

JOHN MILTON, *Paradise Regained.*

Educator—Philosopher—Scientist

Map me no maps.
>> FIELDING, *Rape upon Rape.*

O, what learning is!
>> *Romeo and Juliet.* iii, 3.

Knowledge is power.
>> BACON, *Meditationes Sacræ.*

Deep versed in books.
>> MILTON, *Paradise Regained.* Bk. IV, l. 327.

A progeny of learning.
>> SHERIDAN, *The Rivals.* i, 2.

The march of intellect.
>> SOUTHEY, *Colloquies.* Vol. II. The Doctor.

Education makes the man.
>> CAWTHORNE, *Birth and Education of Genius.*

All jargon of the schools.
>> PRIOR, *Ode on Exodus* iii, 14.

By my penny of observation.
>> *Love's Labour 's Lost.* iii, 1.

Wisdom of our ancestors.
>> BURKE, *Thoughts on Cause of Present Discontent.*

When wine is in, wit is out.
>> Italian saying.

To philosophise is to doubt.
>> MONTAIGNE.

It seems the part of wisdom.
>> COWPER, *The Task.* Bk. IV, l. 336.

I know a hawk from a handsaw.
>> *Hamlet.* ii, 2, l. 394.

Each mind has its own method.
EMERSON, *Essays.* Intellect.

Science is organised knowledge.
SPENCER, *Education.* Ch. 2.

Whose cockloft is unfurnished.
RABELAIS, *Pro. to Fifth Book.*

Small Latin, and less Greek.
BEN JONSON, *To the Memory of Shakespeare.*

An undevout astronomer is mad.
YOUNG, *Night Thoughts.* N. ix, l. 1267.

Doubt is the key of knowledge.
Persian saying.

Fools are the wise man's ladder.
ANON.

Deeper than e'er plummet sounded.
The Tempest. iii, 3.

In earthly mire philosophy may slip.
SCOTT, *The Poacher.*

For I am nothing if not critical.
Othello. ii, 1.

Common sense is not a common thing.
VALAINCOURT.

The best lesson is that of example.
LA HARPE.

Wit and wisdom are born with a man.
SELDEN, *Learning.*

The mind 's the standard of the man.
WATTS, *Horæ Lyricæ.* Bk. II. False Greatness.

Human science is uncertain guess.
PRIOR, *Solomon.* Bk. I, l. 740.

Adversity's sweet milk, philosophy.
Romeo and Juliet. iii, 3, l. 55.

No man can be wise on an empty stomach.
> ELIOT, *Adam Bede.* Bk. X, ch. 2.

No man at one time can be wise and love.
> HERRICK, *Hesperides.* 1. 230.

No beauty 's like the beauty of the mind.
> COOKE, *How a Man may Choose a Good Wife.* v, 3.

The glory of a firm capacious mind,
> HOMER, *Odyssey.* Bk. IV, 1. 262. Pope's trans.

Necessity, the mother of invention.
> WYCHERLEY, *Love in a Wood.* iii, 3.

Study is the apprenticeship of life.
> FLEURY.

Enflamed with the study of learning.
> MILTON, *Tractate of Education.*

O this learning, what a thing it is!
> *Taming of the Shrew.* i, 2, 1. 160.

Ignorance is the mother of all evils.
> MONTAIGNE.

Necessity is the mother of invention.
> FRANCK, *Twin Rivals.*

'T is education forms the common mind.
> POPE, *Moral Essays.* Ep. i, 1. 149.

Knowledge comes, but wisdom lingers.
> TENNYSON, *Locksley Hall.* St. 71.

The march of the human mind is slow.
> BURKE, *Speech on Conciliation of America.*

Philosophy will clip an angel's wings.
> KEATS, *Lamia.*

One science only will one genius fit.
> POPE, *Essay on Criticism.* Pt. I, 1. 60.

Necessity is a severe schoolmistress.
> MONTAIGNE.

Let these describe the undescribable.
> Byron, *Childe Harold.*   Canto iv, st. 53.

Out of too much learning become mad.
> Burton, *Anatomy of Melancholy.*
> Pt. III, sec. 4, memb. 1.

Philosophy is nothing but Discretion.
> Selden, *Table Talk.*   Philosophy.

The heart is wiser than the intellect.
> Holland, *Kathrina.*   Pt. II, st. 9.

There is no knowledge that is not power.
> Emerson, *Society and Solitude.*   Old Age.

For never, never, wicked man was wise.
> Homer, *Odyssey.*   Bk. II, l. 320.   Pope's trans.

A faultless body and a blameless mind.
> Homer, *Odyssey.*   Bk. III, l. 138.   Pope's trans.

And men talk only to conceal the mind.
> Young, *Love of Fame.*   Satire II, l. 207.

Learning is but an adjunct to ourself.
> *Love's Labour's Lost.*   iv, 3.

Stern men with empires in their brains.
> Lowell, *Biglow Papers.*   Series II, No. 2.

There are few things that we know well.
> Vauvenargues.

A little learning is a dangerous thing.
> Pope, *Essay on Criticism.*   Pt. II, l. 15.

Be wisely worldly but not worldly wise.
> Quarles.

Diffused knowledge immortalises itself.
> Mackintosh, *Vindiciæ Gallicæ.*

Where bright-eyed Science watches round.
> Gray, *Ode for Music.*

Study is like the heaven's glorious sun.
> *Love's Labour's Lost.*   i, 1.

Whose little body lodged a mighty mind.
>> HOMER, *Iliad*. Bk. V, 1. 999.   Pope's trans.

Cunning is to wisdom as an ape to a man.
>> PENN.

Strength of mind is exercise, not rest.
>> POPE, *Essay on Man.*   Ep. ii, 1. 104.

Pay as you go is the philosopher's stone.
>> RANDOLPH.

Pursuit of knowledge under difficulties.
>> Title given by Lord BROUGHAM to a book.   1830.

Who are little wise the best fools be.
>> DONNE, *The Triple Fool.*

This is a man's invention and his hand.
>> *As You Like It.*   iv, 3, l. 29.

In youth and beauty wisdom is but rare !
>> HOMER, *Odyssey.*   Bk. VII, 1. 379.   Pope's trans.

Better a witty fool than a foolish wit.
>> *Twelfth Night.*   i, 5, 1. 40 (quoted).

Sweet food of sweetly uttered knowledge.
>> SIDNEY, *Defence of Poesy.*

Catch no more fish than you can salt down.
>> ANON.

Who can direct when all pretend to know ?
>> GOLDSMITH, *The Traveller.*   1. 64.

Some rise by sin, and some by virtue fall.
>> *Measure for Measure.*   ii, 1, 1. 38.

We work to turn our hopes to certainties.
>> COOLIDGE.

Hope is a mine of riches to the poor man.
>> ANON.

One is rich when one is sure of the morrow.
>> CHEVALIER.

He hath indeed better bettered expectation.
Much Ado About Nothing. i, 1.

Serves but to brighten all our future days.
JOHN BROWN, *Barbarossa.*

If wishes were horses, beggars might ride.
ANON.

Some are weather-wise, some are otherwise.
FRANKLIN, *Poor Richard.* 1779.

Like truths of science waiting to be caught.
TENNYSON, *The Golden Year.*

Too much to know is to know naught but fame.
Love's Labour 's Lost. i, 1, l. 92.

As for me, all I know is that I know nothing.
SOCRATES-PLATO, *Phædrus.* Sec. 235.

How prone to doubt, how cautious are the wise !
HOMER, *Odyssey.* Bk. XIII, l. 375. Pope's trans.

Knowledge is more than equivalent to force.
SAMUEL JOHNSON, *Rasselas.* Ch. 13.

In years that bring the philosophic mind.
WORDSWORTH, *Intimations of Immortality.*
St. 10.

Be not a baker if your head be of butter.
Spanish Saying.

Every philosopher is cousin to an atheist.
DE MUSSET.

He was a scholar, and a ripe and good one.
King Henry VIII. iv, 2.

Send thee manly patience with thy learning.
BEAUMONT AND FLETCHER, *Elder Brother.* ii, 3.

I know no disease of the soul but ignorance.
BEN JONSON, *Discoveries.*

Thou wert my guide, philosopher, and friend.

POPE, *Essay on Man*. Ep. iv, 1. 390.

One eare it heard, at the other out it went.

CHAUCER, *Troilus and Creseide*. Bk. IV, 1, 435.

Who is too old to learn is too old to teach.

ANON.

For 't is the mind that makes the body rich.

Taming of the Shrew. iv, 3, 1. 174.

And gladly wolde he lerne, and gladly teche.

CHAUCER, *Canterbury Tales*. Prologue 1. 310.

A little too wise they say do ne'er live long.

MIDDLETON, *The Phœnix.*, i, 1.

Men of polite learning and a liberal education.

HENRY, *Commentaries*. The Acts, ch. 10.

Fair Science frown'd not on his humble birth.

GRAY, *The Epitaph*.

Knowledge is the knowing that we cannot know.

EMERSON, *Society and Solitude*.

And Frenche she spake ful fayre and fetisly.

CHAUCER, *Canterbury Tales*. Prologue, 1. 120.

The elegant simplicity of the three per cents.

STOWELL, *Campbell's Chancellors*.

Of whom to be dispraised were no small praise.

MILTON, *Paradise Regained*. Bk. III, 1. 56.

I will show myself highly fed and lowly taught.

All 's Well that Ends Well. ii, 2.

He who tries to prove too much, proves nothing.

ANON.

Faith, thou hast some crotchets in thy head now.

Merry Wives of Windsor. ii, 1.

Wisdom is to the soul what health is to the body.

DE SAINT-RÉAL.

Measure your mind's height by the shade it casts.
                    BROWNING, *Paracelsus.*   ii.

Not body enough to cover his mind decently with.
            SYDNEY SMITH, *Lady Holland's Memoir.*
                                    v, 1, p. 258.

We know what we are, but know not what we may be.
                            Hamlet.   iv, 5, l. 42.

Knowledge bloweth up, but charity buildeth up.
            BACON, *Rendering of I. Cor.*   viii, 1.

Science seldom renders men amiable ; women, never.
                                    BEAUCHÊNE.

What is all Knowledge, too, but recorded Experience.
            CARLYLE, *Essays.*   On History.

The increase of knowledge increases the need of it.
                                    ANON.

Heaven first taught letters for some wretch's aid.
            POPE, *Eloisa to Abelard.*   l. 51.

All our wisdom consists of but servile prejudices.
                                    ROUSSEAU.

When dunces are satiric, I take it for a panegyric.
                                    SWIFT.

Be wise with speed ; a fool at forty is a fool indeed.
            YOUNG, *Love of Fame.*   Satire ii, l. 281.

No one ever gets wiser by doing wrong, nor stronger.
            RUSKIN, *Queen of the Air.*

There is no other Royal path which leads to geometry.
            EUCLID, *to Ptolemy.*   Bk. II, ch. 4.

The road to knowledge crosses the plains of ignorance.
                                    ANON.

Be wise ; soar not too high to fall ; but stoop to rise.
            MASSINGER, *Duke of Milan.*   i, 2, l. 45.

The wise man gets his wisdom from those who have none.
                            Arabian Saying.

A wise man will make more opportunities than he finds.
BACON.

Learning is not wisdom any more than cloth is clothes.
ANON.

Minds that have little to confer find little to perceive.
WORDSWORTH, *Yes! Thou Art Fair.*

That stone . . . philosophers in vain have so long sought.
MILTON, *Paradise Lost.* Bk. III, l. 60.

What is mind? No matter. What is matter? Never mind.
KEY. On authority of F. J. Furnivall.

Superstition excites storms ; philosophy appeases them.
VOLTAIRE.

To scoff at philosophy is to act as a true philosopher.
PASCAL.

Every fool can find fault that wise men cannot remedy.
ANON.

Speak to me as to thy thinking, as thou dost ruminate.
Othello. iii, 3.

A handful of common sense is worth a bushel of learning.
Spanish Saying.

He gets wisdom cheaply who gets it at another's expense.
PLAUTUS.

None are less eager to learn than they who know nothing.
SUARD.

Wise men learn more from fools than fools from the wise.
CATO.

A wise man sometimes changes his mind, but a fool
never.
Old Saying.

I am rather bound to guard you against loose scholarship.
DOANE, *St. Agnes Addresses.*

8

Knowledge comes of learning well retain'd, unfruitful else.

> DANTE, *Vision of Paradise*. Canto v, l. 41.

Thou shouldst not have been old till thou hadst been wise.

> *King Lear*. i, 5, l. 48.

There 's no art to find the mind's construction in the face.

> *Macbeth*. i, 4, l. 11.

He who binds his soul to knowledge, steals the keys of heaven.

> WILLIS, *Scholar of Thibet Ben Khorat*. ii.

Ripe in wisdom was he, but patient, and simple, and childlike.

> LONGFELLOW, *Evangeline*. Pt. I, iii, l. 11.

There is no necessity for proving the existence of light.

> From the French.

Philosophy, well understood, is an excellent road to heaven.

> CHASTEL.

Even to rebuild the temple the schools must not be closed.

> From the Talmud.

Languages begin by being a music, and end by being an algebra.

> AMPÈRE.

Be wiser than other people if you can, but do not tell them so.

> CHESTERFIELD, *Letters*. Dublin Castle,
> Nov. 19, 1745.

He who pretends to know everything, proves that he knows nothing.

> LE BAILLY.

He that pryeth into the clouds may be struck with a thunderbolt.

ANON.

Double ignorance is where a man is ignorant of his ignorance.

PLATO.

For love is ever the beginning of Knowledge, as fire is of light.

CARLYLE, *Essays.* Death of Goethe.

There is not much to a man who is not wiser to-day than yesterday.

LINCOLN, *Maxims.*

A life of knowledge is not often a life of injury and crime.

SYDNEY SMITH, *Pleasures of Knowledge.*

Education, we are often told, is a drawing out of the faculties.

LOWELL. Harvard anniversary.

Seek, and you will find, in this world, as well as in the next.

CHESTERFIELD, *Letters.* Feb. 16, 1784.

What the fool does in the end, the wise man does in the beginning.

From the Spanish.

It is the path of the passions that has conducted me to philosophy.

ROUSSEAU.

Nothing doth more hurt in a state than that cunning men pass for wise.

BACON.

A prison is never narrow when the imagination can range in it at will.

ANON.

Ideas are a capital that bears interest only in the hands of talent.

RIVAROL.

They have been at a great feast of languages, and stolen the scraps.

Love's Labour 's Lost. v, 1.

Better to sit with a wise man in prison than with a fool in paradise.

ANON.

Sheer necessity, — the proper parent of an art so nearly allied to invention.

SHERIDAN, *The Critic.*

Art imitates nature, and necessity is the mother of invention.

FRANCK, *Northern Memoirs.* 1658, p. 52.

Every addition to true knowledge is an addition to human power.

MANN, *Lectures on Education.* Lec. i.

Science moves but slowly, slowly creeping on from point to point.

TENNYSON, *Locksley Hall.*

Science when well digested is nothing but good sense and reason.

STANISLAUS (Poland), *Maxims.* No. 43.

Nothing can be truer than fairy wisdom. It is as true as sunbeams.

JERROLD, *Jerrold's Wit.* Fairy Tales.

Take the advice of a friend, and submit thy inventions to his censure.

FULLER, *Holy and Profane States.* Bk. III. Fancy.

Few men make themselves masters of the things they write or speak.

SELDEN, *Table Talk.* Learning.

I would by no means wish a daughter of mine to be a
progeny of learning.

SHERIDAN, *The Rivals.* i, 2.

Only by knowledge of that which is not Thyself, shall
thyself be learned.

MEREDITH, *Know Thyself.*

Science is the great antidote to the poison of enthusiasm
and superstition.

ADAM SMITH, *Wealth of Nations.*

Bk. V, pt. iii, art. 3.

Only when genius is married to science can the highest
results be produced.

SPENCER, *Education.* Ch. i.

He had been eight years upon a project for extracting
sunbeams out of cucumbers.

SWIFT, *Gulliver's Travels.* Pt. III, ch. v.

There is in the smallest thing a message for us could we
but read it.

ANON.

By labour and intent study, which I take it to be my portion in this life.

MILTON, *Reason of Church Government.*

Int. Bk. II.

A man of sense carefully avoids any particular character
in his dress.

CHESTERFIELD, *Letters.* Dec. 30, 1748.

The child is wiser in his innocence than the philosopher
in his wisdom.

From the Spanish.

As turning the logs will make a dull fire burn, so changes
of study a dull brain.

LONGFELLOW, *Driftwood. Table Talk.*

I doubt the wisdom of being too wise, and I see much
wisdom in some folly.

HUBBARD, *Philistine.*

There is four hundred times as much learning in the world as there is wisdom.

JOSH BILLINGS.

A fool can ask more questions in an hour than seven wise men can answer in a year.

Old Saying.

Mediocre minds usually condemn what is beyond the reach of their understanding.

ROCHEFOUCAULD.

To be conscious that you are ignorant is a great step to knowledge.

DISRAELI, *Sybil.* Bk. I, ch. v.

Our knowledge is the amassed thought and experience of innumerable minds.

EMERSON, *Letters and Social Aims.*

To discuss an opinion with a fool is like carrying a lantern before a blind man.

DE GASTON.

Every kind of persecution for opinions is incompatible with sound philosophy.

COLTON, *Lacon.*

Angling may be said to be so like the mathematics that it can never be fully learnt.

WALTON, *Complete Angler.* Preface.

A philosopher is a fool who torments himself during life, to be spoken of when dead.

D'ALEMBERT.

A grain of gold will gild a great surface, but not so much as a grain of wisdom.

THOREAU, *Yankee in Canada.*

Doubt is the vestibule which all must pass before they can enter into the temple of wisdom.

COLTON, *Lacon.*

Reflection increases the vigour of the mind, as exercise does the strength of the body.

> LÉVIS.

A kind of semi-Solomon, half-knowing everything, from the cedar to the hyssop.

> MACAULAY (About Brougham), *Life and Letters.* Vol. I, p. 175.

Learning without thought is labour lost ; thought without learning is perilous.

> CONFUCIUS, *Analects.* Bk. II, ch. xv.

This same philosophy is a good horse in the stable, but an arrant jade on a journey.

> GOLDSMITH, *The Good-Natured Man.* Act i.

Knowledge is the only fountain, both of the love and the principles of human liberty.

> WEBSTER, *Address at Bunker Hill,* June 17, 1843.

There are more things in heaven and earth, Horatio, than are dreamt of in your philosophy.

> *Hamlet.* i, 5, 1. 166.

The true, strong, and sound mind is the mind that can embrace equally great things and small.

> JAMES BOSWELL, *Life of Johnson.* 1778.

Philosophy goes no further than probabilities, and in every assertion keeps a doubt in reserve.

> FROUDE, *Short Studies on Great Subjects.*

For I do not distinguish them by the eye, but by the mind, which is the proper judge of the man.

> SENECA, *Of a Happy Life.* Ch. i.

Knowledge, in truth, is the great sun in the firmament. Life and power are scattered with all its beams.

> WEBSTER, *Bunker Hill Monument Address.* 1825.

Pedantry crams our heads with learned lumber, and takes out our brains to make room for it.

> COLTON, *Lacon.*

Life is long enough for him who knows how to use it.
Working and thinking extend its limits.

VOLTAIRE.

The astronomer thinks of the stars, the naturalist of
nature, the philosopher of himself.

FONTENELLE.

Philosophy writes treatises on old age and friendship;
Nature makes those on youth and love.

D'ALEMBERT.

He who creates a desire to learn in a child, does more
than he who forces it to learn much.

ANON.

Thou hast most traitorously corrupted the youth of the
realm in erecting a grammar-school.

King Henry VI. Pt. II, iv, 7.

The riches of scholarship and the benignities of literature defy fortune and outlive calamity.

LOWELL, *Books and Libraries.*

Philosophy triumphs easily over past evils and future
evils, but present evils triumph over it.

ROCHEFOUCAULD, *Maxims.*

Knowledge is, indeed, that which, next to virtue, truly
and essentially raises one man above another.

ADDISON, *The Guardian.* Let. of Alexander, No. 111.

For all knowledge and wonder (which is the seed of
knowledge) is an impression of pleasure in itself.

BACON, *Advancement of Learning.* Bk. I.

The teacher who can give his pupils pleasure in their
work shall be crowned with laurels.

HUBBARD, *Philistine.*

I am no believer in the theory of education which under-
values the separate items that make it up.

DOANE, *St. Agnes Addresses.* 1885.

Only themselves understand themselves, and the like of
themselves, as Souls only understand Souls.
>> WHITMAN, *Children of Adam.*

I shall detain you no longer . . . I will point ye out the
right path of a virtuous and noble education.
>> MILTON, *Tractate of Education.*

It is not the passing through these learnings that hurts
us, but the dwelling and sticking about them.
>> BEN JONSON, *Discoveries.*

A child becomes for his parents, according to the education he receives, a blessing or a chastisement.
>> J. PETIT-SENN.

So much one man can do,
That does both act and know.
>> MARVELL, *On Cromwell's Return from Ireland.*

And he is oft the wisest man,
Who is not wise at all.
>> WORDSWORTH, *Oak and the Broom.*

He never says a foolish thing,
Nor ever does a wise one.
>> EARL OF ROCHESTER, *On Charles II's.*
>> *bedchamber door.*

Earthly godfathers of Heaven's lights
That give a name to every fixed star.
>> *Love's Labour 's Lost.* i, 1.

Stuff the head
With all such reading as was never read.
>> POPE, *The Dunciad.* Bk. IV, l. 247.

Full oft we see
Cold Wisdom waiting on superfluous Folly.
>> *All 's Well that Ends Well.* i, 1, l. 115.

Institute
A course of learning and ingenious studies.
>> *Taming of the Shrew.* i, 1.

Science is a first-rate piece of furniture for a man's upper chamber, if he has common sense on the ground floor.

> HOLMES, *Poet at Breakfast Table.* v.

Knowledge is of two kinds. We know a subject ourselves, or we know where we can find information upon it.

> JAMES BOSWELL, *Life of Johnson.* 1775.

Greece, so much praised for her wisdom, never produced but seven wise men : judge of the number of fools!

> GRÉCOURT.

Friendship

The only rose without thorns is friendship.

MLLE. DE SCUDÉRI.

Friendship

Farewell, my friend.

Winter's Tale. iv, 4.

A favourite has no friend.

GRAY, *On a Favourite Cat Drowned.*

Friends of my better days.

HALLECK, *On death of Jos. R. Drake.*

We met,—'t was in a crowd.

BAYLY, *We Met.*

Most friendship is feigning.

As You Like It. ii, 7, 1. 181.

Friendship 's full of dregs.

Timon of Athens, i, 2, 1. 240.

Prosperity makes few friends.

VAUVENARGUES.

Friendship 's the wine of life.

YOUNG, *Night Thoughts.* N. ii, 1. 582.

True friends are great riches.

ANON.

The vanquished have no friends.

SOUTHEY, *Joan of Arc.* Bk. III, 1. 465.

Friendship is a sheltering tree.

COLERIDGE, *Youth and Age.*

My friends were poor but honest.

All 's Well that Ends Well. i, 3.

Love is the marrow of friendship.

HOWELL, *Familiar Letters.* Bk. I, Sec. i, Let. 17.

125

One is judged by his friendships.

ANON.

Mislike me not for my complexion.
Merchant of Venice. ii, 1.

Better new friend than an old foe.
SPENSER, *Faerie Queene.* Bk. I, canto ii, st. 27.

A true friend is forever a friend.
MACDONALD, *Marquis of Lossie.* Ch. lxxi.

Out upon this half-fac'd fellowship!
King Henry IV. Pt. I, i, 3, 1. 208.

To friendship every burden 's light.
GAY, *The Hare with Many Friends.*

Friends are as dangerous as enemies.
DE QUINCEY, *Essay on Schlosser's Lit'y History.*

A faithful friend loves to the end.

ANON.

Absence makes the heart grow fonder.
BAYLY, *Isle of Beauty.*

Friendly counsel cuts off many foes.
King Henry VI. Pt. I, iii, 1.

Friendship—one soul in two bodies.

PYTHAGORAS.

Friendship is Love without his wings!
BYRON, *L'Amitié est l'Amour sans Ailes.* St. 1.

Love and friendship exclude each other.
DE LA BRUYÈRE, *Manners of the
Present Age.* Ch. v.

Keep good company and you 'll be of them.
From the Chinese.

Friends are not so easily made as kept.
MARQUIS OF HALIFAX, *Maxims of State.* xii.

And out of mind as soon as out of sight.

LORD BROOKE, *Mustapha*.

Friend more divine than all divinities.

ELIOT, *Spanish Gypsy*. Bk. IV.

The union of hearts, the union of hands.

MORRIS, *Flag of our Union*.

Flattery is monstrous in a true friend.

FORD, *The Lover's Melancholy*. i, 1.

He who reckons ten friends has not one.

MALESHERBES.

His heart and hand both open and both free.

Troilus and Cressida. iv, 5.

He that doth lend doth lose his friend.

ANON.

I thought you and he were hand-in-glove.

SWIFT, *Polite Conversation*. Dia. ii.

A friend is worth all hazards we can run.

YOUNG, *Night Thoughts*. N. ii, l. 571.

From wine what sudden friendship springs.

GAY, *Squire and His Cur*.

The only way to have a friend is to be one.

EMERSON, *Essays*. Of Experience.

Friendship stops where borrowing begins.

ANON.

Friends in distress make troubles less.

From the French.

He makes no friend who never made a foe.

TENNYSON, *Idylls of the King*.

Launcelot and Elaine. l. 1109.

A brother is a friend given by nature.

G. LEGOUVÉ.

I do desire we may be better strangers.

As You Like It. iii, 2.

Trust not him that hath once broken faith.

King Henry VI. Pt. III, iv, 4, 1. 30.

A good friend is one's nearest relation.

ANON.

Above our life we love a steadfast friend.

MARLOWE, *Hero and Leander.* Sestiad II.

Women, like princes, find few real friends.

LYTTLETON, *Advice to a Lady.* St. 2.

Better an open enemy than a false friend.

From the German.

A fellow-feeling makes one wondrous kind.

GARRICK, *Prologue on quitting stage.* 1776.

I do know him by his gait ; he is a friend.

Julius Cæsar. i, 3.

True friendship is a plant of slow growth.

WASHINGTON, *Social Maxims.* Friendship.

The only rose without thorns is friendship.

MLLE. DE SCUDÉRI.

Adversity is the touchstone of friendship.

ANON.

Nature teaches beasts to know their friends.

SHAKESPEARE, *Coriolanus.* ii, 1.

I much commend to make a foe into a friend.

ANON.

I was never less alone than when by myself.

GIBBON, *Memoir.* Vol. i.

A friend to everybody is a friend to nobody.

Spanish Saying.

The friends of our friends are our friends.

ANON.

The endearing elegance of female friendship.

SAMUEL JOHNSON, *Rasselas.* Ch. 41.

To God, thy countrie, and thy friend be true.
> VAUGHAN, *Rules and Lessons.* St. 8.

A friend should bear his friend's infirmities.
> *Julius Cæsar.* iv, 3, l. 86.

Neighbours are good when they are neighbourly.
> ANON.

Plenty, as well as want, can separate friends.
> COWLEY, *Davideis.* Bk. III, l. 205.

Angels from friendship gather half their joys.
> YOUNG, *Night Thoughts.* N. ii, l. 575.

I would be friends with you and have your love.
> *Merchant of Venice.* i, 3, l. 139,

Friendship multiplies joys and divides grief.
> ANON.

I would help others, out of a fellow-feeling.
> BURTON, *Anatomy of Melancholy.*
> Democritus to the Reader.

A man dies as often as he loses his friends.
> BACON.

To lose a friend is the greatest of all losses.
> SYRUS.

Fortune makes friends, misfortune tries them.
> ANON.

Who ceases to be a friend, never was a friend.
> ANON.

The joy that is not shared has an early death.
> ANON.

If you would be rid of a bore, lend him money.
> ANON.

A true friendship is as wise as it is tender.
> THOREAU, *Week.*

Old acquaintances are better than new friends.
> DU DEFFAND.

9

Friends tie their purse with a cob-web thread.
ANON.

The friend of him who has no friend—Religion !
JAMES MONTGOMERY, *The Pillow.*

Fate gives us parents ; choice gives us friends.
DELILLE.

Two friends, two bodies with one soul inspir'd.
HOMER, *Iliad.* Bk. XVI, 1. 267.   Pope's trans.

Love has compensations that friendship has not.
MONTAIGNE.

Friendship can smooth the front of rude despair.
CAMBRIDGE, *The Scribleriad.* Bk. I, 1. 196.

If good advice were horses, everyone might ride.
ANON.

Affection is the broadest basis of good in life.
ELIOT, *Daniel Deronda.* Bk. V, ch. 35.

With women, friendship ends when rivalry begins.
From the French.

Where you have friends you should not go to inns.
ELIOT, *Agatha.*

But let not therefore my good friend be grieved !
Julius Cæsar.   i, 2.

True love is rare ; true friendship, still rarer.
LA FONTAINE.

Friendship is a plant that one must often water.
ANON.

Delicacy is to affection what grace is to beauty.
DE MAINTENON.

A treacherous friend is the most dangerous enemy.
FIELDING.

Trust not too much in new friends and old houses.
From the German.

However rare true love, true friendship is rarer.
ROCHEFOUCAULD.

The fewer the friendships, the better the friends.
ANON.

A good companion on the road is better than a coach.
SYRUS.

Friendship is Love, without either flowers or veil.
J. C. AND A. W. HARE, *Guesses at Truth*.

This it is to have a name in great men's fellowship.
Antony and Cleopatra. ii, 7.

A good friend is better than a near relation.
ANON.

I have found that a friend may profess, yet deceive.
BYRON, *Lines to Rev. J. T. Beecher.* St. 7.

Of humblest Friends, bright Creature! scorn not one.
WORDSWORTH, *In a Child's Album*.

No friend's a friend till (he shall) prove a friend.
BEAUMONT AND FLETCHER, *Faithful Friends*.
iii, 3, l. 50.

Poets, like friends to whom you are in debt, you hate.
WYCHERLEY, *The Plain Dealer.* Pro.

Friendship is a disinterested commerce between equals.
GOLDSMITH, *The Good-Natured Man.* i, 1.

Confidence is a plant of slow growth in an aged bosom.
PITT, *Speech.* Jan. 14, 1766.

Make not friends with an angry man or a drinking man.
ANON.

Women sometimes deceive the lover—never the friend.
MERCIER.

One good friendship will outlive forty average loves.
ANON.

Friendship makes more marriages than love does.
From the French.

Reprove your friends secretly and praise them openly.
SYRUS.

Love thyself last : cherish those hearts that hate thee.
King Henry VIII. iii, 2.

A man, sir, should keep his friendship in constant repair.
DR. JOHNSON. In conversing with Sir J. Reynolds.

Give neither counsel nor salt until you are asked for it.
ANON.

The amity that wisdom knits not, folly may easily untie.
Troilus and Cressida. ii, 3, l. 110.

To respect a friend is worse than to be deceived by him.
ROCHEFOUCAULD.

He who has a thousand friends has not a friend to spare.
Persian Saying.

If you would have friends, first learn to do without them.
HUBBARD. *Philistine.*

I have loved my friends as I do virtue, my soul, my God.
THOMAS BROWNE, *Religio Medici.* Pt. II, sec. 5.

Friendship is a shield that blunts the darts of adversity.
DE SAINT-SURIN.

Friendship is the highest degree of perfection in society.
MONTAIGNE.

Tell me your company and I will tell you what you are.
Italian Saying.

Love that which I love, and I will love thee that loves it.
THOREAU, *Early Spring.*

True love may be rare, but true friendship is still rarer.
ANON.

Broken friendship may be soldered, but it is seldom sound.
ANON.

Your companions are your mirror and show you yourself.
ANON.

Before you accept your friend eat a peck of salt with
him.

Scotch Saying.

The fallyng out of faithfull frends, is the renuying of
loue.

RICHARD EDWARDS, *Paradise of Dainty Devices.*

No. 42, st. 1.

And when he is out of sight, quickly also is he out of
mind.

À KEMPIS, *Imitation of Christ.*

He is a weak friend who cannot bear with his friend's
weakness.

ANON.

One seeks new friends only when too well known by old
ones.

DE PUISIEUX.

The man that makes the best friend will make the worst
enemy.

ANON.

A sudden thought strikes me — Let us swear an eternal
friendship.

FRERE, *The Rovers.* i, 1.

Friendship between women is only a suspension, of hos-
tilities.

From the French.

It is chance that makes brothers, but hearts that make
friends.

ANON.

Friendship often ends in love; but love, in friendship—
never.

COLTON, *Lacon.*

It is not flesh and blood, but the heart, that makes
brothers.

SCHILLER.

Procure not friends in haste, neither part with them in haste.

SOLON.

Literary friendship is a sympathy not of manners, but of feelings.

DISRAELI, *Literary Characters*. Ch. 19.

You must therefore love me, myself, if we are to be real friends.

CICERO, *De Finibus*.

Unless you bear with the faults of a friend you betray your own.

SYRUS.

Defend me from my friends ; I can defend myself from my enemies.

VILLARS, *Taking leave of Louis XIV*.

The worst of all countries is the one in which we have no friends.

From the French.

It is impossible to say all that we think, even to our truest friend.

THOREAU, *Week*.

Old friends are best. King James used to call for his old shoes.

SELDEN, *Friends*.

Time sooner or later vanquishes love : friendship alone subdues time.

D'ARCONVILLE.

A good book is the best of friends, the same to-day and forever.

TUPPER, *Proverbial Philosophy*.
Of Reading. l. 14.

Friends are the surest guard for kings, gold in time does wear away.

EDWARDS, *Damon and Pithias*.

Friendship between two women is always a plot against another one.

A. KARR.

Envy lurks at the bottom of the human heart like a viper in its hole.

HONORÉ DE BALZAC.

There is no more agreeable companion than the woman who loves us.

DE ST. PIERRE.

He that wants money, means, and content, is without three good friends.

As You Like It. iii, 2.

We awaken in others the same attitude of mind that we hold toward them.

HUBBARD, *Philistine.*

My friend is that one whom I can associate with my choicest thought.

THOREAU, *Week.*

The worst evil we have to contend with in this world is insincerity.

ANON.

A puppy plays with every pup he meets, but an old dog has few associates.

JOSH BILLINGS.

What is commonly called friendship is only a little more honour among rogues.

THOREAU, *Week.*

Friendships begin with liking or gratitude—roots that can be pulled up.

ELIOT, *Daniel Deronda.* Bk. IV, ch. xxxii.

The condition which high friendship demands is ability to do without it.

EMERSON, *Essays.* Of Friendship.

"Own kin are the worst friends," said the fox when he saw the dogs after him.

ANON.

I believe in sunshine, fresh air, friendship, calm sleep, beautiful thoughts.

HUBBARD, *Philistine.*

The man I meet with is not often so instructive as the silence he breaks.

THOREAU, *Letters.*

Friendship that begins between a man and a woman will soon change its name.

ANON.

What betterer or properer can we call our own than the riches of our friends.

Timon of Athens. i, 2.

To forgive a fault in another is more sublime than to be faultless one's self.

GEORGE SAND.

He who has neither friend nor enemy, is without talents, powers, or energy.

LAVATER.

Descend a step in choosing thy wife ; ascend a step in choosing thy friend.

From the Talmud.

If you would not have your enemy know your secret, tell it not to your friend.

Persian Saying.

So live with thy friend that if he become thine enemy he can do thee no harm.

TULLY.

Pure friendship is something which men of an inferior intellect can never taste.

DE LA BRUYÈRE, *Manners of the Present Age.* Ch. v.

If you want enemies, excel others : if you want friends,
let others excel you.

COLTON, Lacon.

The way to make friendships that will last long is to be
long in making them.

ANON.

Reason is the torch of friendship, judgment its guide,
tenderness its aliment.

DE BONALD.

There are some men whose enemies are to be pitied
much, and their friends more.

COLTON, Lacon.

Thy friend has a friend and thy friend's friend has a
friend, so be discreet.

TALMUD.

Animals are such agreeable friends—they ask no questions, they pass no criticisms.

ELIOT, Spanish Gypsy.   Bk. III.

A woman's friendship is, as a rule, the legacy of love or
the alms of indifference.

ANON.

Happy he who finds a friend ; without that second self
one lives but half of life.

CHÊNEDOLLÉ.

When we do soar, the company grows thinner and thinner
till there is none at all.

THOREAU, Letters.

The friendship of a man is often a support ; that of a
woman is always a consolation.

ROCHEPÈDRE.

Wait not till I invite thee, but observe that I am glad to
see thee when thou comest.

THOREAU, Week.

No one can be provident of his time who is not prudent in the choice of his company.

TAYLOR, *Holy Living and Dying.* Ch. I, sec. i.

Complete success alienates man from his fellows, but suffering makes kinsmen of us all.

HUBBARD, *Philistine.*

It is equally impossible to forget our friends, and to make them answer to our ideal.

THOREAU, *Week.*

Women go further in love than most men, but men go further in friendship than women.

DE LA BRUYÈRE.

For a companion, I require one who will make an equal demand on me with my own genius.

THOREAU, *Week*

Our happiness in this world depends chiefly on the affections we are able to inspire.

DE PRASLIN.

True friendship is like sound health, the value of it is seldom known until it be lost.

COLTON, *Lacon.*

All who joy would win
Must share it,—Happiness was born a twin.

BYRON, *Don Juan.* Canto II, st. 172.

The language of friendship is not words, but meanings. It is an intelligence above language.

THOREAU, *Week.*

Some friendships are made by nature, some by contract, some by interest, and some by souls.

TAYLOR, *Discourse of Nature (etc.) of Friendship.*

True happiness consists not in the multitude of friends, but in the worth and choice.

BEN JONSON, *Cynthia's Revels.* iii, 2.

We need the friendship of a man in great trials ; of a
woman in the affairs of every-day life.

Thomas.

How few friendships would be lasting if we knew what
our best friends say of us in our absence.

Pascal.

I hate the prostitution of the name of friendship to
signify modish and worldly alliances.

Emerson, *Essays*. Of Friendship.

For whoever knows how to return a kindness he has
received must be a friend above all price.

Sophocles, *Philoctetes*.

Moral virtues are the foundation of society in general,
and of friendship in particular.

Chesterfield, *Letters*. July 20, 1749.

In what concerns you much, do not think you have
companions ; know that you are alone in the world.

Thoreau, *Letters*.

False friends, like our shadows, keep close to us in sunshine, only to leave us with the first cloud.

Bovee.

No quality will get a man more friends than a disposition
to admire the qualities of others.

Boswell, *Life of Johnson*. Vol. II, p. 22.

It is a rule in friendship, when Distrust enters in at the
fore-gate, Love goes out at the postern.

Howell, *Familiar Letters*. Bk. I, Sec. v, Let. 20.

We must accept or refuse one another as we are. I
could tame a hyena more easily than my friend.

Thoreau, *Week*.

It is better to sacrifice one's love of sarcasm than to in-
dulge it at the expense of a friend.

Anon.

We know the value of a fortune when we have gained it, and that of a friend when we have lost it.

PETIT-SENN.

Friendship closes its eye, rather than see the moon eclipst; while malice denies that it is ever at the full.

J. C. AND A. W. HARE, *Guesses at Truth.*

For to cast away a virtuous friend, I call as bad as to cast away one's own life, which one loves best.

SOPHOCLES, *Œdipus Tyrannis.*

Many a friend will tell us our faults without reserve, who will not so much as hint at our follies.

CHESTERFIELD, *Letters.* July 1, 1748.

Nature and religion are the bands of friendship, excellence and usefulness are its great endearments.

TAYLOR, *Discourse of Nature (etc.) of Friendship.*

As some heads cannot carry much wine, so it would seem that I cannot bear so much society as you can.

THOREAU, *Letters.*

It is always safe to learn, even from our enemies—seldom safe to venture to instruct, even our friends.

COLTON, *Lacon.*

Doing all we can to promote our friend's happiness is better than to drink continually to his prosperity.

ANON.

There is good sense in the Spanish saying, "Tell me whom you live with, and I will tell you what you are."

CHESTERFIELD, *Letters.* Oct. 12, 1748.

We have three kinds of friends : those who love us; those who are indifferent to us, and those who hate us.

CHAMFORT.

There is no man so friendless but what he can find a
friend sincere enough to tell him disagreeable truths.
BULWER-LYTTON, *What Will He Do with It.*
Bk. II, ch. xiv.

Life is to be fortified by many friendships. To love, and
to be loved, is the greatest happiness of existence.
SYDNEY SMITH, *Of Friendship*   Lady Holland's
Memoir.

Future—Hope—Ambition

Don't never prophesy onless you know !
JAMES RUSSELL LOWELL.

Future—Hope—Ambition

Hope on, hope ever.

ANON.

Hope is a sarcasm.

MERCIER, La fille du prêtre.

To hope is to enjoy.

SAINT-LAMBERT.

Ambition has no rest!

BULWER–LYTTON, Richelieu. iii, 1.

O my prophetic soul!

Hamlet. i, 5.

Nor care beyond to-day.

GRAY, On Distant Prospect of Eton.

Is Man a child of hope?

WORDSWORTH, The Excursion. Bk. V.

Rats desert a sinking ship.

ANON.

Such joy ambition finds.

MILTON, Paradise Lost. Bk. IV, l. 92.

There's a gude time coming.

SCOTT, Rob Roy. Ch. xxxii.

Hope is a lover's staff.

Two Gentlemen of Verona. iii, 1, 1. 246.

The tender leaves of hope.

King Henry VIII. iii, 2.

Ambition is no sluggard.

KEATS, Endymion.

10

Great hopes make great men.

ANON.

Ambition dares not stoop.

BEN JONSON, *Cynthia's Revels.* iv, 1.

Naught venture naught have.

TUSSER, *October's Abstract.*

I have a soul above buttons.

COLMAN (the Younger), *New Hay at Old Market.*

My hopes in heaven do dwell.

King Henry VIII. iii, 2, 1. 458.

Love is wiser than ambition.

CORNWALL, *A Vision.*

Hope tells a flattering tale.

MISS WROTHER, *Universal Songster.*

Hope is the poor man's bread.

Italian Saying.

Hope and fear are inseparable.

ROCHEFOUCAULD.

A high hope for a low heaven.

Love's Labour 's Lost. i, 1.

Patience is the art of hoping.

VAUVENARGUES.

Man proposes, but God disposes.

À KEMPIS, *Imitation of Christ.*

Gay hope is theirs by fancy fed.

GRAY, *On Distant Prospect of Eton.*

Nothing certain but uncertainty.

ANON.

Time rolls his ceaseless course.

SCOTT, *Lady of the Lake.* Canto iii, st. 1.

Hope! thou nurse of young desire.

BICKERSTAFF, *Love in a Village.* i, 1, 1. 1.

Trust no Future, howe'er pleasant!
> LONGFELLOW, *A Psalm of Life.*

The mighty hopes that make us men.
> TENNYSON, *In Memoriam.* lxxxv.

Ambition can creep as well as soar.
> BURKE, *Letters on Regicide Peace.* iii, 1797.

All women are ambitious naturally.
> MARLOWE, *Hero and Leander.* Sestiad i.

Nae man can tether time or tide.
> BURNS, *Tam O'Shanter.*

Hope elevates, and joy brightens.
> MILTON, *Paradise Lost.* Bk. IX, 1. 633.

Hope is the gardener of the heart.
> DE FINOD.

Ambition loves to slide, not stand.
> DRYDEN, *Absalom and Achitophel.* Pt. I, 1. 198.

Hope is a loan made to happiness.
> From the French.

The sickening pang of hope deferr'd.
> SCOTT, *Lady of the Lake.* Canto iii, st. 22.

Success is a fruit slow to ripen.
> ANON.

All hope abandon, ye who enter here.
> DANTE, *Hell.* Canto iii, st. 9.

Hell is paved with good intentions.
> BOSWELL, *Life of Johnson.*

Hope is never ill when faith is well.
> ANON.

Virtue is chok'd with foul ambition.
> *King Henry VI.* Pt. II, ii, 1, 1. 143.

It is to hope, though hope were lost.
> MRS. BARBAULD, *Come Here, Fond Youth.*

Don't never prophesy onless you know!

> LOWELL, *Biglow Papers.*

And mad ambition trumpeteth to all.

> WILLIS, *Poem to Senior Yale Class.* 1827.

Folly ends when genuine hope begins.

> COWPER, *Hope.* 1. 637.

Virtue was never built upon ambition.

> FLETCHER, *Loyal Subject.* iii, 2.

Ambition is the growth of every clime.

> BLAKE, *King Edward the Third.* (Dagworth.)

The never-ending flight of future days.

> MILTON, *Paradise Lost.* Bk. II, l. 221.

Coming events cast their shadows before.

> CAMPBELL, *Lochiel's Warning.*

Fain would I climb, yet fear I to fall.

> RALEIGH, *Poem.*

Hope is the yeast in the bread of life.

> ANON.

I had a dream which was not all a dream.

> BYRON, *Darkness.*

The dream of happiness is real happiness.

> FONTANES.

O world! how many hopes thou dost engulf!

> DE MUSSET.

Hope for the best; prepare for the worst.

> ANON.

Trust on, and think to-morrow will repay.

> DRYDEN, *Aurengzebe.* iv, 1.

Hope is brightest when it dawns from fears.

> SCOTT, *Lady of the Lake.* Canto iv, st. 1.

One of these days is none of these days.

> ANON.

Illusions ruin all those whom they blind.

DE GIRARDIN.

Hope springs exulting on triumphant wing.

BURNS, *Cotter's Saturday Night.* St. 16.

Hope against hope, and ask till ye receive.

MONTGOMERY, *World before the Flood.* Can. v.

Love's despair is but Hope's pining ghost!

COLERIDGE, *The Visionary Hope.*

Ambition, like a torrent, ne'er looks back.

BEN JONSON, *Catiline.* (Cicero.) iii, 11.

Ambition makes more trusty slaves than need.

BEN JONSON, *Sejanus.* i, 1.

You can never plan the future by the past.

BURKE, *Let. to a Member of Nat'l Ass'y.* Vol. IV.

Men would be angels, angels would be gods.

POPE, *Essay on Man.* Ep. i, 1. 126.

'T is distance lends enchantment to the view.

CAMPBELL, *Pleasures of Hope.* Pt. I, 1. 7.

Enjoy what you have ; hope for what you lack.

LÉVIS.

Hope is brightest when it dawns from fears.

SCOTT, *Lady of the Lake.* Canto iv, st. 1.

To-day's egg is better than to-morrow's hen.

Persian Saying.

Every great passion is but a prolonged hope.

FEUCHÈRES.

For hope is but the dream of those that wake.

PRIOR, *Vanity of the World.* Bk. III, 1. 102.

Men at some times are masters of their fates.

Julius Cæsar. i, 2.

But Hope, the charmer, lingered still behind.

CAMPBELL, *Pleasures of Hope.* Pt. I, 1. 40.

He that will not look before must look behind.
                                    From the Gaelic.

Hope elevates, and joy brightens his crest.
        MILTON, *Paradise Lost.* Bk. IX, l. 633.

A misty morning does not signify a cloudy day.
                                                ANON.

Ambition is the only power that combats love.
        COLLEY CIBBER, *Cæsar in Egypt.* Act I.

I'm weary of conjectures,—this must end 'em.
        JOSEPH ADDISON, *Cato.* v, I.

Hope dead lives nevermore, no, not in heaven.
        CHRISTINA ROSSETTI, *Dead Hope.*

Ambition is but Avarice on stilts and masked.
        LANDOR, *Imaginary Conversations.*

Hope travels through, nor quits us when we die.
        POPE, *Essay on Man.* Ep. ii, l. 273.

Ill-weav'd ambition, how much art thou shrunk!
        King Henry IV. Pt. I, v, 4, l. 88.

Too low they build who build beneath the stars.
        YOUNG, *Night Thoughts.* N. viii, l. 225.

The best of prophets of the future is the past.
        BYRON, *Letter of Jan. 28, 1821.*

What makes life dreary is the want of a motive.
        ELIOT, *Daniel Deronda.* Bk. VIII, ch. 65.

Castles in the air cost a vast deal to keep up.
                                    BULWER-LYTTON.

The world was all before them, where to choose.
        MILTON, *Paradise Lost.* Bk. I, l. 642.

The loss of illusions is the death of the soul.
                                            CHAMFORT.

We know what we are, but know not what we may be.
        Hamlet. iv, 5.

A gift in the hand is better than two promises.

LA FONTAINE.

Where there is no hope there can be no endeavour.

JOHNSON, *The Rambler*. No. 110.

Nothing resembles yesterday so much as to-morrow.

ANON.

But what will not ambition and revenge descend to?

MILTON, *Paradise Lost*. Bk. IX, 1. 168.

Nothing becomes him so ill that he would do well.

Love's Labour's Lost. ii, 1.

To worry about to-morrow is to be unhappy to-day.

ANON.

No man is born without ambitious worldly desires.

CARLYLE, *Essays*. Schiller.

True hope is swift, and flies with swallow's wings.

King Richard III. v. 2, 1. 23.

That what will come, and must come, shall come well.

ARNOLD, *Light of Asia*. Bk. VI, 1. 274.

And Hope enchanted smiled, and waved her golden hair.

COLLINS, *Ode on the Passions*. 1. 3.

If at great things thou wouldst arrive, get riches first.

MILTON, *Paradise Regained*. Bk. II, 1. 426.

The miserable have no other medicine but only hope.

Measure for Measure. iii, 1, 1. 2.

No use in crossing the stream till you get to it.

LINCOLN, Maxims.

Past and to come seem best ; things present worst.

King Henry IV. Pt. II, i, 3, 1. 108.

True hope is swift, and flies with swallow's wings.

King Richard III. v, 2.

Attempt not to hatch more eggs than can be covered.

ANON.

For the future is of more consequence than the past.
>> DOANE, *St. Agnes Addresses.*

The present is withered by our wishes for the future.
>> E. SOUVESTRE.

Doubt follows white-winged Hope with a limping gait.
>> BALZAC.

Who tries to live by hope is likely to die by hunger.
>> ANON.

He who hath lost confidence hath little else to lose.
>> BOISTE.

Hope is a good anchor, but it needs something to grip.
>> ANON.

Never leave that till to-morrow which you can do to-day.
>> FRANKLIN, *Review of Pennsylvania.*

We never live : we are always in expectation of living.
>> VOLTAIRE.

Men inherit their own past and devise their own future.
>> ANON.

It is a great obstacle to happiness to expect too much.
>> FONTENELLE.

A life without a purpose is as a ship without a rudder.
>> ANON.

Better a sparrow in the hand than an eagle on the wing.
>> Spanish Saying.

Above the cloud with its shadow is the star with its light.
>> HUGO.

Hope, deceitful as it is, carries us agreeably through life.
>> ROCHEFOUCAULD.

Hope may suffice for a breakfast, but serves as a poor supper.
>> ANON.

The man that feeds on hope must needs have a slender appetite.
>> ANON.

Hope makes a good travelling companion, but a poor banker.

> ANON.

In all the wedding cake, hope is the sweetest of the plums.

> JERROLD, *Jerrold's Wit.*   The Catspaw.

How much one must have suffered to be weary even of hope!

> PAULINE.

We have but one instant to live, and we have hopes for years.

> FLÉCHIER.

He that hews above his height may have chips in his eyes.

> ANON.

Should we condemn ourselves to ignorance to preserve hope?

> SOUVESTRE.

Great things often result from little words of encouragement.

> ANON.

The thought of eternity consoles us for the shortness of life.

> MALESHERBES.

There is nothing that fear or hope does not make men believe.

> VAUVENARGUES.

I believe we are now living in Eternity as much as we ever shall.

> HUBBARD, *Philistine.*

Ambition, in a private man a vice, is, in a prince, the virtue.

> MASSINGER, *Bashful Lover.*   i, 2.

I charge thee, fling away ambition. By that sin fell the angels.

King Henry VIII. iii, 2, l. 437.

If you cannot have what you wish, wish for what you can have.

ANON.

Applause is the spur of noble minds, the end and aim of weak ones.

COLTON, *Lacon.*

The energies of the soul slumber in the vague reveries of hope.

MME. GUIZOT.

The past gives us regret, the present sorrow, and the future fear.

MME. DE LAMBERT.

To be happy is not to possess much, but to hope and to love much.

LAMENNAIS.

What we gain by experience is not worth what we lose in illusion.

PETIT-SENN.

There 's hope a great man's memory may outlive his life half a year.

Hamlet. iii, 2, l. 137.

Prospective happiness! it is the only real happiness in the world.

DE MUSSET.

Hope is a lure. There is no hand that can retain a wave or a shadow.

HUGO.

Dost thou love life, then do not squander time, for that is the stuff life is made of.

FRANKLIN, *Poor Richard.*

The very substance of the ambitious is merely the shadow
of a dream.

Hamlet.   ii, 2, l. 264.

'T is a common proof, that lowliness is young ambition's
ladder.

Julius Cæsar.   ii, 1, l. 21.

Where peace and rest can never dwell, hope never
comes, that comes to all.

MILTON, *Paradise Lost.*   Bk. I, l. 65.

Things which you don't hope happens more frequently
than things which you do hope.

PLAUTUS, *Mostellaria.*   i, 3, l. 71.

Ambition has its disappointments to sour us, but never
the good fortune to satisfy us.

FRANKLIN, *On True Happiness.*

Penn. Gazette, Nov. 20, 1735.

Most people would succeed in small things if they were
not troubled with great ambitions.

LONGFELLOW, *Drift-Wood.*   Table Talk.

To hope till hope creates
From its own wreck the thing it contemplates.

SHELLEY, *Prometheus.*   iv. last stanza.

The setting of a great hope is like the setting of the sun.
The brightness of our life is gone.

LONGFELLOW, *Hyperion.*   Bk. I, ch. 1.

But still there clung
One hope, like a keen sword on starting threads uphung.

BYRON, *Revolt of Islam.*

Hope says to us at every moment : Go on ! go on ! and
leads us thus to the grave.

DE MAINTENON.

The ambitious do not belong to themselves : they are the
slaves of the world.

From the French.

Is not the attitude of expectation somewhat divine? —
a sort of home-made divineness?

> THOREAU, *Letters.*

Those who endeavour to excel all, are at least sure of
excelling a great many.

> CHESTERFIELD, *Letters.* June, 1742.

Shallow men speak of the past, wise men of the present,
and fools of the future.

> DU DEFFAND.

Success too often sanctions the worst and the wildest
schemes of human ambition.

> COLTON, *Lacon.*

A wise man takes a step at a time; he establishes one
foot before he takes up the other.

> From the Sanskrit.

I am Sir Oracle,
And when I ope my lips let no dog bark.

> *Merchant of Venice.* i, 1.

There is no man easier to deceive than he who hopes:
for he aids in his own deceit.

> BOSSUET.

Hope is so sweet with its golden wings, that, at his last
sigh, man still implores it.

> DE LA PENA.

Happiness is the shadow of man: remembrance of it
follows him; hope of it precedes him.

> PETIT-SENN.

It's better to love to-day than to-morrow. A pleasure
postponed is a pleasure lost.

> A. RICARD.

Let us remember, that no horizon, no sky line, no
mountain range limits or bounds our aims.

> WM. CROSWELL DOANE, *St. Agnes Addresses.*

Hope, like the sun . . . . as we journey towards it,
  casts the shadow of our burden behind us.

SMILES.

After your death you were better have a bad epitaph
  than their ill report while you live.

Hamlet. ii, 2, 1. 545.

O, that a man might know
The end of this day's business ere it come !

Julius Cæsar. v, 1.

Hope ! hope, you miserable. There is no infinite mourn-
  ing, no incurable evils, no eternal hell !

HUGO.

An you had an eye behind you, you might see more
  detraction at your heels than fortunes before you.

Twelfth Night. ii, 5.

Come what come may,
Time and the hour runs through the roughest day.

Macbeth. i, 3.

The moment past is no longer : the future may never be :
  the present is all of which man is the master.

ROUSSEAU.

Young, one is rich in all the future that he dreams ; old,
  one is poor in all the past he regrets.

ROCHEPÈDRE.

I see, but cannot reach, the height
That lies forever in the light.

LONGFELLOW, *Golden Legend.* Pt. II.

To know that which before us lies in daily life,
Is the prime wisdom.

MILTON, *Paradise Lost.* Bk. viii, 1. 192.

Strange cozenage, none would live past years again,
Yet all hope pleasure in what yet remain.

DRYDEN, *Aurengzebe.*

And may this consecrated hour
With better hopes be filled !
> HELEN M. WILLIAMS, *Trust in Providence.*

One plows, another sows ;
Who will reap no one knows.
> ANON.

We 'll shine in more substantial honours,
And to be noble we 'll be good.
> THOMAS PERCY, *Reliques,* Winifreda.

Hope, of all ills that men endure,
The only cheap and universal cure.
> COWLEY, *For Hope.*

We must take the current when it serves,
Or lose our ventures.
> *Julius Cæsar.*   iv, 3.

Men's evil manners live in brass ; their virtues
We write in water.
> *King Henry VIII.*   iv, 2.

The evil that men do lives after them ;
The good is oft interred with their bones.
> *Julius Cæsar.*   iii, 2.

Things past belong to memory alone ;
Things future are the property of hope.
> HOME, *Agis* (Lysander).   Act ii.

Love, the brightest jewel of a crown,
That fires ambition, and adorns renown.
> LEE, *Sophonisba.*   i, 2.

Love is not much unlike ambition ;
For in them both all lets must be remov'd.
> COOKE, *How a Man may Choose.*   iii, 2.

Work without hope draws nectar in a sieve,
And hope without an object cannot live.
> COLERIDGE, *Work without Hope.*   St. 2.

Hope springs eternal in the human breast ;
Man never *is*, but always *to be* blest.

>   POPE, *Essay on Man.*   Ep. i, 1. 95.

What reinforcements we may gain from hope ;
If not, what resolution from despair.

>   MILTON, *Paradise Lost.*   Bk. I, 1. 190.

Here may he reign secure, and in my choice
To reign is worth ambition, though in Hell.

>   MILTON, *Paradise Lost.*   Bk. I, 1. 261.

And makes us rather bear those ills we have
Than fly to others that we know not of.

>   *Hamlet.*   iii, 1, 1. 76.

I laugh, for hope hath happy place with me,
If my bark sinks, 't is to another sea.

>   CHANNING, *A Poet's Hope.*   St. 13.

While there is life there's hope (he cried),
Then why such haste?—so groan'd and died.

>   GAY, *Sick Man and the Angel.*

Who bids me Hope, and in that charming word
Has peace and transport to my soul restor'd.

>   LYTTLETON, *Progress of Love.*   Hope.
>   Eclogue, ii, 1. 41.

Joy is the ray of sunshine that brightens and opens
those two beautiful flowers, Confidence and Hope.

>   SOUVESTRE.

Beware of desperate steps.   The darkest day,
Live till to-morrow, will have passed away.

>   COWPER, *Needless Alarm.*

For wheresoe'er I turn my ravished eyes,
Gay gilded scenes and shining prospects rise.

>   ADDISON, *Letter from Italy.*

Hope, like the gleaming taper's light.
Adorns and cheers our way.

>   GOLDSMITH, *The Captivity.*

Catch, then, O catch the transient hour ;
Improve each moment as it flies.

SAMUEL JOHNSON, *Winter.*

Our hopes, like towering falcons, aim
At objects in an airy height.

PRIOR, *To Hon. Charles Montague.*

Visions of glory, spare my aching sight !
Ye unborn ages, crowd not on my soul !

GRAY, *The Bard.*

Yet who would tread again the scene
He trod through life before ?

MONTGOMERY, *Falling Leaf.*

To live in hearts we leave behind,
Is not to die.

CAMPBELL, *Hallowed Ground.*

O fading honours of the dead !
O high ambition, lowly laid !

SCOTT, *Lay of Last Minstrel.* Canto. ii, st. 10.

All my ambition is, I own,
To profit and to please, unknown.

COTTON, *Visions in Verse.*

One only hope my heart can cheer,
The hope to meet again.

LINLEY, *Song.*

But see how oft ambition's aims are cross'd,
And chiefs contend 'til all the prize is lost !

POPE, *Rape of the Lock.* Canto v, 1. 108.

Our greatest good, and what we least can spare,
Is hope : the last of all our evils, fear.

ARMSTRONG, *Art of Preserving Health.*

Bk. IV, 1. 318.

Auspicious Hope! in thy sweet garden grow
Wreaths for each toil, a charm for every woe.
> CAMPBELL, *Pleasures of Hope.* Pt. I, 1. 45.

Oh, blindness to the future, kindly giv'n,
That each may fill the circle mark'd by heaven.
> POPE, *Essay on Man.* Ep. i, 1. 85.

Cease every joy, to glimmer in my mind,
But leave,—oh! leave the light of Hope behind!
> CAMPBELL, *Pleasures of Hope.* Pt. II, 1. 375.

But hope will make thee young, for Hope and Youth
Are children of one mother, even Love.
> SHELLEY, *Revolt of Islam.* Canto viii, st. 27.

Youth fades; love droops; the leaves of friendship fall;
A mother's secret hope outlives them all.
> HOLMES, *A Mother's Secret.*

Races, better than we, have leaned on her wavering
promise,
Having naught else but Hope.
> LONGFELLOW, *Children of Lord's Supper.* 1. 230.

How like a mountain devil in the heart
Rules the unreined ambition!
> WILLIS, *Parrhasius.*

When Fortune means to men most good,
She looks upon them with a threatening eye.
> *King John.* iii, 4.

The baby figure of the giant mass
Of things to come.
> *Troilus and Cressida.* i, 3.

To speed to-day, to be put back to-morrow;
To feed on hope, to pine with feare and sorrow.
> SPENSER, *Mother Hubberds Tale.*

The miserable have no other medicine,
But only hope.
> *Measure for Measure.* iii, 1.

Better aim at a star than shoot down a well ;
You'll hit higher.

ANON.

If you can look into the seeds of time,
And say which grain will grow and which will not.

Macbeth. i, 3.

Making forty thousand wishes
Will never fill your pail with fishes.

ANON.

By the street of By and By
One arrives at the house of Never.

CERVANTES.

But I know that while the mariner wafts along the
golden year,
Broader continents of action open up in every sphere.

STEDMAN, *Flood-Tide.*

We dream such beautiful dreams, that we often lose all
our happiness when we perceive that they are only
dreams.

From the French.

Virtue is enlarged and infinite in her hopes, inasmuch
as they extend beyond present things, even to
eternal.

COLTON, *Lacon.*

Man spends his time in reasoning on the past, in com-
plaining of the present, and in trembling for the
future.

RIVAROL.

In eternal cares we spend our years, ever agitated by
new desires ; we look forward to living, and yet
never live.

FONTENELLE.

There are many things that are thorns to our hopes
until we have attained them, and envenomed arrows
to our hearts, when we have.

COLTON, *Lacon.*

If we exhaust our income in schemes of ambition, we
shall purchase disappointment ; if in law, vexation ;
if in luxury, disease.

COLTON, *Lacon.*

If you have built castles in the air, your work need not
be lost ; that is where they should be.   Now put the
foundations under them.

THOREAU, *Walden.*

Our minds are as different as our faces ; we are all
travelling to one destination—happiness ; but none
are going by the same road.

COLTON, *Lacon.*

Hope, whose habitation is manifestly terrestrial, and
whose very existence must, I conceive, be lost, in
the overwhelming realities of futurity.

COLTON, *Lacon.*

Poets are the hierophants of an unapprehended inspira-
tion ; the mirrors of the gigantic shadows which
futurity casts upon the present.

SHELLEY, *Defence of Poetry.*

Lawyer—Legal—Justice

Arguments very seldom convince.
ELBERT HUBBARD, *Philistine*.

Lawyer—Legal—Justice

Law is a lottery.

ANON.

Law is king of all.
DEAN ALFORD, *School of the Heart.* Lesson Sixth.

Neode hap no lawe.
LANGLAND, *Piers the Plowman.* Passus 23, l. 10.

Love knoweth no lawes.

LYLY, *Euphues.*

Necessity knows no law.
PUBLIUS SYRUS, *Maxims.* 553.

Beauty is a good client.

ANON.

Old father antic, the law.
King Henry IV. Pt. I, i, 2.

So you shall pay your fees.
Winter's Tale. i, 2.

The guilty catch themselves.

ANON.

Order is Heaven's first law.
POPE, *Essay on Man.* Ep. iv, l. 49.

Who spares vice wrongs virtue.
PUBLIUS SYRUS, *Maxims.*

To go to law is to go to sea.

ANON.

Where law ends, tyranny begins.
CHATHAM, *Speech on Wilkes' Case.* Jan. 9, 1770.

Report me and my cause aright.

Hamlet.   v. 2.

Don 't fight over a cheese-mite.

ANON.

Arguments very seldom convince.

HUBBARD, *Philistine.*

Face to face clears many a case.

ANON.

Fools, for arguments, use wagers.

ANON.

The more laws, the more offences.

ANON.

Make not thyself judge of any man.

LONGFELLOW.

Don 't throw good money after bad.

ANON.

Advise none to marry or go to law.

ANON.

Justice delayed is justice denied.

GLADSTONE.

Never argue with a child or a fool.

ANON.

I am a mortal man again, a Lawyer.

BEAUMONT AND FLETCHER, *Little French Lawyer.*

Law-makers must not be Law-breakers.

ANON.

One lie needs seven to wait upon it.

ANON.

The gladsome light of jurisprudence.

COKE, *First Institute.*

A sense of justice is a noble fancy.

TEGNER, *Frithofs' Saga.*   Canto viii.

Before you decide hear the other side.

ANON.

A snapper-up of unconsidered trifles.

Winter's Tale.   iv, 2.

Self-defence is Nature's eldest law.

DRYDEN, *Absalom and Achitophel.*   Pt. I, 1. 458.

The Law, our kingdom's golden chaine.

DEKKER, *Satiro-Mastix.*

To err is human, to forgive divine.

POPE, *Essay on Criticism.*   Pt. III, 525.

These nice sharp quillets of the law.

King Henry VI.   Pt. I, i, 1.

Possession is nine points of the law.

ANON.

Lawyers and woodpeckers have long bills.

ANON.

The best cause requires a good pleader.

ANON.

The law is a sort of hocus-pocus science.

MACKLIN, *Love à la Mode.*   ii, 1.

Law hath a sharp claw and a hungry maw.

ANON.

He who commits no crime requires no law.

ANTIPHANES.

Justice is one thing, law is another.

ANON.

Multiplying laws multiplies criminals.

ANON.

Justice without wisdom is impossible.

FROUDE, *Party Politics.*

Who has many servants has many thieves.

Dutch Saying.

'T is but half a judge's task to know.
> POPE, *Essay on Criticism.*   Pt. III, 1. 2.

Vice is as degrading as it is criminal.
> CHESTERFIELD, *Letters.*   Aug. 7, 1749.

Never argue for victory, but for verity.
> ANON.

Drink and lawing lead to the almshouse.
> ANON.

Possession is eleven points in the law.
> COLLEY CIBBER, *Woman's Wit.*   Act i.

I 'll cavil on the ninth part of a hair.
> *King Henry IV.*   Pt. I, iii, 1.

Such virtue is there in a robe and gown !
> DRYDEN, *Pro. to Troilus and Cressida.*

A lie, like a note, must be met at last.
> ANON.

A liar is sooner caught than a cripple.
> Italian Saying.

The majesty and power of law and justice.
> *King Henry IV.*   Pt. II, v, 2.

Who breaks no law is subject to no king.
> CHAPMAN, *Revenge of Bussy d'Ambois.*   iv, 1.

Forbear to judge, for we are sinners all.
> *King Henry VI.*   Pt. II, iii, 3, 1. 31.

Lawyers' houses are built on fools' heads.
> ANON.

And princely counsel in his face yet shone.
> MILTON, *Paradise Lost.*   Bk. II, 1. 300.

Lawyers are needful to keep us out of law.
> ANON.

Crime, as well as virtue, has its degrees.
> RACINE.

A fool with judges, amongst fools a judge.

> COWPER, *Conversations*.

A wise lawyer seldom goes to law himself.

> ANON.

The law 's made to take care o' raskills.

> ELIOT, *Mill on the Floss*.   Bk. III, ch. 4.

He thinks too much : such men are dangerous.

> *Julius Cæsar*.   i, 2.

They reck no laws that meditate revenge.

> KYD, *The Spanish Tragedy*.   Act i.

In too much controversy the truth is lost.

> Old Saying.

Every true man's apparel fits your thief.

> *Measure for Measure*.   iv, 2.

Who always tells me a lie never cheats me.

> Spanish Saying.

Don't go to law for the wagging of a straw.

> ANON.

Argument makes three enemies to one friend.

> ANON.

The lawyer grows fat, but his client is lean.

> ANON.

Don't hang a man and then try him afterwards.

> ANON.

Courts, not mobs, must execute the penalties of the law.

> McKINLEY, *Message*.   Dec. 5, 1899.

Arguments that prove too much prove nothing.

> COLTON.   *Lacon*.

The welfare of the people is the highest law.

> Latin translation.

The law : It has honoured us ; may we honour it.

> WEBSTER.   May 10, 1847.

Law is a bottomless pit ; keep far from it.

ANON.

Choose an old physician and a young lawyer.

ANON.

He who allows oppression shares the crime.

DARWIN, *Loves of the Plants.* Canto iii, 1. 458.

The cold neutrality of an impartial judge.

BURKE, *Pref. to Brissot's Address.* Vol. V, p. 67.

Condemn the fault, and not the actor of it.

Measure for Measure. ii, 2.

Show me a liar and I will show you a thief.

ANON.

No man 's a faithful judge in his own cause.

MASSINGER, *The Bashful Lover.* ii, 7.

He that goes to law holds a wolf by the ears.

BURTON.

Still you keep o' the windy side of the law.

Twelfth Night. iii, 4, 1. 181.

Every man loves justice at another man's house.

ANON.

Do not show all you know at the very first go.

ANON.

Walking humbly before God, dealing justly and mercifully.

MCKINLEY, *Speech.* New Orleans, 1901.

Thou then would'st make mine enemy my judge !

SHELLEY, *Prometheus Unbound.* iii, 1.

He thought as a sage, though he felt as a man.

BEATTIE, *The Hermit.*

And courts to courts return it round and round.

POPE, *Dunciad.* Pt. II, 1. 272.

Give no man counsel or physic till he asks it.

ANON.

A single fact is worth a cartload of argument.

ANON.

There is a higher law than the Constitution.

SEWARD, *Speech*. March 11, 1850.

Where justice reigns, 't is freedom to obey.

MONTGOMERY, *Greenland*. Canto iv.

The world is not thy friend nor the world's law.

Romeo and Juliet. v, 1.

His conduct still right with his argument wrong.

GOLDSMITH, *Retaliation*. 1. 46.

They who possess the prince possess the laws.

DRYDEN, *Absalom and Achitophel*. Pt. I, 1. 476.

We have strict statutes and most biting laws.

Measure for Measure. i, 3, 1. 19.

With all his crimes broad blown, as flush as May.

Hamlet. iii, 3.

A lean compromise is better than a fat lawsuit.

From the French.

Costs me more money than my share oft comes to.

BEN JONSON, *The Alchemist*.

He hears but half who hears but one side only.

ÆSCHYLUS.

The law of heaven and earth is life for life.

BYRON, *The Curse of Minerva*. St. 15.

Oh 't is a blessed thing to have rich clients.

BEAUMONT AND FLETCHER, *Spanish Curate*.

I stand for judgment: answer: shall I have it?

Merchant of Venice. iv, 1, 1. 103.

Laws grind the poor, and rich men rule the law.

GOLDSMITH, *The Traveller*. 1. 386.

We surgeons of the law do desperate cures, Sir.

BEAUMONT AND FLETCHER, *Spanish Curate*.

Lawyers and painters can soon make black white.

ANON.

Plead much, read more, dine late or not at all.

POPE, *Satires.*

The law of love is better than the love of law.

ANON.

A lawyer and a cart-wheel must be well greased.

From the German.

Curse on all laws but those which love has made.

POPE, *Eloisa to Abélard.* l. 74.

Even the dog is honest when meat is out of reach.

ANON.

Into courts of law and courtings go cautiously.

ANON.

A knock-down argument : 't is but a word and a blow.

DRYDEN, *Amphitryon.* i, 1.

That lawyer is honest who has hair on his teeth.

ANON.

A fox should not be on the jury at a goose's trial.

ANON.

The first thing we do, let 's kill all the lawyers.

King Henry VI. Pt. II, iv, 2, l. 84.

He that has the worst cause makes the most noise.

ANON.

If the judge be your accuser, may God be your help.

ANON.

Dread an action at law as you would a lion's paw.

ANON.

Litigious terms, fat contentions, and flowing fees.

MILTON, *Prose Works.* Vol. I. Of Education.

The judge is condemned when the guilty is acquitted.

SYRUS.

He that goes to law for a sheep often loses his cow.

From the German.

Hide nothing from thy minister, physician, and lawyer.

ANON.

Justice, sir, is the great interest of man on earth.

WEBSTER, *On Mr. Justice Story.* *1845.*

We condemn vice and extol virtue only through interest.

ROCHEFOUCAULD.

Mercy to the criminal may be cruelty to the innocent.

ANON.

Argument with a fool shows that there are two of them.

ANON.

There is no free state where the laws are not supreme.

ARISTOTLE.

Give the benefit of doubt till the truth is fully out.

ANON.

Justice tempered with too much mercy becomes injustice.

ANON.

Give a lawyer the reins and he 'll drive you to the devil.

ANON.

When beauty is at the bar, blind men make the best jury.

ANON.

There is no virtue so truly great and godlike as justice.

ADDISON, *The Guardian.* No. 99.

A lie which is half a truth is ever the blackest of lies.

TENNYSON, *The Grandmother.* viii.

We must never assume that which is incapable of proof.

LEWES, *Physiology of Common Life.* Ch. xiii.

The verdict oft acquits the raven and condemns the dove.

JUVENAL.

Give a knave your finger and he will take your whole
hand.

Dutch Saying.

A peasant between two lawyers is a fish between two
cats.

ANON.

Remember, when the judgment's weak the prejudice
is strong.

KANE O'HARA, *The Midas.* i, 4.

Sin has many tools but a lie is a handle that fits them
all.

HOLMES.

A lie and a snake, unless soon killed, breed a hundred-
fold.

ANON.

Who knows only his own side of the case knows little of
that.

MILLS.

Equity is a roguish thing ; for Law we have a measure,
know what to trust to.

SELDEN, *Table Talk.* Equity.

The only thing certain about litigation is its uncertainty.

BOVEE.

We hand folk over to God's mercy and show none ourselves.

ELIOT, *Adam Bede.* Ch. xiii.

They have been grand-jurymen since before Noah was a
sailor.

Twelfth Night. iii, 2, 1. 16.

It must be a very bad cause if the lawyer is ashamed
of it.

ANON.

Law and Equity, which God hath joined, let no man
put asunder.

COLTON, Lacon.

Custom which is before all law, Nature which is above all
art.

DANIEL, An Apology for Rhime.

Who knows enough to keep out of the law is a good
lawyer.

ANON.

Equity is according to the conscience of him that is
chancellor.

SELDEN, Table Talk.   Equity.

That law is best which leaves the least discretion to the
judge.

From the Latin.

He who has left a rogue behind him has made a good day's
journey.

German Saying.

If you argue, pray that it may be with those who can
understand you.

ANON.

In answering an opponent, arrange your ideas, but not
your words.

COLTON, Lacon.

When both sides find fault you have probably meted out
justice.

ANON.

Use every man after his desert, and who should 'scape
whipping?

Hamlet.   ii, 2.

Lawyers' gowns are lined with the wilfulness of their
clients.

ANON.

When the state is most corrupt, then the laws are most multiplied.

TACITUS.

If you pity a rogue you are no great friend of honest men.

ANON.

To judge wisely I suppose we must know how things appear to the unwise.

ELIOT, *Daniel Deronda.* Bk. IV, ch. 29.

A lawyer is a cat that is called in to help mice to settle their quarrels.

ANON.

A lie will go around the world while truth is pulling on its boots.

ANON.

With an aspect of iron, that when I come to woo ladies I fright them.

King Henry V. v, 2.

Falsehood is never so successful as when she baits her hook with truth.

COLTON, *Lacon.*

The mere repetition of the Cantilena of lawyers cannot make it law.

SCOTT, *O'Connell vs. the Queen.*

A thread will tie an honest man better than a rope will tie a rogue.

Scotch Saying.

A liar's punishment is not being believed when he speaks the truth.

ANON.

To go to law is to kindle a fire to warm others and singe ourselves.

ANON.

To live by the bar you must live like a hermit, and work
like a horse.

ELDON.

A lie is like a snowball; the farther you roll it, the
larger it becomes.

LUTHER.

Little thieves are hanged by the neck and great thieves
by the purse.

ANON.

The urging of that word, judgment, hath bred a kind
of remorse in me.

King Richard III. i, 4, 1. 109.

'T is like the breath of an unfee'd lawyer; you gave me
nothing for 't.

King Lear. i, 4, 1. 142.

I do not know the method of drawing up an indictment
against an whole people.

BURKE, *Conciliation of America.* Speech.

A man may wear out a suit of clothes, but a suit at law
may wear a man out.

ANON.

Wilt make haste to give up thy verdict because thou wilt
not lose thy dinner.

MIDDLETON, *A Trick to Catch the Old One.* iv, 5.

Substantial fearless souls that will swear suddenly, that
will swear anything.

BEAUMONT AND FLETCHER, *Spanish Curate.*

I have found you an argument, I am not obliged to find
you an understanding.

BOSWELL, *Life of Johnson.* An. 1784.

Save a rogue from the gallows and he will steal your pig
the same night.

ANON.

Lawyers are always more ready to get a man into troubles than out of them.

GOLDSMITH, *The Good-Natured Man.* Act iii.

Let us consider the reason of the case. For nothing is law that is not reason.

POWELL, *Coggs vs. Bernard.*

If a man deceives me once, shame on him ; if he deceive me twice, shame on me.

ANON.

Society does not punish those who sin, but those who sin and conceal not wisely.

HUBBARD, *Philistine.*

For my own part, I judge of every man's truth by his degree of understanding.

CHESTERFIELD, *Letters.* Sept. 21, 1747.

In law there 's many a loss without a gain, but never a gain without a loss.

ANON.

Corruption is like a ball of snow: when once set a rolling, it must increase.

COLTON, *Lacon.*

"Virtue in the middle," said the Devil as he seated himself between two lawyers.

ANON.

A criminal : one who does by illegal means what all the rest of us do legally.

HUBBARD, *Philistine.*

Corruption abounding in the commonwealth, the commonwealth abounded in laws.

TACITUS, *Annals.* Bk. III, p. 160.

Let a man keep the law,—any law,—and his way will be strewn with satisfaction.

EMERSON, *Prudence.*

Justice is that virtue of the soul which is distributive according to desert.

ARISTOTLE, *Metaphysics*.   On Virtues and Vices.

A lie has no legs and cannot stand ; but it has wings, and can fly far and wide.

WARBURTON.

He draweth out the thread of his verbosity finer than the staple of his argument.

Love's Labour 's Lost.   v, 1.

Next to sound Judgment, Diamonds and Pearls are the rarest things to be met with.

LA BRUYÈRE, *Characters and Manners*.

Of Judgments.

Justice discards party, friendship, kindred, and is therefore always represented as blind.

ADDISON, *The Guardian*.   No. 99.

For variety they may swear truth, else 't is not much look'd after.

BEAUMONT AND FLETCHER, *Spanish Curate*.   iii.

Law and equity are two things which God hath joined, but which man hath put asunder.

COLTON, *Lacon*.

Reason is the life of the law ; nay, the common law itself is nothing else but reason.

COKE, *First Institute*.

We have just enough religion to make us hate, but not enough to make us love one another.

SWIFT, *Thoughts on Various Subjects*.

Can one better expiate his sins than by enlisting his experience in the service of morals?

DE BERNARD.

We often injure our cause by calling in that which is weak, to support that which is strong.

COLTON, *Lacon*.

He who saith there is no such thing as an honest man,
you may be sure is himself a knave.

BISHOP BERKELEY.

Laws are like cobwebs, which may catch small flies, but
let wasps and hornets break through.

SWIFT, *Essay on Faculties of the Mind.*

The lawyer is a gentleman who rescues your estate from
your enemies, and keeps it to himself.

BROUGHAM.

After an existence of nearly twenty years of almost in-
nocuous desuetude these laws are brought forth.

CLEVELAND, *Message.* March 1, 1886.

Who goes to law should have three bags : one of papers,
one of money, and one of patience.

From the French.

The law is the last result of human wisdom acting upon
human experience for the benefit of the public.

SAMUEL JOHNSON, *Johnsoniana.* Anecdotes, 58.

Laws should be clear, uniform, precise ; to interpret
them is nearly always to corrupt them.

VOLTAIRE.

When two dogs strive for a bone and the third runs away
with it, there 's a lawyer among the dogs.

ANON.

Laws should never be in contradiction to usages ; for if
the usages are good, the laws are valueless.

VOLTAIRE.

We can only escape the arbitrariness of the judge by
placing ourselves under the despotism of the law.

NAPOLEON.

Every item in the decalogue can be legally broken, and
the chief business of the lawyer is to tell you how.

HUBBARD, *Philistine.*

I know no method to secure the repeal of bad or obnoxious laws so effective as their stringent execution.

GRANT, *Inaugural Address.* March 4, 1869.

Our human laws are but the copies, more or less imperfect, of the eternal laws so far as we can read them.

FROUDE, *Short Studies on Great Subjects.*

Four things belong to a judge : to hear courteously, to answer wisely, to consider soberly, and to decide impartially.

SOCRATES.

A jeer and a sneer
Never prove a case clear.

ANON.

He who holds no laws in awe,
He must perish by the law.

BYRON, *Occasional Pieces.* Mournful Ballad.

When anger in the bosom lies,
Justice out the window flies.

ANON.

Fond of doctors, little health :
Fond of lawyers, little wealth.

ANON.

No man e'er felt the halter draw,
With good opinion of the law.

TRUMBULL, *McFingal.* Canto iii, 1. 489.

If lying were a capital crime,
The hangman would work overtime.

ANON.

Dazzle mine eyes? or do I see
Two glorious Suns of Chancery?

PRAED, *Eve of Battle.*

O, what a tangled web we weave
When first we practice to deceive !

SCOTT, *Marmion.* Canto vi, st. 17.

And he that gives us in these days
New Lords may give us new laws.
                    WITHER, *Contented Man's Morrice.*

What is law, if those who make it
Become the forwardest to break it?
                    BEATTIE, *Wolf and Shepherd.*

The thief at every sound doth jump,
And sees an officer in every stump.
                                        ANON.

If with the law you once begin,
'T will strip you to the very skin.
                                        ANON.

Who will not mercie unto others show,
How can he mercie ever hope to have?
          SPENSER, *Faerie Queen.* Bk. VI, canto i, st. 42.

With books and money placed for show,
Like nest-eggs to make clients lay.
                    BUTLER, *Hudibras.* Pt. III, l. 624.

Fools and churls make lawyers rich ;
Concessions fair jump o'er the ditch.
                                        ANON.

    Pity is the virtue of the law,
And none but tyrants use it cruelly.
                    Timon of Athens.   iii, 5.

Don't spend ten precious pounds in court
To get by law a paltry groat.
                                        ANON.

Justice, while she winks at crimes,
Stumbles on innocence sometimes.
          BUTLER, *Hudibras.*   Pt. I, canto ii, l. 1177.

Bold of your worthiness, we single you
As our best-moving fair solicitor.
                    Love's Labour 's Lost.   ii, 1, l. 28.

When law can do no right,
Let it be lawful that law bar no wrong.
King John.   iii, 1, 1. 185.

The good needs fear no law,
It is his safety and the bad man's awe.
MASSINGER, *The Old Law.*   v, 1, 1. last.

Who to himself is law, no law doth need,
Offends no law, and is a king indeed.
CHAPMAN, *Bussy D'Ambois.*   ii, 1.

Laws, in great rebellions lose their end,
And all go free, when multitudes offend.
ROWE, *Lucan's Pharsalia.*   Bk. V, 1. 364.

Had you heard him first
Draw it to certain heads, then aggravate !
BEN JONSON, *Volpone.*

The wretch that often has deceived,
Though truth he speaks is ne'er believed.
PHÆDRUS.

I am armed with more than complete steel,
The justice of my quarrel.
MARLOWE, *Lust's Dominion.*

The hungry judges soon the sentence sign,
And wretches hang that jurymen may dine.
POPE, *Rape of the Lock.*   Canto iii, 1. 21.

The universal cause
Acts to one end, but acts by various laws.
POPE, *Essay on Man.*   Ep. iii, 1. 1.

To offend, and judge, are distinct offices
And of opposed natures.
Merchant of Venice.   ii, 9, 1. 61.

Before I be convict by course of law,
To threaten me with death is most unlawful.
King Richard III.   i, 4, 1. 192.

Custom, that unwritten law,
By which the people keep even kings in awe.

D'AVENANT, *Circe.* ii, 3.

Military—Naval—Heroism

By sea and land I'll fight.
SHAKESPEARE, *Antony and Cleopatra.*

Military—Naval—Heroism

As sure as a gun.
DRYDEN, *Spanish Friar.*

Let us do or die.
BURNS, *Bannockburn.*

Let us have peace.
GRANT. Accepting nomination, May 20, 1868.

I 'll fight at sea.
Antony and Cleopatra. iii, 7.

Fear has many eyes.
CERVANTES, *Don Quixote.* Pt. III, ch. 6.

How goes the enemy?
REYNOLDS, *The Dramatist.*

As certain as a gun.
BUTLER, *Hudibras.* Pt. I.

All hell broke loose.
MILTON, *Paradise Lost.* Bk. IV, l. 918.

Thus am I doubly armed.
ADDISON, *Cato.* v, 1.

I 'll not budge an inch.
Taming of the Shrew.

Rashness is not valour.
ANON.

The Empire means peace.
LOUIS NAPOLEON, *Speech at Bordeaux.* 1852.

I war not with the dead.
HOMER, *Iliad.* Bk. VII, l. 485, Pope's trans.

The churchyard's peace.
> SCHILLER, *Don Carlos.*   iii, 10, 220.

The brazen throat of war.
> MILTON, *Paradise Lost.*   Bk. XI, 1. 713.

Far off his coming shone.
> MILTON, *Paradise Lost.*   Bk. VI, 1. 768.

Men hate where they hurt.
> ANON.

Gashed with honourable scars.
> MONTGOMERY, *Battle of Alexandria.*

My voice is still for war.
> ADDISON, *Cato.*   ii, 1.

There is war in the skies.
> OWEN MEREDITH, *Lucile.*   Pt. I, canto iv, st. 12.

Are you good men and true?
> *Much Ado About Nothing.*   iii, 3.

I came, saw, and overcame.
> *King Henry IV.*   Pt. II, iv, 3, 1. 45.

Every man meets his Waterloo at last.
> PHILLIPS, *Speech.*   Nov. 1, 1859.

Foolish fears double danger.
> ANON.

I have peppered two of them.
> *King Henry IV.*   Pt. I, ii, 4.

I came, I saw, I conquered.
> JULIUS CÆSAR.

Boldly ventured is half won.
> ANON.

Silence is the soul of war.
> PRIOR, *Ode in Imitation of Horace.*
> Bk. III, Ode 2.

A very valiant trencher-man.
> *Much Ado About Nothing.*   i, 1.

Hold the Fort! I am coming.
> GEN. WM. T. SHERMAN.   Signal to Gen. Corse,
> > Oct. 5, 1864.

Every bullet has its billet.
> WILLIAM III. (attributed to.)

Trouble often shows the man.
> ANON.

My sentence is for open war.
> MILTON, *Paradise Lost.*   Bk. II, l. 51.

By sea and land I'll fight.
> *Antony and Cleopatra.*   iv, 2.

The always wind-obeying deep.
> *Comedy of Errors.*   i, 1, l. 64.

I will die in the last ditch.
> WILLIAM OF ORANGE.   Words to Buckingham.

Velvet paws hide sharp claws.
> ANON.

One brave deed makes no hero.
> WHITTIER, *The Hero.*

A thing devised by the enemy.
> *King Richard III.*   v, 3.

My nearest and dearest enemy.
> MIDDLETON, *Anything for a Quiet Life.*   v, 1.

Moneys are the sinews of war.
> FULLER, *The Good Soldier.*

I would fain die a dry death.
> *The Tempest.*   i, 1.

The law is silent during war.
> CICERO, *Oratio Pro Annio Milone.*   iv.

A plague of all cowards, I say.
> *King Henry IV.*   Pt. I, ii, 4.

Women's jars breed men's wars.

FULLER, *The Wise Statesman.*

All battle is misunderstanding.

BACON.

I bring you peace with honour.

BEACONSFIELD.

Our antagonist is our helper.

BURKE, *Revolution in France.*

See the conquering hero comes.

THOMAS MORELL.

Instinct is a great matter : I was a coward on instinct.

King Henry IV. Pt. I, ii, 4.

What, drawn, and talk of peace ?

Romeo and Juliet. i, 1.

All delays are dangerous in war.

DRYDEN, *Tyrannic Love.* i, 1.

The hastie man never wanteth woe.

HEYWOOD, *Proverbs.* Bk. I, ch. 2.

Obey orders, if it breaks owners.

Old Saying.

Despair will make a coward brave.

ANON.

We must bring you to our captain.

Two Gentlemen of Verona. v, 3.

The vanquish'd have no friends.

SOUTHEY, *Joan of Arc.* Bk. III, 1. 465.

War is not as onerous as servitude.

VAUVENARGUES.

Peace the offspring is of Power.

TAYLOR, *A Thousand Years.*

Revenge is an expensive luxury.

ANON.

A weak invention of the enemy.
> CIBBER, *Richard III.*   v, 3.   (Altered by.)

Courage mounteth with occasion.
> *King John.*   ii, 1.

Trust not the ship to one rope.
> ANON.

Words are women, deeds are men.
> HERBERT, *Jacula Prudentum.*

The victory of endurance born.
> BRYANT, *The Battle-Field.*   St. 8.

Beware the fury of a patient man.
> DRYDEN, *Absalom and Achitophel.*   Pt. I, 1. 1005.

The greatest enemy to man is man.
> BURTON, *Anatomy of Melancholy.*
> Pt. I, sec. i, memb. 1, subs. 1.

Defeat is a tonic to a brave man.
> ANON.

An Austrian army awfully arrayed.
> ANON, in *Wheeler's Magazine.*
> Winchester, Eng., 1828.

All but fools know fear sometimes.
> HEINRICH HEINE.

How partial is the voice of Fame !
> PRIOR, *Epigram on Partial Fame.*

A great ship must have deep water.
> ANON.

Fling but a stone, the giant dies.
> MATTHEW GREEN, *The Spleen.*   1. 93.

Be careful, but not full of care.
> ANON.

Fought all his battles o'er again.
> DRYDEN, *Alexander's Feast.*   1. 65.

Bless the hand that gave the blow.

> DRYDEN, *Spanish Friar.*

Battle's magnificently stern array.

> BYRON, *Childe Harold.*   Canto iii, st. 28.

In a calm sea every man is a pilot.

> ANON.

Painful labour both by sea and land.

> *Taming of the Shrew.*   v, 2.

It is a theme as fluent as the sea.

> *King Henry V.*   iii, 7.

Every hero becomes a bore at last.

> EMERSON, *Uses of Great Men.*

A sword less hurt does, than a pen.

> WM. KING, *Eagle and Robin.*   1. 82.

Many little leaks may sink a ship.

> FULLER, *Holy and Profane States.*   Good Servant.

We shall never war except for peace.

> McKINLEY, *Speech.*   El Paso, May 6, 1901.

War is not of life the sum.

> BRET HARTE, *Hark! I hear the Tramp.*

Each able to sustain a nation's fate.

> DRYDEN, *Annus Mirabilis.*

From spoil protect the sons of peace.

> GEORGE CRABBE.

Let your discretion be your tutor.

> *Hamlet.*   iii, 2.

Courage in danger is half the battle.

> PLAUTUS.

Self-defence is Nature's eldest law.

> DRYDEN, *Absalom and Achitophel.*   Pt. I, 1. 458.

The Guard dies, but never surrenders.

> ROUGEMONT.

Simple duty has no place for fear.
> WHITTIER, *Abraham Davenport.*

Armed at point exactly, cap-a-pie.
> *Hamlet.* i, 2, 1. 200

A tyrant's hand, a coward's heart.
> ANON.

The sex is ever to a soldier kind.
> HOMER, *Odyssey.* Bk. XIV, 1. 246. Pope's trans.

For courage mounteth with occasion.
> *King John.* ii, 1.

Courage needs eyes as well as arms.
> ANON.

Ran on embattled armies clad in iron.
> MILTON, *Samson Agonistes.*

The lion is not so fierce as painted.
> FULLER, *At Expecting Preferment.*

A mighty hunter, and his prey was man.
> POPE, *Windsor Forest.*

The brave only know how to forgive.
> STERNE, Sermon XII.

Every bullet hath a lighting place.
> GASCOIGNE, *The Fruites of Warre.*

Every bullet has got its commission.
> DIBDIN, *The Benevolent Tar.*

Security is mortal's chiefest enemy.
> *Macbeth.* iii, 5.

Guilty consciences make men cowards.
> VANBRUGH, *Provok'd Wife.* v, 6.

Such renown as time shall ne'er decry.
> *Pericles.* iii, 2.

Or as it were the pageants of the sea.
> *Merchant of Venice.* i, 1.

The Army's at the door and in disguise.
>BUCKINGHAM, *The Rehearsal.*

I have a kind of alacrity in sinking.
>*Merry Wives of Windsor.*   iii, 5.

Trouble is soon enough when it comes.
>ANON.

To unpathed waters, undreamed shores.
>*Winter's Tale.*   iv, 3.

Heaven gives its favourites—early death.
>BYRON, *Childe Harold.*   Canto iv, st. 102.

Whistling aloud to bear his courage up.
>BLAIR, *The Grave.*

I 've done my duty, and I 've done no more.
>FIELDING, *Tom Thumb the Great.*

Find a cruel man and you see a coward.
>ANON.

It is magnificent, but it is not war.
>BOSQUET, *On Charge of Light Brigade.*

A hundred times in life a coward dies.
>ANON.

The fortune of war is always doubtful.
>SENECA, *Phœnissæ.*   vi, 9.

Blood is the god of war's rich livery.
>MARLOWE, *Tamburlaine the Great.*   Pt. II, iii, 2.

So ends the bloody business of the day.
>HOMER, *Odyssey.*   Bk. XXII, l. 516.   Pope's trans.

Praise the sea, but keep on the land.
>HERBERT, *Jacula Prudentum.*

Danger, the spurre of all great mindes.
>CHAPMAN, *Revenge of Bussy d'Ambois.*   v, 1.

Fortune gives her hand to the bold man.
>VIRGIL.

Dire is the omen when the valiant fear.
> Rowe, *Lucan's Pharsalia.* Bk. VII, 1. 506.

The good seaman is known in bad weather.
> Anon.

Blue, darkly, deeply, beautifully blue.
> Southey, *Madoc in Wales.* Pt. V.

Old men for counsel, young men for war.
> Anon.

True fame is neither bought nor sought.
> Anon.

When one will not, two can not quarrel.
> Spanish Saying.

To whom God will, there be the victory.
> *King Henry VI.* Pt. III, ii, 5, 1. 15.

Come not within the measure of my wrath.
> *Two Gentlemen of Verona.* v, 4.

Unbounded courage and compassion joined.
> Addison, *The Campaign.* 1. 216.

Courage should have eyes as well as arms.
> Anon.

Better an unjust peace than a just war.
> From the Latin.

The angel, Pity, shuns the walks of war.
> Darwin, *Loves of the Plants.* Canto iii, 1. 398.

It was a slaughter rather than a battle.
> Schiller, *Die Jungfrau von Orleans.* i, 9.

Cooped in their wingèd sea-girt citadel.
> Byron, *Childe Harold.* Canto ii, st. 28.

The better part of valour is discretion.
> *King Henry IV.* Pt. I, v, 4.

Eternal vigilance is the price of liberty.
> Curran, *Speech.* Dublin, 1790.

God always favours the heaviest battalions.

VOLTAIRE.

A fair complexion is unbecoming in a sailor.

ANON.

Everyone who does the best he can is a hero.

JOSH BILLINGS.

Yet I love glory :—glory 's a great thing.

BYRON, *Don Juan.* Canto viii.

Arms which to man ne'er-dying Fame afford.

CONGREVE.

To see great Hector in his weeds of peace.

Troilus and Cressida. iii, 3.

A hero's love is as delicate as a maiden's.

THOREAU, *Week.*

A man's best gift to his country — his life's blood.

MCKINLEY, *Speech.* San Francisco, May 23, 1901.

Bravery escapes more dangers than cowardice.

SÉGUR.

A revolution is the lava of a civilisation.

VICTOR HUGO.

God nerve the hero's arm in the fearful fight.

STEDMAN, *Alice of Monmouth.*

Methought I saw a thousand fearful wrecks.

King Richard III. i, 4.

Cry " Havock ! " and let slip the dogs of war.

Julius Cæsar. iii, 1.

Better lose the anchor than the whole ship.

Dutch Saying.

He jests at scars that never felt a wound.

Romeo and Juliet. ii, 2.

Fools rush in where angels fear to tread.

POPE, *Essay on Criticism.* Pt. III, 1. 66.

I will kill thee a hundred and fifty ways.
>> *As You Like It.*   v, 1.

Seldom comes glory till a man be dead.
>> HERRICK, *Hesperides.*   1. 265.

A man of courage is also full of faith.
>> CICERO, *Tusculan Disputations.*   Bk. III, ch. 8.

The harder match'd the greater victory.
>> *King Henry VI.*   Pt. III, v, 1.

Ne'er to meet, ne'er to part, is peace.
>> YOUNG, *Night Thoughts.*   N. v, 1. 1058.

Nothing but peace and gentle visitation.
>> *Love's Labour 's Lost.*   v, 2.

The wounds of civil war are deeply felt.
>> LUCAN, *Pharsalia.*   i, 32.

Advice to persons about to fight : Don 't !
>> ANON.

We have met the enemy and they are ours.
>> PERRY, *Letter to Gen. Harrison.*   Sept. 10, 1813.

Covering discretion with a coat of folly.
>> *King Henry V.*   ii, 4.

The paths of glory lead but to the grave.
>> GRAY, *Elegy in a Country Churchyard.*

Havoc, let loose the dogs of war, halloo !
>> FIELDING, *Tom Thumb.*   ii, 1.

Courage scorns the death it cannot shun.
>> DRYDEN, *Conquest of Granada.*   Pt. II, iv, 2.

There 's no erring twice in love and war.
>> POMFRET, *Love Triumphant over Reason.*   1. 88.

Fearless minds climb soonest unto crowns.
>> *King Henry VI.*   Pt. III, iv, 7.

All are not soldiers that wear red coats.
>> ANON.

By uniting we stand, by dividing we fall.
DICKINSON, *The Liberty Song.*

Grim-visag'd war hath smooth'd his wrinkled front.
King Richard III. i, 1, 1. 9.

The rising world of waters dark and deep.
MILTON, *Paradise Lost.* Bk. III, 1. 11.

Even war is better than a wretched peace.
TACITUS, *Annales.* iii, 44.

Fie, my Lord, fie! a soldier, and afear'd?
Macbeth. v, 1, 1. 41.

Be always valourous, but seldom venturous.
ANON.

We have scotch'd the snake, not kill'd it.
Macbeth. iii, 2.

Ships are but boards, sailors are but men.
Merchant of Venice. i, 3.

He wants worth who dares not praise a foe.
DRYDEN, *Conquest of Granada.* Act ii.

Danger deviseth shifts; wit waits on fear.
Venus and Adonis. St. 115.

Like Douglas conquer, or like Douglas die.
HOME, *Douglas.* v, 1, 1. 100.

Hail to the chief who in triumph advances!
SCOTT, *Lady of the Lake.* Canto ii, st. 19.

There never was a good war or a bad peace.
FRANKLIN, *Letter to Quincy.* Sept. 11, 1773.

Drummer, strike up, and let us march away.
King Henry VI. Pt. III, iv, 7, 1. 50.

In avoiding Scylla we fall into Charybdis.
GUALTIER, *Alexandreis.* v.

The hell of waters! where they howl and hiss.
BYRON, *Childe Harold.* Canto iv, st. 69.

Renowned for their deeds as far from home.
>> *King Richard II.*   ii, 1.

A moderate pension shakes full many a sage.
>> BYRON, *Don Juan.*   Canto viii.

Welcome, brave captain and victorious lord.
>> *King Henry VI.*   Pt. I, iii, 4.

Then is all safe, the anchor's in the port.
>> *Titus Andronicus.*   iv, 4.

He would not flatter Neptune for his trident.
>> *Coriolanus.*   iii, 1.

Hath pass'd in safety through the narrow seas.
>> *King Henry VI.*   Pt. III, iv, 8.

From heart of very heart, great Hector, welcome.
>> *Troilus and Cressida.*   iv, 5.

The best of armour is to keep out of gunshot.
>> BACON.

We can die but once to save our country.
>> ADDISON, *Cato.*   iv, 4.

Don't shout till you're out of the wood.
>> ANON.

'T is next to conquer, bravely to defend.
>> GARTH, *The Dispensary.*   Canto iii, l. 222.

Better face a danger than be always in fear.
>> ANON.

Men at some time are masters of their fates.
>> *Julius Cæsar.*   i, 2.

To be tender-minded does not become a sword.
>> *King Lear.*   v, 3.

Savage bears keep at peace with one another.
>> JUVENAL, *Satire.*   xv, 164.

He who hath no heart should have good heels.
>> ANON.

One murder makes a villain, millions a hero.
PORTEUS.

For self is not to be destroyed, but conquered.
DOANE, *St. Agnes Addresses.*

A lion among ladies is a most dreadful thing.
Midsummer Night's Dream.   iii, 1.

We 'll have a swashing and a martial outside.
As You Like It.   i, 3.

It is time to fear when tyrants seem to kiss.
Pericles.   i, 2.

Still, in thy right hand, carry gentle peace.
King Henry VIII.   iii, 2.

Sail like my pinnace to these golden shores.
Merry Wives of Windsor.   i, 3.

He dares to die for his country or his friends.
HORACE, *Carmina.*   IV, ix, 51.

Nor heed the storm that howls along the sky.
SMOLLETT, *Ode to Independence.*

He serves me most who serves his country best.
POPE, *Iliad.*   Bk. X.

Whistling to keep myself from being afraid.
DRYDEN, *Amphitryon.*

Judge not of a ship as she lies on the stocks.
ANON.

Many would run away if they had courage enough.
ANON.

War is a fire struck in the Devil's tinder-box.
HOWELL, *Familiar Letters.*   Bk. II, let. 43.

The loudest to threaten are the last to thrash.
ANON.

Peace rules the day where reason rules the mind.
COLLINS, *Oriental Eclogues.*   Eclogue 1.

Whilst breezy waves toss up their silvery spray.
> HOOD, *Ode to the Moon.*

In war the olive branch of peace is of use.
> OVID, *Epistolæ ex Ponto.*   I, i, 31.

For where no hope is left, is left no fear.
> MILTON, *Paradise Regained.*   Bk. III, l. 206.

War seldom enters but where wealth allures.
> DRYDEN, *Hind and Panther.*   Pt. II, l. 706.

Blood only serves to wash ambition's hands.
> BYRON, *Don Juan.*   Canto ix, st. 59.

When is a man strong, until he feels alone?
> BROWNING, *Colombe's Birthday.*   Act iii.

Self conquest is the greatest of victories.
> PLATO.

There are few die well that die in a battle.
> *King Henry V.*   iv, 1, l. 148.

The crystal-pointed tents from hill to hill.
> STEDMAN, *Alice of Monmouth.*   xi.

There are heroes in evil as well as in good.
> ROCHEFOUCAULD, *Maxims.*   No. 194.

'T is not the fight that crowns, but the end.
> HERRICK, *Hesperides.*   l. 341.

There were no heroes, were there no martyrs.
> LYTTON, *Last of the Barons.*   Bk. I, ch. 5.

None but yourself who are your greatest foe.
> LONGFELLOW, *Michael Angelo.*   Pt. II, 3.

Wise men and gods are on the strongest side.
> SEDLEY, *Death of Marc Antony.*   iv, 2.

Advantage is a better soldier than rashness.
> *King Henry V.*   iii, 5.

The body of a dead enemy always smells sweet.
> VESPASIAN (attributed to).

Conquest pursues where courage leads the way.
GARTH, *The Dispensary.* Canto iv, l. 99.

Better die with the sword than by the sword.
DANIEL, *Civil War.* Bk. VII, ch. 26.

You will hardly conquer, but conquer you must.
OVID, *Metamorphoses.* ix, 509.

War, that mad game the world so loves to play.
SWIFT, *Ode to Sir William Temple.*

It showed discretion, the best part of valour.
BEAUMONT AND FLETCHER,
King and No King. iv, 3.

He who considers too much will perform little.
SCHILLER, *William Tell.* iii, 1.

Who bravely dares must sometimes risk a fall.
SMOLLETT, *Advice.* l. 208.

Here's to the pilot that weathered the storm.
CANNING, *The Pilot.*

Heroes as great have died, and yet shall fall.
HOMER, *Iliad.* Bk. XV, l. 157. Pope's trans.

Be bolde, Be bolde, and everywhere, Be bolde.
SPENSER, *Faerie Queene.* Bk. III, canto xi, st. 54.

He that will use all winds, must shift his sail.
FLETCHER, *Faithful Shepherdess.* iii, 3.

Lords of the wide world and wild, watery seas.
Comedy of Errors. ii, 1.

The man of courage knows not when he is beaten.
ANON.

Famous throughout the world for warlike praise.
SPENSER, *Faerie Queene.*

A man who will not flee will make his foes flee.
ANON.

More have been drowned in the bowl than in the sea.
From the German.

Revenge converts a little right into a great wrong.
> From the German.

When Fortune favours, none but fools will dally.
> DRYDEN, *Epi. VIII.* To the Duke of Guise.

Between two blades, which bears the better temper.
> *King Henry VI.* Pt. I, ii, 4.

He conquers twice who conquers himself in victory.
> SYRUS, *Maxims.*

On Fame's eternall beadroll worthie to be fyled.
> SPENSER, *Faerie Queene.* Bk. IV, canto ii, st. 32.

War its thousands slays, Peace its ten thousands.
> BEILBY PORTEUS, *Death.* 1. 178.

War, war, is still the cry, " War even to the knife ! "
> BYRON, *Childe Harold.* Canto i, st. 86.

A man without courage is a knife without an edge.
> ANON.

Early and provident fear is the mother of safety.
> BURKE, *Speech on Petition of Unitarians.*

Courage from hearts, and not from numbers, grows.
> DRYDEN, *Annus Mirabilis.* lxxvi.

Victory follows me, and all things follow victory.
> SCUDÉRI, *L'Amour Tyrannique.*

It is in great dangers that we see great courage.
> REGNARD, *Le Légataire.*

When Greeks joined Greeks, then was the tug of war!
> LEE, *Rival Queens.* iv, 2.

A leaden sword in an ivory scabbard is still lead.
> ANON.

Cowards father cowards, and base things sire base.
> *Cymbeline.* iv, 2.

Dangers breed fears, and fears more dangers bring.
> BAXTER, *Love Breathing Thanks and Praise.*
> Pt. III

And high above the fight the lonely bugle grieves.
MELLIN, *Bunker Hill.*

The days of peace and slumberous calm are fled.
KEATS, *Hyperion.* Bk. II.

Despise your enemy, and you'll soon be beaten.
ANON.

The clatter of arms drowns the voice of the law.
MONTAIGNE, *Essais.* iii.

It's poor foolishness to run down your enemies.
ELIOT, *Adam Bede.* Bk. VI, ch. 53.

Peace rules the day where reason rules the mind.
COLLINS, *Eclogue II.* Hassan. 1. 68.

An equal doom clipp'd Time's blest wings of peace.
PETRARCH, *To Laura in Death.* Sonnet xlviii, 1. 18.

Better little man for friend than great man for foe.
ANON.

Breathe soft, ye winds ! ye waves, in silence sleep !
GAY, *To a Lady.* Ep. i, 1. 17.

Peace be to me, and every one that dares not fight.
Love's Labour's Lost. i, 1.

They shall have wars and pay for their presumption.
King Henry VI. Pt. III, iv, 1, 1. 114.

Let's march without the noise of threat'ning drum.
King Richard II. iii, 3, 1. 51.

We Germans fear God, but nothing else in the world.
BISMARCK, In the Reichstag. 1887.

Quarrels seldom last long, with wrong all on one side.
ROCHEFOUCAULD.

He that hath learned to obey will know how to command.
SOLON.

We kind o' thought Christ went agin war an' pillage.
LOWELL, *Biglow Papers.* No. 3.

When you obey your superior you instruct your inferior.
ANON.

There is no person who is not dangerous for someone.
MME. DE SÉVIGNÉ, *Lettres.*

Abolish fear and you can accomplish whatever you wish.
HUBBARD, *Philistine.*

Noble deeds that are concealed are most esteemed.
PASCAL, *Pensées.* I, ix, 21.

An old warrior is never in haste to strike the blow.
METASTASIO.

Many would be cowards if they had sufficient courage.
ANON.

Even in the hero's heart discretion is the better part.
CHURCHILL, *The Ghost.* Pt. I, 1. 232.

Be bold, but not too bold; be strong, but not headstrong.
ANON.

Out of this nettle, danger, we pluck this flower, safety.
King Henry IV. Pt. I, ii, 3.

When our actions do not, our fears do make us traitors.
Macbeth. iv, 2.

Millions for defence, but not one cent for tribute.
PINCKNEY, When Ambassador to French Republic.
1796.

It is sweet and glorious to die for one's country.
HORACE, *Carmina.* III, ii, 13.

I die content, I die for the liberty of my country.
LE PELLETIER (attributed to).

It costs more to revenge injuries than to bear them.
WILSON, *Maxims.* No. 303.

Peace, dear nurse of arts, plenties, and joyful births.
King Henry V. v, 2, 1. 34.

The blood of the soldier makes the glory of the general.
ANON.

He is foolish to blame the sea who is shipwrecked twice.

SYRUS.

Thy head is as full of quarrels as an egg is full of meat.

Romeo and Juliet. iii, 1, l. 23.

Scorn the last word in a quarrel, secure the first after it.

ANON.

Fierce warres, and faithfull loves shall moralise my song.

SPENSER, *Faerie Queene.* Intro., st. 1.

What my tongue speaks my right drawn sword may prove.

King Richard II. i, 1.

Better never to have been born than to live without glory.

NAPOLEON.

This goin' ware glory waits ye haint one agreeable feetur.

LOWELL, *Biglow Papers.*

'T was for the good of my country that I should be abroad.

GEO. FARQUHAR, *Beaux Stratagem.*

Though thy enemy seem a mouse, yet watch him like a lion.

ANON.

You may relish him more in the soldier than in the scholar.

Othello. ii, 1.

It is cowardly to fly from a living enemy or to abuse a dead one.

From the Danish.

Nothing so easy as revenge ; nothing so grand as forgiveness.

ANON.

Nature—Art—Seasons

Nature is the art of God.

SIR THOMAS BROWNE, *Religio Medici*.   Sec. 16.

Nature—Art—Seasons

Art is power.

> LONGFELLOW, *Hyperion.* Bk. III, ch. 5.

Ants never sleep.

> EMERSON, *Nature.* Ch. 4.

Arts that polish life.

> MILTON, *Paradise Lost.* Bk. XI.

Ill weede growth fast.

> HEYWOOD, *Proverbs.*

Summer's parching heat.

> *King Henry VI.* Pt. II, i, 1, 1. 81.

Smooth waters run deep.

> Scotch Proverb.

Nature means necessity.

> BAILEY, *Festus.* Dedication.

The boyhood of the year.

> TENNYSON, *Sir Launcelot.* St. 3.

Nature is the art of God.

> BROWNE, *Religio Medici.* Pt. I, sec. 16.

The woods have many ears.

> MUNDAY AND CHETTLE, *Death of Earl of Huntingdon.* i, 2.

Who can paint like Nature?

> THOMSON, *Seasons.* Spring. 1. 465.

Flowers worthy of Paradise.

> MILTON, *Paradise Lost.*

Art is the child of Nature.
> LONGFELLOW, *Keramos.*

Rustic herald of the Spring.
> AKENSIDE, *Ode III.* To the Cuckoo.

Nature's unchanging harmony.
> SHELLEY, *Queen Mab.* ii.

Architecture is frozen music.
> SCHELLING, *Philosophy of Art.* 1. 576.

Keep your weather eye open.
> ANON.

Over the hills and far away.
> GAY, *Beggar's Opera.* i, 1.

It never rains but it pours.
> ANON.

The ripest fruit first falls.
> *King Richard II.* ii, 1, 1. 153.

Rouse the lion from his lair.
> SCOTT, *The Talisman.* Heading ch. 6.

Autumn nodding o'er the plain.
> THOMSON, *Seasons.* Autumn. 1. 2.

Follow nature, and not fashion.
> CHESTERFIELD, *Letters.* March, 1747.

The natural alone is permanent.
> LONGFELLOW, *Kavanagh.* Ch. 13.

Rich with the spoils of nature.
> BROWNE, *Religio Medici.* Pt. I, sec. 13.

Infantine Art, divinely Artless.
> BROWNING, *Red Cotton Nightcap Country.* ii.

And every dew-drop paints a bow.
> TENNYSON, *In Memoriam.* Pt. CXXII.

Art is the perfection of Nature.
> BROWNE, *Religio Medici.* Sec. 16.

When the sunne shineth, make hay.

HEYWOOD, *Proverbs.* Bk. I, ch. 3.

A fine cage never feeds a bird.

From the French.

A brotherhood of venerable Trees.

WORDSWORTH. Sonnet composed at Castle ——.

Nothing in Nature is unbeautiful.

TENNYSON, *The Lover's Tale.* 1. 348.

Art is long and time is fleeting.

LONGFELLOW, *A Psalm of Life.*

Nature's first great title-mind.

CROLY, *Pericles and Aspasia.*

When yellow waves the heavy grain.

BURNS, *The Vision.*

For the rain it raineth every day.

Twelfth Night. v, 1.

A good garden may have some weeds.

ANON.

The poetry of earth is never dead.

KEATS, *Grasshopper and Cricket.*

To the earth the plow seems cruel.

ANON.

The never idle workshop of Nature.

ARNOLD, *Elegiac Poems.* Ep.

There are no grotesques in nature.

BROWNE, *Religio Medici.* Pt. XV.

A picture is a poem without words.

CORNIFICIUS, *Anet. ad Her.* iv, 28.

The sunrise wakes the lark to sing.

CHRISTINA G. ROSSETTI, *Bird Raptures.* 1. 1.

Some touch of Nature's genial glow.

SCOTT, *Lord of the Isles.* Canto iii, st. 14.

Nature is always wise in every part.
> THURLOW, *Select Poems.*   Harvest Moon.

Nature vicarye of the Almighty Lord.
> CHAUCER, *Parlement of Foules.*   1. 379

How soon prospers the vicious weed.
> FLETCHER, *Apollyonist.*   Canto iii, st. 4.

The busy lark, the messenger of day.
> CHAUCER, *Knight's Tale.*   1. 1493.

Spring is the painter of the earth.
> ALCUIN.

A day in April never came so sweet!
> *Merchant of Venice.*   ii, 9.

Falling leaves are Nature's sermons.
> ANON.

The sea is certainly common to all.
> PLAUTUS, *Rudens.*   IV, iii, 36.

Art may err, but Nature cannot miss.
> DRYDEN, *The Cock and Fox.*

Nature, the Handmaid of God Almighty.
> HOWELL, *Familiar Letters.*   Bk. II, let. 6.

Framed in the prodigality of nature.
> *King Richard III.*   i, 2.

Art curbs Nature, Nature guideth Art.
> MARSTON, *Scourge of Villainy.*

Architecture is the work of nations.
> RUSKIN, *Sculpture.*

He that sips many arts drinks none.
> ANON.

A bird in a cage is not half a bird.
> HENRY WARD BEECHER.

God Almightie first planted a garden.
> BACON, *Essay XLVI.*   Of Gardens.

All nature wears one universal grin.

> FIELDING, *Tom Thumb the Great.* i, 1.

Self-defense is Nature's eldest law.

> DRYDEN, *Absalom and Achitophel.* Pt. I, 1. 458.

The uncertain glory of an April day !

> *Two Gentlemen of Verona.* i, 3.

A little bird needs but a small nest.

> ANON.

O Winter ! ruler of the inverted year.

> COWPER, *The Task.* Winter Evening.
> Bk. IV, 1. 120.

Stern Winter loves a dirge-like sound.

> WORDSWORTH, *On the Power of Sound.* St. 12.

Pictures must not be too picturesque.

> EMERSON, *Of Art.*

Nature's tears are reason's merriment.

> *Romeo and Juliet.* iv, 5.

Nature stamp'd us in a Heavenly mould.

> CAMPBELL, *Pleasures of Hope.* i.

Art indeed is long, but Life is short.

> MARVELL, *On death of Lord Hastings.*

Death, kind Nature's signal of retreat.

> JOHNSON, *Vanity of Human Wishes.* 1. 362.

Earth, air, and ocean, glorious three.

> MONTGOMERY, *On Women.*

Nature in him was almost lost in Art.

> COLLINS, *To Sir Thomas Hammer.*

Who lives to Nature rarely can be poor.

> YOUNG, *Night Thoughts.* N. vi, 1. 530.

And liquid lapse of murmuring streams.

> MILTON, *Paradise Lost.* Bk. VIII, 1. 263.

Forests have ears, and fields have eyes.

> LONGFELLOW, *Saga of King Olaf.* viii.

All Nature is but Art, unknown to thee.
POPE, *Essay on Man.* Ep. i, 1. 289.

The perfection of art is to conceal art.
QUINTILIAN.

The fellow mixes blood with his colours.
RENI GUIDO, *Uttered of Rubens.*

As full of spirit as the month of May.
King Henry IV. Pt. I, iv, 1.

Spare, woodman, spare the beechen tree!
CAMPBELL, *The Beech-Tree's Petition.*

Soft silken primrose fading timelessly.
MILTON, *On Death of an Infant.*

To shoot at crows is powder flung away.
GAY. Ep. iv, 1. last.

A kiss from my mother made me a painter.
WEST.

The course of Nature is the art of God.
YOUNG, *Night Thoughts.* N. ix, 1. 1280.

If folly grow romantic, I must paint it.
POPE, *Moral Essays.* Ep. ii, 1. 15.

A rosebud set with little wilful thorns.
TENNYSON, *The Princess.* Pro.

Keep not from sowing for fear of the birds.
ANON.

The statue lies hid in the block of marble.
ADDISON.

To hold, as 't were, the mirror up to nature.
Hamlet.

If Winter comes, can Spring be far behind?
SHELLEY, *Ode to West Wind.* Pt. V.

There's rosemary, that 's for remembrance.
Hamlet. iv, 5.

Nature needs little ; opinion exacts much.

ANON.

Expect St. Martin's summer, halcyon days.

King Henry VI. Pt. I, i, 2.

Nature's licensed vagabond, the swallow.

TENNYSON, *Queen Mary.* v, 1.

Wines work when vines are in the flower.

BUTLER, *Hudibras.* Pt. II, canto i, 1. 286.

The world globes itself in a drop of dew.

EMERSON, *Compensation.*

To-morrow to fresh woods and pastures new.

MILTON, *Lycidas.*

Most subject is the fattest soil to weeds.

King Henry IV. Pt. II, iv, 4.

By the bird's song ye may learn the nest.

TENNYSON, *Geraint and Enid.*

Not without art, but yet to Nature true.

CHURCHILL, *The Rosciad.* 1. 699.

And the cold marble leapt to life a God.

MILMAN, *The Belvedere Apollo.*

Every form as nature made it is correct.

PROPERTIUS, *Elegia.* II, xviii, 25.

And the spring comes slowly up this way.

COLERIDGE, *Christabel.* Pt. I.

The ripest peach is highest on the tree.

RILEY, *The Ripest Peach.*

Nature 's God's, Art is man's instrument.

OVERBURY, *A Wife.* St. 8.

It was Homer who gave laws to the artist.

WAYLAND, *The Iliad and the Bible.*

I only feel, but want the power to paint.

JUVENAL, *Satiræ.* vii, 56.

Art is difficult, transient is her reward.
SCHILLER, *Wallenstein.* Pro., l. 40.

Use can almost change the stamp of Nature.
Hamlet. iii, 4.

Look here, upon this picture, and on this.
Hamlet. iii, 4, l. 53.

The Indian Summer, the dead Summer's soul.
CLEMMER, *Presence.* l. 62.

The universe is but one vast symbol of God.
CARLYLE, *Sartor Resartus.* Bk. III, ch. 3.

His faithful dog salutes the smiling guest.
CAMPBELL, *Pleasures of Hope.* Pt. I, l. 86.

Nature teaches beasts to know their friends.
Coriolanus. ii, 1.

Apples and crabs may grow on the same tree.
BAXTER, *Hypocrisy.*

Far from the madding crowd's ignoble strife.
GRAY, *Elegy in Country Churchyard.*

I bring fresh showers for the thirsty flowers.
SHELLEY, *The Cloud.* vi.

Distinct as the billows, yet one as the sea.
MONTGOMERY, *The Ocean.* St. 6.

Change of weather is the discourse of fools.
ANON.

Squat like a toad, close at the ear of Eve.
MILTON, *Paradise Lost.* Bk. IV, l. 800.

See, Winter comes, to rule the varied year.
THOMSON, *Seasons.* Winter. l. 1.

But Winter lingering chills the lap of May.
GOLDSMITH, *The Traveller.* l. 172.

Cussing the weather is mighty poor farming.
ANON.

I was never less alone than when by myself.
GIBBON, *Memoir.*

Who loves a garden, loves a greenhouse too.
COWPER, *The Task.* The Garden. 1. 566.

Lauk! what a monstrous tail our cat has got!
CAREY, *Dragon of Wantley.* ii, 1.

Art can never give the rules that make an art.
BURKE, *On Sublime and Beautiful.*

All passes. Art alone enduring stays to us.
DOBSON.

How hard it is to hide the sparks of Nature!
Cymbeline. iii, 3, 1. 79.

The fur that warms a monarch, warm'd a bear.
POPE, *Essay on Man.* Ep. iii, 1. 44.

One touch of Nature makes the whole world kin.
Troilus and Cressida. iii, 3, 1. 175.

Nature is seldom in the wrong, custom always.
MONTAGU, *Letter to Miss A. Wortley.* 1709.

Fruits that blossom first will first be ripe.
Othello. ii, 3, 1. 383.

Far from the gay cities, and the ways of men.
HOMER, *Odyssey.* Bk. XIV, 1. 410. Pope's trans.

The sleeping and the dead are but as pictures.
Macbeth. ii, 2.

Love the sea? I dote upon it—from the beach.
JERROLD, *Jerrold's Wit.* Love of the Sea.

Eat the fruit and don't inquire about the tree.
ANON.

Smooth runs the water where the brook is deep.
King Henry IV. Pt. II, iii, 1.

Though Nature's sternest painter, yet the best.
BYRON, *English Bards and Scotch Reviewers.*

It is not strength but art obtains the prize.
>> POPE, *Iliad.*

Come, gentle Spring! ethereal Mildness! come.
>> THOMSON, *Seasons.* Spring. 1. i.

O fairest flower, no sooner blown but blasted.
>> MILTON, *On Death of an Infant.*

God made the country and man made the town.
>> COWPER, *The Task.* The Sofa.

Nature hath framed strange fellows in her time.
>> *Merchant of Venice.* i, i.

And those who paint 'em truest praise 'em most.
>> ADDISON, *The Campaign.* 1. last.

Sweet as the primrose peeps beneath the thorn.
>> GOLDSMITH, *Deserted Village.* 1. 329.

Hills peep o'er hills, and Alps on Alps arise!
>> POPE, *Essay on Criticism.* Pt. II, 1. 32.

Use Greek art as a first, not a final, teacher.
>> RUSKIN, *Queen of the Air.*

Thou hast seen a farmer's dog bark at a beggar?
>> *King Lear.* iv, 6, 1. 159.

Drive the natural away, it returns at a gallop.
>> DESTOUCHES, *Glorieux.* v, 3.

Art is indeed not the bread but the wine of life.
>> RICHTER.

The hawthorn-trees blow in the dew of the morning.
>> BURNS, *The Chevalier's Lament.*

All Nature's diff'rence keeps all Nature's peace.
>> POPE, *Essay on Man.* Ep. iv, 1. 51.

Strength levels grounds, Art makes a garden there.
>> HERBERT, *Church Militant.*

Every dog hath his day, and every man his hour.
>> ANON.

The wolf loses his teeth, but not his inclination.

> Spanish Saying.

It is n't the biggest trees that bear the most fruit.

> ANON.

It is not the worst fruit on which the wasp lights.

> BUERGER.

Small herbs have grace, great weeds do grow apace.

> *King Richard III.* ii, 4.

A barleycorn is better than a diamond to a crow.

> ANON.

He best can paint them who shall feel them most.

> POPE, *Eloisa and Abelard.* 1. ult.

Solitude is the voice of Nature that speaks to us.

> SAND.

God the first garden made, and the first city Cain.

> COWLEY, *Stanzas to J. Eveleyn, Esq.*

He who has been bitten by a snake is afraid of an eel.

> ANON.

The eyes are charmed by paintings, the ears by music.

> CICERO, *Academici.* iv, 7.

Man is Creation's masterpiece. But who says so? Man!

> GAVARNI.

One is never criminal in obeying the voice of Nature.

> BALZAC.

Men do nothing excellent but by imitation of Nature.

> ROUSSEAU.

The world looks not the same to the eagle and its prey.

> ANON.

In our fine arts not imitation but creation is the aim.

> EMERSON, *Art.*

Birds with bright plumage do not always make good pie.

> ANON.

When we go for berries we must not retreat from briers.
ANON.

All the arts of pleasure grow when suckled by freedom.
SCHILLER, *Der Spaziergang*. 1. 22.

Love is a religion of which the great pontiff is Nature.
ANON.

All things are artificial ; for Nature is the Art of God.
BROWNE, *Religio Medici*. Sec. 16.

Nature never makes excellent things for mean or no uses.
LOCKE, *Essay on Human Understanding*.
Bk. II, ch. i, sec. 15.

Nothing is great but the inexhaustible wealth of Nature.
EMERSON, *Resources*.

A little stream as well as a river may quench the thirst.
ANON.

Dead he is not, but departed, —for the artist never dies.
LONGFELLOW, *Nuremberg*. St. 13.

Nature alone is antique, and the oldest art a mushroom.
CARLYLE, *Sartor Resartus*. Bk. II, ch. 3.

Divine Nature gave the fields, human art built the cities.
VARRO, *De re Rustica*. iii, 1.

That the soul of our grandam might haply inhabit a
bird.
Twelfth Night. iv, 2.

What we call a gentleman is no longer the man of
nature.
DIDEROT.

Beneath the milk-white thorn that scents the evening
gale.
BURNS, *Cotter's Saturday Night*.

When spring unlocks the flowers to paint the laughing soil.

> HEBER, *Hymn for Seventh Sunday after Trinity.*

Illusion on a ground of truth is the secret of the fine arts.

> JOUBERT.

We never know the worth of water until the well runs dry.

> ANON.

It is my temper and I like it the better to affect all harmony.

> BROWNE, *Religio Medici.*

Nowadays, those who love nature are accused of being romantic.

> CHAMFORT.

Plant the crab-tree where you will, it will never bear pippins.

> ANON.

It is only at the tree loaded with fruit that people throw stones.

> From the French.

Life without industry is guilt. Industry without art is brutality.

> HUBBARD, *Philistine.*

A great fondness for animals often results from a knowledge of men.

> From the French.

Nature has given man no better thing than shortness of life.

> PLINY THE ELDER, *Historia Naturalis.* vii, 51, 3.

Every dew-drop and rain-drop had a whole heaven within it.

> LONGFELLOW, *Hyperion.* Bk. III, ch. 7.

Nature is a mutable cloud which is always and never the same.

> EMERSON, *Essay.* History.

For one swallow does not make spring, nor yet one fine day.

> ARISTOTLE, *Ethics.* i, 6.

Painters and poets have equal license in regard to everything.

> HORACE, *Ars Poetica.* ix.

Custom which is above all law, Nature which is above all art.

> DANIEL, *An Apology for Rhime.*

When well apparel'd April on the heel of limping winter treads.

> *Romeo and Juliet.* i, 2.

Flowers, leaves, fruit are therefore air-woven children of light.

> MOLESCHOTT, *Licht und Leben.* p. 29.

A crowd is not company; and faces are but a gallery of Pictures.

> BACON, *Essay XXVII.* Of Friendship.

Art may make a suit of clothes : but Nature must produce a man.

> HUME, *Essay XV.* The Epicurean.

Nature has given us the seeds of knowledge, not knowledge itself.

> SENECA, *Epistolæ Ad Lucilium.* cxx.

There are many more fishes in the sea than were ever taken out of it .

> ANON.

It is good to lend to God and the soil ; they pay good interest.

> Danish Saying.

No matter how much you feed a wolf he will always return to the forest.

ANON.

To me high mountains are a feeling, but the hum of human cities torture.

BYRON, *Childe Harold*, Canto iii, st. 72.

Clipping the tiger's claws never makes him lose his taste for blood.

ANON.

One's own thistle field is dearer to him than his neighbour's garden of roses.

From the German.

The rock that resists a crowbar gives way to the roots of the tender plant.

TAMIL.

God gives to every bird its food, but does not throw it into the nest.

HOLLAND.

He who hunts for flowers will find flowers; he who loves weeds may find weeds.

BEECHER.

The conscious utterance of thought by speech or action, to any end is art.

EMERSON, *Art*.

Things perfected by nature are better than those finished by art.

CICERO, *De Natura Deorum*. ii, 34.

Certainly nothing is unnatural that is not physically impossible.

SHERIDAN, *The Critic*. ii, 1.

Art is a natural product of humanity, as vegetation is a product of the soil.

L'EVEQUE, *Spiritualism in Art*.

15

Youth and Will may resist excess, but Nature takes revenge in silence.

DE MUSSET.

Great men are seldom over scrupulous in the arrangement of their attire.

CHARLES DICKENS, *Pickwick Papers.* Ch. ii.

I pray that the life of this spring and summer may ever lie fair in my memory.

THOREAU, *Early Spring.*

In order to manage an ungovernable beast, he must be stinted in his provender.

Queen Elizabeth.

A bear never knows until he is muzzled how many people are not afraid of him.

ANON.

To pay homage to beauty is to admire Nature ; to admire Nature is to worship God.

ANON.

You may turn Nature out of doors with violence, but she will still return.

HORACE, *Epistolæ.* i, 10, 24.

The only good copies are those which exhibit the defects of bad originals.

ROCHEFOUCAULD, *Maxims.* No. 136.

Arts that represent the mind were ever reputed nobler than those that serve the body.

BEN JONSON, *Discoveries.*

The province of art is not to present a specific message, but to impart a feeling.

HUBBARD, *Philistine.*

The science of Nature initiates the human mind into the secret thoughts of Divinity.

MME. D'AGOULT.

A cow is a very good animal in the field ; bu we turn
her out of a garden.

> BOSWELL, *Life of Johnson*. An. 1772.

Where the katydid works her chromatic reed on the wal-
nut-tree over the well.

> WHITMAN, *Leaves of Grass*. Pt. XXXIII, st. 196.

Beauty is the first gift Nature gives to women, and the
first she takes from her.

> MÉRÉ.

Picture is the invention of heaven, the most ancient and
the most akin to nature.

> BEN JONSON, *Discoveries*.

All nature is your congratulation, and you have cause
momentarily to bless yourself.

> THOREAU, *Walden*.

Greater completion marks the progress of art, absolute
completion its decline.

> RUSKIN, *Seven Lamps of Architecture*.
> Pt. XXX, ch. iv.

A blade of grass is always a blade of grass, whether in
one country or another.

> SAMUEL JOHNSON, *Mrs. Piozzi's Anecdotes
> of Johnson*. p. 100.

All kinds of nonsense are talked to you, now-a-days,
ingeniously and irrelevantly, about art.

> RUSKIN, *Queen of the Air*.

It has been the providence of nature to give this creature
nine lives instead of one.

> PILPAY, *Fable III*.

Animals are such agreeable friends — they ask no questions, they pass no criticisms.

> ELIOT, *Mr. Gilfil's Love Story*. Ch. vii.

See one promontory (said Socrates of old), one mountain,
one sea, one river, and see all.

BURTON, *Anat. of Melancholy.* Pt. I, sec. ii,
memb. 4, subsec. 1.

I desire everything in its proper season, that neither the
men nor the times be out of temper.

BROWNE, *Religio Medici.*

Shall I not have intelligence with the earth? Am I not
partly leaves and vegetable mould myself?

THOREAU, *Walden.*

Whenever the faculties of men are at their fulness, they
must express themselves by art.

RUSKIN, *Crown of Wild Olive.* War. 93.

Piety in art — poetry in art — Puseyism in art — let us be
careful how we confound them.

MRS. JAMESON, *Memoirs and Essays.*
House of Titian.

Let us a little permit Nature to take her own way ; she
better understands her own affairs than we.

MONTAIGNE, *Essays.* Experience.

As the arts advance towards their perfection the science
of criticism advances with equal pace.

BURKE, *On Taste.*

Virtue, as it is understood by the world, is a constant
struggle against the laws of nature.

DE FINOD.

I do not know of any poetry to quote which adequately
expresses this yearning for the Wild.

THOREAU, *Excursions.*

Greek art, and all other art, is fine when it makes a
man's face as like a man's face as it can.

RUSKIN, *Queen of the Air.*

The morning wind forever blows, the poem of creation
is uninterrupted ; but few are the ears that hear it.
THOREAU, *Walden.*

The business of Art is not to represent things as Nature
makes them, but as she ought to make them.
RAPHAEL (attributed to).

I am not satisfied with ordinary windows. I must have a
true sky-light, and that is outside the village.
THOREAU, *Letters.*

Art is the right hand of Nature. The latter has only
given us being, the former has made us men.
SCHILLER, *Fiesco.* ii, 17.

Now every field and every tree is in bloom. The woods
are in full leaf, and the year in its highest beauty.
VIRGIL, *Ecloga.* iii, 56.

The elephant hath joints, but none for courtesy : his legs
are legs for necessity, not for flexure.
Troilus and Cressida. ii, 3, 1. 97.

We see spiders, flies, or ants entombed and preserved
forever in amber, a more than royal tomb.
BACON, *Historia Vitæ et Mortis.*

Nature, which is the time-vesture of God, and reveals
Him to the wise, hides Him from the foolish.
CARLYLE, *Sartor Resartus.* Bk. III, ch. viii.

There are three things that I have always loved and have
never understood : Painting, Music, and Women.
FONTENELLE.

I have lately got back to that glorious society, called
Solitude, where we meet our friends continually.
THOREAU, *Letters.*

The truly great are by universal suffrage exempted from
these trammels, and may live or dress as they please.
COLTON, *Lacon.*

How can a man comprehend great matters, that breaketh
his minde too much to small observations?

BACON, *Essay LII.* Of Ceremonies.

He had a head which statuaries loved to copy, and a foot
the deformity of which the beggars in the street
mimicked.

MACAULAY, *On Moore's Life of Byron.*

He only is a great man who can neglect the applause of
the multitude, and enjoy himself independent of its
favour.

STEELE, *Spectator.* No. 554.

Those who make their dress a principal part of themselves, will, in general, become of no more value
than their dress.

HAZLITT, *Political Essays.* On Clerical Character.

Reminiscences—Old Age—Memory

'T is greatly wise to talk with our past hours.

EDWARD YOUNG, *Night Thoughts*. ii, 1. 376.

Reminiscences—Old Age—Memory

I wept for memory.
C. G. ROSSETTI, *Song, She Sat and Sang Always.*

Slow-consuming age.
GRAY, *Ode on Eton College.* St. 9.

Old friends are best.
SELDEN, *Table Talk.* Friends.

Our hour is fully out.
Antony and Cleopatra. iv, 9.

In the brave old days.
MACAULAY, *Lays of Ancient Rome.*

I bear a charmed life.
Macbeth. v, 8, 1. 12.

Actions are our epochs.
BYRON, *Manfred.* ii, 1.

Thou tedious old fools.
Hamlet. ii, 2.

Old head and young hand.
ANON.

Time hath a taming hand.
NEWMAN, *Persecution.* 1. ult.

Briefly thyself remember.
King Lear. iv, 6, 1. 233.

Old foxes want no tutor.
ANON.

Time can tarry for no man.
BEAUMONT AND FLETCHER, *Scornful Lady.* v.3.

233

What 's past is prologue.

The Tempest. ii, 1, 1. 253.

Old oxen have stiff horns.

ANON.

Life is but a day at most.

BURNS, *Friars' Carse Hermitage.*

I, the heir of all the ages.

TENNYSON, *Locksley Hall.*

Old men are twice children.

RANDOLPH, *Jealous Lovers.* iii, 6.

An old man is twice a child.

Hamlet. ii, 2, 1. 404.

Be old young, and old long.

ANON.

Memory, bosom spring of joy.

COLERIDGE, *Domestic Peace.*

The Wisdom of our ancestors.

BACON (according to Lord Brougham).

An old man 's twice a child.

MASSINGER, *Bashful Lover.* iii, 1.

Quoth the raven, " Nevermore."

POE, *The Raven.*

Old sacks want much patching.

ANON.

All times when old are good.

BYRON, *The Age of Bronze.* i.

Steeped to the lips in memory.

LONGFELLOW, *Goblet of Life.*

Tide and time for no man stay.

SOMERVILLE, *The Scented Miser.*

The past, at least, is secure.

WEBSTER, On Foot's Resolution.

When age is in the wit is out.
> *Much Ado About Nothing.* iii, 5.

Fretting cares make grey hairs.
> ANON.

Rivetted, screw'd to my memory.
> *Cymbeline.* ii, 2.

Our past has gone into history.
> McKINLEY, *Speech.* Memphis, April 30, 1901.

Remembered joys are never past.
> MONTGOMERY, *The Little Cloud.*

Few persons know how to be old.
> ROCHEFOUCAULD, *Maxims and Moral Sentences.*
> No. 448.

Liars should have good memories.
> Old Proverb.

Old age is an incurable disease.
> SENECA, *Epistolæ Ad Lucilium.* cviii, 29.

Old foxes are not easily caught.
> ANON.

A man is never too old to learn.
> MIDDLETON, *Mayor of Queenborough.* v, 1.

Memory, the warder of the brain.
> *Macbeth.* i, 7.

No man can call again yesterday.
> ANON.

Let the dead Past bury its dead.
> LONGFELLOW, *A Psalm of Life.*

Men are still children at sixty.
> AUBERT.

My life is one demd horrid grind.
> DICKENS, *Nicholas Nickleby.* Vol. II, ch. xxxii.

Old dogs are in no hurry to bark.
> ANON.

Asleep in the lap of legends old.

KEATS, *Eve of St. Agnes.*

Prefer old heads and young hands.

ANON.

The silver livery of advised age.

King Henry VI. Pt. II, v, 2.

Once more who would not be a boy ?

BYRON, *Childe Harold.* Canto ii, 23.

Remembrance oft may start a tear.

BURNS. Verses written under great grief.

Old birds are not caught by chaff.

ANON.

The eternal landscape of the past.

TENNYSON, *In Memoriam.* Pt. XLVI.

There is no fool like an old fool.

ANON.

How ill white hairs become a fool.

King Henry IV. Pt. II, v, 5, 1. 52.

O good grey head which all men knew.

TENNYSON, *On Death of Duke of Wellington.* St. 4.

His saying was : live and let live.

SCHILLER, *Wallenstein's Lager.* vi, 106, 110.

Cows forget that they were calves.

ANON.

Time and wind stay no man's pleasure.

SOUTHWELL, *St. Peter's Complaint.*

Procrastination is the thief of time.

YOUNG, *Night Thoughts.* N. i, 1. 393.

By our remembrances of days foregone.

All's Well that Ends Well. i, 3.

All our tastes are but reminiscences.

LAMARTINE.

We have some salt of our youth in us.
Merry Wives of Windsor. ii, 3.

The dust we tread upon was once alive.
BYRON, *Sardanapalus.* iv, 1, 1. 66.

How noiseless falls the foot of time.
SPENCER, *To Lady A. Hamilton.*

Though old and wise, yet still advise.
ANON.

Hunt half a day for a forgotten dream.
WORDSWORTH, *Hart-Leap Well.*

The very life which we enjoy is short.
SALLUST, *Catilina.* i.

Remembrance and reflection how allied !
POPE, *Essay on Man.* Ep. i, 1. 225.

The very staff of my age, my very prop.
Merchant of Venice. ii, 2.

Still are the thoughts to memory dear.
SCOTT, *Rokeby.* Canto i, st. 32.

Sorrows remembered sweeten present joy.
POLLOK, *Course of Time.*

O, call back yesterday, bid time return.
King Richard II. iii, 2.

But where are the snows of yester year ?
VILLON, *Ballade des Dames du Temps Jadis.*

May I attain to a youth never attained!
THOREAU, *Early Spring.*

Old men for counsel, young men for war.
ANON.

And make each day a critic on the last.
POPE, *Essay on Criticism.* Pt. iii, 1. 12.

He was not of an age, but for all time !
BEN JONSON, *Underwoods.* xii.
To Shakespeare's Memory.

For you and I are past our dancing days.
Romeo and Juliet. i, 5.
Men are but children of a larger growth.
DRYDEN, *All for Love.* iv, 1.
The days of rejoicing are gone forever.
DU LORENS, *Le Tableau Parlant.*
Old heads will not suit young shoulders.
ANON.
Time conquers all, and we must Time obey.
POPE, *Pastorals.* Winter. 1. 88.
May you live all the days of your life.
SWIFT, *Polite Conversation.* Dia. ii.
A youth of frolics, an old age of cards.
POPE, *Moral Essays.* Ep. ii, 1. 244.
We lift our heads, a race of other days.
SPRAGUE, *Centennial Ode.*
Our lives are but marches to the grave.
BEAUMONT AND FLETCHER, *Humourous Lieutenant.*
iii, 5, 1. 76.
When an old dog barks he giveth counsel.
ANON.
The inaudible and noiseless foot of Time.
All 's Well that Ends Well. v, 3.
My eyes make pictures when they are shut.
COLERIDGE, *A Day-Dream.*
Where once my careless childhood strayed.
GRAY, *Distant Prospect of Eton.*
And send him many years of sunshine days !
King Richard II. iv, 1.
She thinks I am too old, and she too young.
STODDARD, *Liber Amoris.*
Prudent youth is better than rash old age.
ANON.

Repent what's past ; avoid what is to come.
Hamlet. iii, 7, l. 149.

The memory of the just survives in Heaven.
WORDSWORTH, *The Excursion.* Bk. VII.

To vanish in the chinks that Time has made.
ROGERS, *Pæstum.*

The bitter past, more welcome is the sweet.
All's Well that Ends Well. v. 3.

Nor cast one longing ling'ring look behind.
GRAY, *Elegy.* St. 22.

An old dog is not to be coaxed with a crust.
CERVANTES.

How sharp the point of this remembrance is !
The Tempest. v, 1, l. 137.

Men shut their doors against a setting sun.
Timon of Athens. i, 2, l. 129.

Must understand his own age and the next.
LOWELL, *A Glance Behind the Curtain.*

Old men are testy and will have their way.
SHELLEY, *The Cenci.* i, 2.

My life is like a stroll upon the beach.
THOREAU, *Week on Concord and Merrimack.*

He seems to be a man sprung from himself.
TIBERIUS. See *Annals of Tacitus*, Bk. XI, sc. 21.

Life is not measured by the time we live.
CRABBE, *The Village.* Bk. II.

It matters not how long we live, but how.
BAILEY, *Festus.* Sc. Wood and Water.

A man's life 's no more than to say " One."
Hamlet. v, 2, l. 74.

In a certain sense all men are historians.
CARLYLE, *Essays.* On History.

Learn that the present hour alone is Man's.
> SAMUEL JOHNSON, *Irene.* iii, 2, l. 33.

To live is not a blessing, but to live well.
> SENECA, *Epistolæ Ad Lucilium.* lxx.

How short is life! how frail is human trust!
> GAY, *Trivia.* Bk. III, l. 235.

Whose life is a bubble, and in length a span.
> BROWNE, *Britannia Pastorals.* Bk. I, song 2.

Be in their flowing cups freshly remembered.
> *King Henry V.* iv, 3, l. 55.

Old men are as anxious to live as the young.
> ANON.

Backward, flow backward, O tide of the years !
> ELIZABETH ALLEN, *Rock Me to Sleep.*

Against three score have something in store.
> ANON.

Whose yesterdays look backward with a smile.
> YOUNG, *Night Thoughts.* N. ii, l. 322.

Time will run back, and fetch the age of gold.
> MILTON, *Hymn on Christ's Nativity.* l. 135.

'T is greatly wise to talk with our past hours.
> YOUNG, *Night Thoughts.* ii, l. 376.

Thyself no more deceive, thy youth hath fled.
> PETRARCH, *To Laura in Death.* Sonnet LXXXII.

Let us respect white hair—especially our own.
> PETIT-SENN.

Begin to patch up thine old body for heaven.
> *King Henry VI.* Pt. II, ii, 4, l. 193.

Young saint, old devil ; young devil, old saint.
> Old Saying.

Old tunes are sweetest, and old friends surest.
> ANON.

In life's morning march, when my bosom was young.
                    CAMPBELL, *Soldier's Dream.*

Young twigges are sooner bent than old trees.
                    LYLY, *Euphues and his England.*

Shall I never see a bachelor of three-score again?
                    Much Ado About Nothing. i, 1.

They say women and music should never be dated.
                    GOLDSMITH, *She Stoops to Conquer.* Act iii.

Past and to come seems best ; things present worse.
                    King Henry IV. Pt. II, i, 3, 1. 108.

The best of prophets of the future is the past.
                    BYRON, *Letter.* Jan. 28, 1821.

As we grow old, we grow more foolish and more wise.
                    ROCHEFOUCAULD.

Old age comes on apace to ravage all the clime.
                    BEATTIE, *The Minstrel.* Bk. I, st. 25.

How ill white hairs become a fool and a jester.
                    King Henry IV. Pt. II, 7, 5.

Every moment of life is a step toward the grave.
                    CRÉBILLON, *Tite et Bérénice.* i, 5.

As you are old and reverend, you should be wise.
                    King Lear. i, 4, 1. 261.

To live in hearts we leave behind is not to die.
                    CAMPBELL, *Hallowed Ground.*

There are worse losses than the loss of youth.
                    INGELOW, *The Star's Monument.*

The part of life which we really live is short.
                    SENECA, *De Brevitate Vitæ.* ii.

I know nothing about it ; I am my own ancestor.
                    JUNOT. Duc d'Abrantes, when asked about
                                        his ancestry.

So that my life be brave, what though not long?
                    WILLIAM DRUMMOND, *Sonnet.*

Let life be short; else shame will be too long.
King Henry V. iv, 5, 1. 23.

This also, that I live, I consider a gift of God.
Ovid, *Tristium.* i, 1, 20.

Music revives the recollections it would appease.
De Staël, *Corinne.* Bk. IX, ch. ii.

Make haste to live, and consider each day a life.
Seneca, *Epistolæ ad Lucilium.* ci.

That life is long, which answers life's great end.
Young, *Night Thoughts.* N. v, 1. 773.

History casts its shadows far into the land of song.
Longfellow, *Outre-Mer.* Ancient Spanish Ballads.

We extol ancient things, regardless of our own times.
Tacitus, *Annales.* ii, 88.

The hour which gives us life begins to take it away.
Seneca, *Hercules Furens.* viii, 74.

A well-written life is almost as rare as a well-spent one.
Carlyle, *Essays.* Jean P. F. Richter.

Old age makes the head white, but not always wise.
Anon.

Old Time the clock setter, that bald sexton Time.
King John. iii, 1.

Memory is the treasury and guardian of all things.
Cicero, *De Oratore.* i, 5.

Thus the whirligig of time brings in his revenges.
Twelfth Night. v, 1.

Never mind who was your grandfather; what are you?
Anon.

Thou speakest of times that long have passed away.
Schiller, *Don Carlos.* i, 2, 48.

Be old when young, that you may be young when old.
Anon.

They only have lived long, who have lived virtuously.

> SHERIDAN, *Pizarro.* iv, 1.

Life, if thou knowest how to use it, is long enough.

> SENECA, *De Brevitate Vitæ.* ii.

Rashness is the error of youth, timid caution of age.

> COLTON, *Lacon.*

Confidence is a plant of slow growth in an aged bosom.

> CHATHAM, *Speech.* Jan. 14, 1766.

Old age is honourable, but youthful pride is abominable.

> ANON.

Life is not mere living, but the enjoyment of health.

> MARTIAL, *Epigrammata.* vi, 70, 15.

Actions of the last age are like almanacs of the last year.

> DENHAM, *The Sophy.*

'T is happy for him that his father was born before him.

> SWIFT, *Polite Conversation.* Dia. iii.

One life ;—a little gleam of Time between two Eternities.

> CARLYLE, *Hero as a Man of Letters.*

Every man's life is a fairy-tale written by God's fingers.

> ANDERSEN. Pref. to Works.

Men are like wine ; age sours the bad and improves the good.

> CICERO.

A great career is a dream of youth realised in mature age.

> DE VIGNY.

Time whereof the memory of man runneth not to the contrary.

> BLACKSTONE, *Commentaries.* Bk. I,
> ch. xviii, sec. 472.

Tradition wears a snowy beard, Romance is always young.

> WHITTIER, *Mary Garvin.*

A new broom sweeps well, but an old one is best for the corners.

ANON

Life is a fatal complaint, and an eminently contagious one.

HOLMES, *Poet at the Breakfast Table.* xii.

Gone — glimmering through the dream of things that were.

BYRON, *Childe Harold.* Canto ii, st. 2.

When we are old, we must do more than when we were young.

GOETHE, *Sprüche in Prosa.* iii.

Youth is a blunder; Manhood a struggle; Old Age a regret.

DISRAELI, *Coningsby.* Bk. III, ch. i.

Every man desires to live long; but no man would be old.

SWIFT, *Thoughts on Various Subjects.*

These who have ensured their remembrance by their deserts.

VIRGIL, *Æneid.* vi, 664.

What exile from his country is able to escape from himself?

HORACE, *Carmina.* ii, 16, 19.

When men grow old, they become more foolish and more wise.

ROCHEFOUCAULD, *Maximes.*

The life of the dead is placed in the memory of the living.

CICERO, *Philippicæ.* ix, 5.

No greater woe can be than to remember happy days in misery.

DANTE, *Inferno.* v, 121.

The powerful hold in deep remembrance all ill-timed pleasantry.

TACITUS, *Annales.* v, 2.

Of all ruins, the ruin of man is the saddest to contemplate.

GAUTIER.

Superfluity comes sooner by white hairs, but competency lives longer.

Merchant of Venice. i, 2, 1. 8.

Some smack of age in you, some relish of the saltness of time.

King Henry IV. Pt. II, i, 2, 1. 91.

We do not count a man's years, until he has nothing else to count.

EMERSON, *Society and Solitude.* Old Age.

What old men can do always falls short of what they desire.

RICARD.

Every man carries in his soul a sepulchre — that of his youth.

FIRMEZ.

Memory records services with a pencil, injuries with a graver.

DE SÉGUR.

He who boasts of his descent, praises the deeds of another.

SENECA, *Hercules Furens.* cccxl.

Look in the chronicles, we came in with Richard conqueror.

Taming of the Shrew. Ind.

" My nobility," said he, " begins in me, but yours ends in you."

IPHICRATES, *Apothegms of Kings.*

Nature has given to man nothing of more value than shortness of life.

> PLINY (the Elder), *Historia Naturalis.* vii, 5, l. 3.

This body is not a home, but an inn ; and that only for a short time.

> SENECA, *Epistolæ ad Lucilium.* cxx.

Memory, in widow's weeds, with naked feet stands on a tombstone.

> DE VERE, *Widowhood.*

We dread old age, which we are not sure of being able to attain.

> LA BRUYÈRE, *Les Caractères.* xi.

The past gives us regret, the present sorrow, and the future fear.

> DE LAMBERT.

Thou should'st not have been old before thou had'st been wise.

> *King Lear.* i, 5.

Recollection is the only paradise out of which we can not be driven.

> ANON.

To remember—to forget : alas ! this is what makes us young or old.

> DE MUSSET.

A youth without fire is followed by an old age without experience.

> COLTON, *Lacon.*

Pleasure is the flower that passes ; remembrance, the lasting perfume.

> BOUFFLERS.

Though I still call you a boy, I consider you no longer as such.

> CHESTERFIELD, *Letters.* Nov. 24, 1749.

Who of us has not regretted that age when laughter was
ever on the lips !

> ROUSSEAU.

A man loves the meat in his youth that he cannot endure
in his age.

> *Much Ado About Nothing*. ii, 3.

Ofttimes the test of courage becomes rather to live than
to die.

> ALFIERI, *Oreste*. iv, 2.

Youth is the period of happiness, but only Age is aware
of the fact.

> ANON.

Remembrances embellish life, but forgetfulness alone
makes it possible.

> CIALDINI. Penned in an album.

To look back to antiquity is one thing, to go back to it is
another.

> COLTON, *Lacon*.

Memory was given to mortals so that they might have
roses in December.

> ANON.

What makes old age so sad is, not that our joys but that
our hopes cease.

> RICHTER, *Titan*. Zykel, 34.

Young men think old men are fools ; but old men know
young men are fools.

> CHAPMAN, *All Fools*. v, 1.

Love, for old men, is sun on the snow : it dazzles more
than it warms them.

> J. PETIT-SENN.

It is not easy to straighten in the oak the crook that grew
in the sapling.

> Gaelic Saying.

Experience teaches that a good memory is generally joined to a weak judgment.

MONTAIGNE, *Essais.* i, 9.

Old age is a tyrant who forbids, upon pain of death, all the pleasures of youth.

ROCHEFOUCAULD, *Maximes.* 461.

Two-thirds of life are spent in hesitating, and the other third in repenting.

SOUVESTRE.

Perhaps the remembrance of these things will prove a source of future pleasure.

VIRGIL, *Æneid.* i, 203.

Who would venture upon the journey of life, if compelled to begin it at the end.

DE MAINTENON.

Benevolence rejuvenates the heart, exercise, the memory, and remembrance, life.

DE LÉSPINASSE.

Kindness is the only charm permitted to the aged : it is the coquetry of white hair.

FEUILLET.

When young, we trust ourselves too much, and we trust others too little when old.

COLTON, *Lacon.*

Badness of memory every one complains of, but nobody of the want of judgment.

ROCHEFOUCAULD, *Reflections and Maxims.* No. 463.

I swear she's no chicken ; she's on the wrong side of thirty, if she be a day.

SWIFT, *Polite Conversation.* Dia. i.

For my eightieth year warns me to pack up my baggage before I leave life.

VARRO, *De Re Rustica.* i, 1.

Content with his past life, let him take leave of life like a satiated guest.

HORACE, *Satiræ.* i, 1, 118.

Few sons attain the praise of their great sires, and most their sires disgrace.

HOMER, *Odyssey.* Bk. II, l. 315. Pope's trans.

The life given us by nature is short ; but the memory of a well-spent life is eternal.

CICERO, *Philippicæ.* xiv, 12.

People will not look forward to posterity, who never look backward to their ancestors.

BURKE, *Reflections on Revolution in France.* p. 48.

Nature has lent us life at interest, like money, and has fixed no day for its payment.

CICERO, *Tusculanarum Disputationum.* i, 39.

No one has lived a short life who has performed its duties with unblemished character.

CICERO, *Tusculanarum Disputationum.* i, 45.

I shall cheerfully bear the reproach of having descended below the dignity of history.

MACAULAY, *History of England.* Vol. I, ch. i.

It is a vice common to all, that in old age we are too much attached to worldly interests.

TERENCE, *Adelphi.* v, 8, 30.

Title and ancestry render a good name more illustrious, but an ill one more contemptible.

ADDISON.

Learn a craft when you are young, that you may not have to live by craft when you are old.

ANON.

To live long is almost everyone's wish, but to live well is the ambition of a few.

HUGHES, *The Lay Monastery.* No. 18.

Shallow men speak of the past, wise men of the present, and fools of the future.

Du Deffand.

I thank God I am as honest as any man living that is an old man and no honester than I.

Much Ado About Nothing. iii, 3.

It is very funny to see a puppy run after his tail, but it is a fool trick in an old dog.

Anon.

Happiness is the shadow of man : remembrance of it follows him ; hope of it precedes him.

Petit-Senn.

Life is a kind of Sleep : old men sleep longest, nor begin to wake but when they are to die.

La Bruyère, *Manners of Present Age.*
On Men. Ch. ii.

What would we not give to still have in store the first blissful moment we ever enjoyed !

Rochepèdre.

Youth is presumptuous, old age is timid : the former aspires to live, the latter has lived.

Mme. Roland.

A life spent worthily should be measured by a nobler line,—by deeds, not years.

Sheridan, *Pizarro.*

About one-half of a man's life is devoted to rectifying the mistakes of the other half.

Anon.

Discouragement is of all ages : in youth it is a presentiment, in old age a remembrance.

Balzac.

We hope to grow old and we dread old age ; that is to say, we love life and flee from death.

La Bruyère, *Les Caractères.* xi.

The short space of life forbids us to lay plans requiring a long time for their accomplishment.

HORACE, *Carmina.* i, 4, 15.

The heart of youth is reached through the senses ; the senses of age are reached through the heart.

RÉTIF DE LA BRETONNE.

The moment past is no longer : the future may never be : the present is all of which man is the master.

ROUSSEAU.

To make love when one is young and fair is a venial sin : it is a mortal sin when one is old and ugly.

DE BERNIS.

To him whose elastic and vigorous thought keeps pace with the sun, the day is a perpetual morning.

THOREAU, *Walden.*

I am young ; I have passed but the half of the road of life, and, already weary, I turn and look back !

DE MUSSET.

An old man in his rudiments is a disgraceful object. It is for youth to acquire, and for age to apply.

SENECA, *Epistolæ ad Lucilium.* xxxvi, 4.

It is a tedious thing to be always beginning life ; they live badly who always begin to live.

SENECA, *Epistolæ ad Lucilium.* xxiii.

Birth and ancestry, and that which we have not ourselves achieved, we can scarcely call our own.

OVID, *Metamorphoses.* xiii, 140.

Who can think wise or stupid things at all that were not thought already in the past.

GOETHE, *Faust.* ii, 2, 1.

I love everything that 's old : old friends, old times, old manners, old books, old wine.

GOLDSMITH, *She Stoops to Conquer.* i, 1.

Memory (is) like a purse,—if it be over-full that it cannot shut, all will drop out of it.

FULLER, *Holy and Profane States.* Bk. II.
Of Memory.

Old wood best to burn, old wine to drink, old friends to trust, and old authors to read.

BACON (quoted by), Apothegm 97.

What has been sown in the mind of the youth blooms and fructifies in the sun of riper years.

MERCIER.

Young, one is rich in all the future that he dreams ; old, one is poor in all the past he regrets.

ROCHEPÈDRE.

O sweet past ! sometimes remembrance raises thy long veil, then we weep in recognising thee !

LOUISE LABÉ.

To be seventy years young is sometimes far more cheerful and hopeful than to be forty years old.

HOLMES. On 70th birthday of Julia W. Howe,
May 27, 1889.

The erection of a monument is superfluous ; the memory of us will last, if we have deserved it in our lives.

PLINY (the Younger), *Epistolæ.* ix, 19.

We will not anticipate the past; so mind, young people,—our retrospection will be all to the future.

SHERIDAN, *The Rivals.* iv, 2.

The seeds of repentance are sown in youth by pleasure, but the harvest is reaped in age by pain.

COLTON, *Lacon.*

Age is not all decay ; it is the ripening, the swelling, of the fresh life within, that withers and bursts the husk.

MACDONALD, *The Marquis of Lossie.* Ch. 40.

The Right Honourable gentleman is indebted to his
memory for his jests and to his imagination for
his facts.

SHELLEY, *Speech in reply to Mr. Dundas.*

If the past is not to bind us, where can duty lie? We
should have no law but the inclination of the
moment.

ELIOT, *Mill on the Floss.* Bk. VI, ch. 14

Statesman—Politician—Patriotism

I have immortal longings in me.

Antony and Cleopatra.   v, 2.

Statesman—Politician—Patriotism

I am the State.

Att'd to Louis XIV., in Dulaure's *History of Paris*.
1863. p. 387.

Did steer humanity.

Antony and Cleopatra. v, 1.

They laugh that win.

Othello. v, 1.

Duty determines destiny.

MCKINLEY, *Jubilee Speech.* Chicago, Oct. 19, 1898.

Remorse begets reform.

COWPER, *The Task.* Book V, 1. 618.

The balance of power.

WALPOLE, *Speech.* 1741.

The swinish multitude.

BURKE, *On the French Revolution.*

Who can refute a sneer?

PALEY, *Moral Philosophy.* Book V, ch. ix.

O, reform it altogether.

Hamlet. iii, 2.

The insolence of office.

Hamlet. iii, 1.

Petition me no petitions.

FIELDING, *Tom Thumb the Great.*

Everybody cannot be first.

ANON.

Victory of common sense.

GEN'L J. MEREDITH READ, *Speech on
McKinley's Election.* 1896.

Talkers are no great doers.

> *King Richard III.* i, 3.

The very pink of perfection.

> GOLDSMITH, *She Stoops to Conquer.* i, 1.

'T is only noble to be good.

> TENNYSON, *Lady Clara Vere de Vere.*

Policy sits above conscience.

> *Timon of Athens.* iii, 2.

A plague o' both your houses.

> *Romeo and Juliet.* iii, 1.

I 'll make you eat your words.

> ANON, *The Play of Stuckley.* 1. 428.

Beware of bees in your bonnet.

> ANON.

I am the very pink of courtesy.

> *Romeo and Juliet.* ii, 4.

I have immortal longings in me.

> *Antony and Cleopatra.* v, 2.

And to be noble we 'll be good.

> PERCY, *Winifrede* (old ballad of).

Party spirit is an evil spirit.

> ANON.

Our supreme governors, the mob.

> WALPOLE, *Letters to Sir Horace Mann.*
>
> Sept. 7, 1743.

Broken with the storms of state.

> *King Henry VIII.* iv, 2.

The dignity and height of honour.

> *King Richard III.* iv, 4.

The public is just a great baby.

> RUSKIN (quoted by), *Sesame and Lilies.*
>
> Sec. 1, 1. 40.

Calumny will sear virtue itself.

> *Winter's Tale.* ii, 1.

The many fail : The one succeeds.
> TENNYSON, *The Day Dream.*

A rotten case abides no handling.
> *King Henry IV.* Part II, iv, 1.

Cohesive power of public plunder.
> CALHOUN, *Speech.* May 27, 1836.

The special head of all the land.
> *King Henry IV.* Part I, iv, 4.

Hasty climbers have sudden falls.
> ANON.

High places have their precipices.
> ANON.

Drest in a little brief authority.
> *Measure for Measure.* ii, 2.

Party honesty is party expediency.
> CLEVELAND, *N. Y. Com'l Advertiser.* Sept. 19, 1889.

Men make laws ; women make manners.
> DE SÉGUR.

I know it, and am ready to take the consequence.
> GEORGE READ, *Reply to Jos. Galloway,*
> *Signing Declaration.*

To be great is to be misunderstood.
> EMERSON, *Self-Reliance.*

I am not in the roll of common men.
> *King Henry IV.* Pt. I, iii, 1.

Union gives strength to the humble.
> SYRUS, *Maxims.*

More authority, dear boy, name more !
> *Love's Labour 's Lost.* i, 2.

Things ill-got had ever bad success.
> *King Henry VI.* Pt. III, ii, 2.

My poverty but not my will consents.
> *Romeo and Juliet.* v, i.

The mind 's the standard of the man.

WATTS, *False Greatness.*

General notions are generally wrong.

LADY MONTAGU, *Letter to Mr. W. Montagu.*
March 28, 1710.

Great talkers are never great actors.

MIDDLETON, *Blurt, Master Constable.* i, 1.

Join we together for the public good.

King Henry VI. Pt. II, i, l. 1.

And skill in thee now grew authority.

BEN JONSON, *Underwoods.*

True poets are the guardians of state.

ROSCOMMON, *Essay on Translated Verse.*

Nations, like men, have their infancy.

BOLINGBROKE, *Of the Study of History.* Letter iv.

A hated government does not last long.

SENECA, *Phœnissæ.* vi, 60.

Resolved to ruin or to rule the state.

DRYDEN, *Absalom and Achitophel.* Pt. I, l. 174.

Who elevates himself isolates himself.

RIVAROL.

Every little fish would become a whale.

Danish Saying.

An injustice to one is a menace to all.

MONTESQUIEU.

The worst men give oft the best advice.

HANNAH MORE, *Florio.* Pt. I.

Thank God, I—I also—am an American !

WEBSTER, *Speech.* Completing Bunker Hill
Monument, June 17, 1843.

It takes greatness to discern greatness.

ANON.

In records that defy the tooth of time.
YOUNG, *The Statesman's Creed.*

Men in great place, are thrice servants.
BACON, *Essay XI.* Of Great Place.

States are great engines moving slowly.
BACON, *Advancement of Learning.* Bk. II.

The good receiv'd, the giver is forgot.
CONGREVE, *To Lord Halifax.* 1. 39.

A solemn sacrifice performed in state.
POPE, *Essay on Morals.* Ep. iv.

By saying nothing you may pass for wise.
ANON.

Let them obey that know not how to rule.
King Henry VI. Pt. II, v, 1.

A mediocre speech can never be too short.
DE LAMBERT.

Our country is the common parent of all.
CICERO, *Orationes in Catilinam.* i, 7.

Where inward dignity joins outward state.
YOUNG, *Love of Fame.*

Our federal Union : it must be preserved.
JACKSON, *Toast.* Jefferson's birthday, 1830.

Yet I love glory :—glory 's a great thing.
LORD BYRON, *Don Juan.* Canto viii.

Great let me call him, for he conquered me.
YOUNG, *The Revenge.* i, 1.

Base men by his endowments are made great.
King Richard III. ii, 3.

Do not look great things, but live them.
ANON.

Independence now and Independence forever.
WEBSTER, *Eulogy on Adams and Jefferson.*

None think the great unhappy but the great.
> YOUNG, *Love of Fame.* Satire i, 1. 238.

With promise of high pay and great rewards.
> *King Henry VI.* Pt. III, ii, 1.

Such strong renown as time shall ne'er decry.
> *Pericles.* iii, 2.

In admiring greatness we rise to its level.
> ANON.

What Reason weaves, by Passion is undone.
> POPE, *Essay on Man.* Ep. ii, 1. 42.

Woe to the crown that doth the cowl obey !
> WORDSWORTH, *Ecclesiastical Sonnets.* Pt. i, 29.

Protection and patriotism are reciprocal.
> CALHOUN, *Speech.* In House of Representatives, 1812.

Be thou familiar, but by no means vulgar.
> *Hamlet.* i, 3.

A pleasant smiling cheek, a speaking eye.
> MARLOWE, *Hero and Leander.* Sestiad i.

Some falls are means the happier to arise.
> *Cymbeline*, iv, 2.

The noblest mind the best contentment has.
> SPENSER, *Faerie Queene.* Bk. I, can. i, st. 35.

He who talks much cannot always talk well.
> GOLDONI, *Pamela.* i, 6.

Great men's vices are esteem'd as virtues.
> MARMION, *Holland's Leaguer.* i, 1.

Trust not him that hath once broken faith.
> *King Henry VI.* Pt. III, iv, 4.

Ambassadors are the eye and ear of states.
> GUICCIARDINI, *Storia d'Italia.*

Just man, by whom impartial laws were given.
> THOMAS TICKELL, *On death of Addison.*

Earthly fame is Fortune's frail dependent.
WORDSWORTH, *Poems to National Independence.*

Pt. II, 19.

Frank, haughty, rash,— the Rupert of debate.
LYTTON, *The New Timon.*

But with the morning cool reflections came.
SCOTT, *Chronicles of the Canongate.* Ch. iv.

The lion is not so fierce as they paint him.
HERBERT, *Jacula Prudentum.*

Patriotism is the last refuge of a scoundrel.
BOSWELL, *Life of Johnson.* 1775.

There is a higher law than the Constitution.
SEWARD, *Speech.* March 11, 1850.

No really great man ever thought himself so.
HAZLITT.

Something is rotten in the state of Denmark.
Hamlet. i, 4, 1. 90.

An honest politician is one who stays bought.
T. B. REED.

Seek honour first, and pleasure lies behind.
CHATTERTON, *The Tournament.* xxiii.

Discretion of speech is more than eloquence.
BACON, *Essay XXXII.* Of Discourse.

The world knows nothing of its greatest men.
HENRY TAYLOR, *Philip von Artevelde.* Pt. I, i, 5.

Great men by small means oft are overthrown.
HERRICK, *Hesperides.* 1. 488.

Thou speakest a word of great moment calmly.
GOETHE, *Iphigenia auf Tauris.* I, 3, 88, 1.

And bears his blushing honours thick upon him.
King Henry VIII. iii, 2.

Upon this land a thousand, thousand blessings.
King Henry VIII. v, 5.

For sufferance is the badge of all our tribe.
Merchant of Venice. i, 3.

Honour is the most capricious in her rewards.
COLTON, *Lacon.*

The applause of list'ning senates to command.
GRAY, *Elegy in a Country Churchyard.* St. 16.

The heart of a Statesman should be in his head.
NAPOLEON I.

How dear is the fatherland to all noble hearts!
VOLTAIRE, *Tancrède.* iii, 1.

Jealousy is a secret avowal of our inferiority.
MASSILLON.

Rocks whereon greatest men have oftest wrecked.
MILTON, *Paradise Regained.* Bk. II, l. 228.

Farewell! a long farewell, to all my greatness!
King Henry VIII. iii, 2.

Count not your chickens before they be hatch'd.
Old Proverb.

It is not good to be better than the very worst.
SENECA, *Epistolæ ad Lucilium.*

A politician, . . . one that would circumvent God.
Hamlet. v, 1.

Laws grind the poor, and rich men rule the law.
GOLDSMITH, *The Traveller.* l. 386.

Their cause I plead,—plead it in heart and mind.
GARRICK, *Prologue.* On quitting stage. 1776.

A king should prefer his country to his children.
SENECA, *Troades.* 332.

Free trade is not a principle, it is an expedient.
DISRAELI, *On import duties.* April 25, 1843.

The greatest happiness of the greatest number.
PRIESTLEY.

Those that think must govern those that toil.
GOLDSMITH, *The Traveller*. l. 372.

They 're only truly great who are truly good.
CHAPMAN, *Revenge for Honour*. Act. v.

Why, this it is, when men are rul'd by women.
King Richard III. i, 1, l. 62.

My dearest meed, a friend's esteem and praise.
BURNS, *The Cotter's Saturday Night*.

A noble cause doth ease much a grievous case.
SIDNEY, *Arcadia*. Book I.

They only babble who practise not reflection.
SHERIDAN, *Pizarro*. i, i.

Great heights are hazardous to the weak head.
BLAIR, *The Grave*. l. 293.

Greatness and goodness are not means but ends.
COLERIDGE, *Literary Remains*. Reproof.

What thin partitions sense from thought divide.
POPE, *Essay on Man*. Ep. i, l. 226.

Politeness costs nothing, and gains everything.
LADY MONTAGU, *Letters*.

He who loves not his country, can love nothing.
BYRON, *The Two Foscari*. iii, i.

Oh ! what a crowded world one moment may contain !
HEMANS, *The Last Constantine*. lix.

A reforming age is always fertile of impostors.
MACAULAY, *Essay on Moore's Life of Bryon*.

He preferred to be good, rather than to seem so.
SALLUST, *Catilina*. liv.

What is the short meaning of this long harangue ?
SCHILLER, *Piccolomini*. i, 2, 100.

is more than a crime ; it is a political fault.
FOUCHÉ, *Memoirs of Fouché*.

The mould of a man's fortune is in his own hands.
BACON, *Essay XI.* On Fortune.

Speech was given to man to disguise his thoughts.
TALLEYRAND, in Barère's *Mémoires.*

Our words have wings, but fly not where we would.
ELIOT, *The Spanish Gypsy.* Book III.

Expect not praise without envy until you are dead.
COLTON, *Lacon.*

They only employ words to disguise their thoughts.
VOLTAIRE, *Dia. XIV.* Le Chapon et la Poularde.

A noble manhood, nobly consecrated to men, never dies.
MCKINLEY, *Speech.* Albany, February 12, 1895.

His conduct still right, with his argument wrong.
GOLDSMITH, *Retaliation.* 1. 46.

Too poor for a bribe, and too proud to importune.
GRAY, on his own character.

They rose, but at their height could seldom stay.
DRYDEN, *Epi. Conquest of Granada.*

And wrinkles, the d——d democrats, won't flatter.
BYRON, *Don Juan.* Canto x, st. 24.

The mouse thinks to cast a shadow like an elephant.
ANON.

It is the act of a bad man to deceive by falsehood.
CICERO, *Oratio pro Murena.* xxx.

A great man marvels that the world calls him great.
ANON.

Liberty exists in proportion to wholesome restraint.
WEBSTER, *Speech.* May 10, 1847.

I have done the state some service and they know it.
Othello. v, 2.

A Conservative Government is an organised hypocrisy.
DISRAELI, *Speech.* March 15, 1847.

To envy anybody is to confess ourselves his inferior.

MLLE. DE LESPINASSE.

I have touched the highest point of all my greatness.

King Henry VIII. iii, 2.

Our differences are policies, our agreements principles.

McKINLEY, *Speech.* Des Moines, 1901.

It is a condition which confronts us—not a theory.

CLEVELAND, *Presidential Message.* 1887.

A mugwump is a person educated beyond his intellect.

HORACE PORTER, bon-mot in Cleveland-Blaine
campaign, 1884.

Orators without judgment are horses without bridles.

ANON.

Oh, that eternal want of peace which vexes public men !

TENNYSON, *Will Waterproof's Lyrical Monologue.*

Men have less lively perception of good than of evil.

LIVY, *Annales.* xxx, 21.

He serves his party best who serves the country best.

HAYES, *Inaugural Address.* March 5, 1877.

Our country is that spot to which our heart is bound.

VOLTAIRE, *Le Fanatisme.* i, 2.

Don't be loud as a bull's roar, and weak as a bulrush.

ANON.

Ill can he rule the great that cannot reach the small.

SPENSER, *Faerie Queene.* Book V, canto ii, st. 51.

My country is the world, and my religion is to do good.

PAINE, *Rights of Man.* Ch. v.

The community has no bribe that will tempt a wise man.

THOREAU, *Yankee in Canada.*

The legislator who meets some evils, half subdues them.

COLTON, *Lacon.*

Party is the madness of the many for the gain of a few.

ANON.

Who bathes in worldly joyes, swimmes in a world of fears.
FLETCHER, *The Purple Island.* Canto viii, st. 7.

This is the period of my ambition : O this blessed hour !
Merry Wives of Windsor. iii, 3.

A brave man's country is wherever he chooses his abode.
QUINTUS CURTIUS RUFUS, *De Rebus Gestis.* vi, 4, 13.

The love of country is more powerful than reason itself.
OVID, *Epistolæ ex Ponto.* i, 3, 29.

A great name without merit is like an epitaph on a coffin.
DE PUISIEUX.

Jealousy is the homage that inferiority pays to merit.
DE PUISIEUX.

The noble lord is the Prince Rupert of Parliamentary
discussion.
DISRAELI, *Speech.* April, 1844.

And he that gives us in these days new lords may give us
new laws.
WITHER, *Contented Man's Morrice.*

Some men build their reputations on other persons'
wrecks.
ANON.

What a singular destiny has been that of this remarkable
man !
MACAULAY, *On Boswell's Life of Johnson.*

Our country is the world—our countrymen are all mankind.
GARRISON, " *Liberator's* " *motto.* 1837-39.

My foot is on my native heath, and my name is Mac-
Gregor.
SCOTT, *Rob Roy.* Ch. xxxiv.

Censure is the tax a man pays to the public for being
eminent.
SWIFT, *Thoughts on Various Subjects.*

A giant on close acquaintance often proves a common man on stilts.

> ANON.

The best government is that which teaches us to govern ourselves.

> ANON.

The public! why, the public's nothing better than a great baby.

> CHALMERS, *Letters.*

Be wiser than other people if you can; but do not tell them so.

> CHESTERFIELD, *Letters.* Dublin Castle, Nov. 19, 1745.

Greatness is never thrust upon a man that leads an aimless life.

> ANON.

Call you that backing of your friends? A plague upon such backing!

> *King Henry IV.* Pt. I, ii, 4.

Take a straw and throw it up in the air; you may see by that which way the wind is.

> SELDEN, *Libels.*

It is an irrepressible conflict between opposing and enduring forces.

> SEWARD, *Speech.* October 25, 1858.

This republic can never fail, so long as the citizen is vigilant.

> McKINLEY, *Speech.* Redlands, Cal., May 8, 1901.

Republics end through luxury; monarchies through poverty.

> MONTESQUIEU, *De l'Esprit.* vii, ch. 4.

Applause is the spur of noble minds, the end and aim of weak ones.

> COLTON, *Lacon,*

A nickname is the hardest stone that the devil can throw at a man.

HAZLITT, *Political Essays.* On Court Influence.

I know that whoever is king, I will always be the subject.

JOHN ROSS, *Reply to Revolutionary Patriots.*

That is the best government which desires to make the people happy.

MACAULAY, on Mitford's *History of Greece.* 1824.

What government is the best? That which teaches us to govern ourselves.

GOETHE, *Sprüche in Prosa.* iii.

It is the prerogative of great men only to have great defects.

ROCHEFOUCAULD, *Maxims.*

The trappings of a monarchy would set up an ordinary commonwealth.

SAMUEL JOHNSON, *Life of Milton.*

I have considered the pension list of the republic a roll of honour.

CLEVELAND, *Veto.* Pension of Mary A.
Dougherty, July 5, 1888.

I was born an American; I live an American; I shall die an American!

WEBSTER, *Speech.* At laying of corner-stone,
Bunker Hill. June 17, 1825.

There are no points of the compass on the chart of true patriotism.

WINTHROP, *Letter to Boston Commercial Club.*
June 12, 1879.

Excess of praise has generally as little foundation as excess of calumny.

HERRING, *Letter to W. Duncombe.* Nov. 5, 1753.

Attack is the reaction ; I never think I have hit hard unless it rebounds.

BOSWELL, *Life of Johnson.*

The real leaders do not always march at the head of the procession.

ANON.

Celebrity : the advantage of being known to those who do not know us.

CHAMFORT.

Many have lived on a pedestal, who will never have a statue when dead.

BÉRANGER.

That man is great who can use the brains of others to carry on his work.

DONN PIATT.

Man thinks, and, at once, becomes the master of the beings that do not think.

BUFFON.

People of a low, obscure education cannot stand the rays of greatness.

CHESTERFIELD, *Letters.*   May 17, 1748.

The most dangerous flattery is the inferiority of those who surround us.

SWETCHINE.

"Committee" is a noun of multitude, signifying many, but not signifying much.

ANON.

Great men are seldom over scrupulous in the arrangement of their attire.

DICKENS, *Pickwick Papers.*   Ch. ii.

A republic is not founded on virtue, but on the ambition of its citizens.

VOLTAIRE.

I know no South, no North, no East, no West, to which
I owe any allegiance.

CLAY, Speech of 1848.

Let our object be : our country, our whole country, and
nothing but our country.

WEBSTER, Speech. At laying of corner-stone,
Bunker Hill, June 17, 1825.

Great men seem to be a part of the infinite, brothers of
the mountain and the seas.

INGERSOLL.

Posthumous fame is a plant of tardy growth, for our body
must be the seed of it.

COLTON, Lacon.

As long as I count the votes what are you going to do
about it? Say.

TWEED, The Ballot in 1871.

Stand by the Stars and Stripes. Above all, stand for
Liberty, whatever happens.

DANA, Art of Newspaper Making.

He had a head to contrive, a tongue to persuade, and a
hand to execute any mischief.

CLARENDON, History of the Rebellion.

They see nothing wrong in the rule that to the victors
belong the spoils of the enemy.

MARCY, Speech in U. S. Senate. Jan., 1832.

There is but one side, happily, now, and we are all
together on that side.

MCKINLEY, Speech. Corinth, April 30, 1901.

Great thoughts, great feelings came to him, like instincts
unawares.

HOUGHTON, The Men of Old.

Whatever may be the issue we shall share one common
danger, one safety.

VIRGIL, Æneid. ii, 709.

The publick weal requires that a man should betray, and
lye, and massacre.

MONTAIGNE, *Essays*. Of Profit and Honesty.

The great are only great because we are on our knees.
Let us rise up.

PRUD'HOMME, *Revolutions de Paris*. Motto.

Be thou as chaste as ice, as pure as snow, thou shalt not
escape calumny.

Hamlet. iii, 1.

To be honest, as this world goes, is to be one man picked
out of ten thousand.

Hamlet. ii, 2.

By union the smallest states thrive, by discord the greatest
are destroyed.

SALLUST, *Jugurtha*. x.

The public is a bad guesser, "stiff in opinion," and
almost "always in the wrong."

DE QUINCEY, *Essays*. Protestantism.

Some are born great, some achieve greatness, and some
have greatness thrust upon 'em.

Twelfth Night. ii, 5.

To preserve the life of citizens, is the greatest virtue in
the father of his country.

SENECA, *Octavia*. 444.

I love reform better than its modes. There is no history
of how bad became better.

THOREAU, *Letters*.

In a change of government, the poor seldom change
anything except the name of their master.

PHÆDRUS, *Fabulæ*. i, 15.

The great men of the world, like the lights of a city, are
not valued till gone out.

ANON.

We like to know the weaknesses of eminent persons : it consoles us for our inferiority.

DE LAMBERT.

To succeed, the candidate must be a gentleman by nature, and a scholar by education.

COLTON, *Lacon*.

The great man is not so great as folks think, and the dull man not so stupid as he seems.

HUBBARD, *Philistine*.

Promises retain men better than services.   For them, hope is a chain, and gratitude a thread.

PETIT-SENN.

The deterioration of a government begins almost always by the decay of its principles.

MONTESQUIEU, *De l'Esprit*.   viii, ch. I.

Sink or swim, live or die, survive or perish, I give my hand and my heart to this vote.

WEBSTER, *Eulogy on Adams and Jefferson*.

No solid South, no solid North, save when solid for the flag and the Union.

McKINLEY, *Speech*.   Tuscumbia, April 30, 1901.

Anarchy is no more an expression of " social discontent," than picking pockets or wife-beating.

THEODORE ROOSEVELT, *Message*.   Dec. 3, 1901.

He smote the rock of the national resources, and abundant streams of revenue gushed forth.

WEBSTER, *Speech on Hamilton*.   March 10, 1831.

The prudent man may direct a state ; but it is the enthusiast who regenerates it, or ruins.

LYTTON, *Rienzi*.   Bk. I, ch. viii.

Councillors of state sit plotting and playing their high chess-game whereof the pawns are men.

CARLYLE, *Sartor Resartus*.   Bk. I, ch. 3.

The people's government, made for the people, made by
the people, and answerable to the people.
WEBSTER, *Second Speech on Foot's Resolution*.
Jan. 26, 1830.

Though the people support the government, the government should not support the people.
CLEVELAND, *Veto, Texas Seed Bill*. Feb. 16, 1887.

A proud man is always hard to be pleased, because he
hath too great expectations from others.
BAXTER, *Christian Ethics*.

One learns taciturnity best among people who have none,
and loquacity among the taciturn.
RICHTER, *Hesperus*.

We join ourselves to no party that does not carry the flag
and keep step to the music of the Union.
CHOATE, *Letter to a Worcester Whig Convention*.
Oct. 1, 1855.

That is the best government which desires to make the
people happy, and knows how to make them happy.
MACAULAY, on Mitford's *History of Greece*. 1824.

Loves to hear himself talk, and will speak more in a min-
ute than he will stand to in a month.
Romeo and Juliet. ii, 4.

The good, alas! are few: they are scarcely as many as
the gates of Thebes or the mouths of the Nile.
JUVENAL, *Satiræ*. xiii, 26.

Great men undertake great things because they are great,
and fools because they think them easy.
VAUVENARGUES.

A great name is like an eternal epitaph engraved by the
admiration of men on the road of time.
SOUVESTRE.

A difference of opinion, though in the merest trifles, alienates the minds, especially of high rank.

CHESTERFIELD, *Maxims.*

The upright, if he suffer calumny to move him, fears the tongue of man more than the eye of God.

COLTON, *Lacon.*

It is more easy to forgive the weak who have injured us, than the powerful whom we have injured.

COLTON, *Lacon.*

The American people never ran away from a difficult question or from a well-defined duty.

MCKINLEY, *Speech.* Redlands, May 8, 1901.

Glory is a shroud that posterity often tears from the shoulders of those who wore it when living.

BÉRANGER.

High positions are like the summit of high, steep rocks : eagles and reptiles alone can reach them.

NECKER.

A disposition to preserve, and an ability to improve, taken together, would be my standard of a statesman.

BURKE, *Reflections on Revolution in France.*

In the opinion of all men he would have been regarded as capable of governing, if he had never governed.

TACITUS, *Annales.* i, 49.

Woman, I tell you, is a microcosm ; and rightly to rule her requires as great talents as to govern a state.

FOOTE, *The Devil upon Two Sticks.* i, 1.

I consider biennial elections as a security that the sober, second thought of the people shall be law.

AMES, *Speech.* January, 1788.

Deliberate with caution, but act with decision, and yield with graciousness, or oppose with firmness.

COLTON, *Lacon.*

To judge of the real importance of an individual, one should think of the effect his death would produce.

LÉVIS.

The chief want, in every state that I have been into, was a high and earnest purpose in its inhabitants.

THOREAU, *Yankee in Canada.*

A meditation on the conduct of political societies made old Hobbes imagine that war was the state of nature.

BURKE, *Vindication of Society.*

Why don't you show us a statesman who can rise up to the emergency, and cave in the emergency's head?

ARTEMUS WARD, *Things in New York.*

And having looked to Government for bread, on the very first scarcity they will turn and bite the hand that fed them.

BURKE, *Thoughts and Details on Society.*

Vol. v, p. 156.

The infant, on first opening his eyes, ought to see his country, and to the hour of his death never lose sight of it.

ROUSSEAU.

Visible governments are the toys of some nations, the diseases of others, the harness of some, the burdens of more.

RUSKIN, *Sesame and Lilies.* Lec. I, 42.

Our country. In her intercourse with foreign nations may she always be in the right, but our country, right or wrong.

STEPHEN DECATUR, *Toast at Norfolk.*

April, 1816.

When one is intensely interested in a certain cause, the tendency is to associate particularly with those who take the same view.

THEODORE ROOSEVELT, *The Rough Riders.* p. 1.

Woman—Love

The sum of earthly bliss.
> JOHN MILTON, *Paradise Lost.* Book VIII.

Woman—Love

Love is blind.
> BEN JONSON, *The Poetaster.* iv, 2.

Rules the rost.
> GASCOIGNE, *The Steele Glas.*

I saw and loved.
> GIBBON, *Autobiographic Memoirs.* p. 48.

Love hath wings.
> COWLEY, *Answer to Invitation to Cambridge.* iii.

Love has a tide.
> HELEN HUNT, *Verses.* Tides.

Mothers make men.
> ANON.

Love conquers all.
> BYRON, *Childe Harold.* Canto ii, st. 63.

Too sweet to last.
> WM. JONES, *Turkish Ode to Neshishi.*

Look ere ye leape.
> HEYWOOD, *Proverbs.* Bk. I, ch. ii.

Content in virtue.
> MULGRAVE. His family motto.

Can one love twice?
> TENNYSON, *Enoch Arden.*

Tetchy and wayward.
> *King Richard III.* iv, 4.

By virtue and toil.
> DUNDONALD. His family motto.

281

Fat, fair, and forty.

> SCOTT, *St. Ronan's Well.* Ch. vii.

Love—sweet misery.

> DE MUSSET.

Hot love soon colde.

> HEYWOOD, *Proverbs.* Bk. I, ch. ii.

Love is kin to duty.

> MORRIS, *The Epic of Hades.* Psyche.

By virtue and faith.

> EARL OF OXFORD. Family motto.

A bevy of fair women.

> MILTON, *Paradise Lost.* Bk. XI, l. 582.

Let us live and love.

> CATULLUS, *Carmina.* v, 1.

Love is always blind.

> POPE, *January and May.*

Love's night is noon.

> *Twelfth Night.* iii, 1.

Love me, love my dog.

> Old Proverb.

Sweets to the sweet.

> *Hamlet.* v, 1.

Sweet girl graduates.

> TENNYSON, *The Princess.* Prologue.

Pity 's akin to love.

> SOUTHERN, *Oroonoko.* ii, 1.

Love begins with love.

> LA BRUYÈRE, *Characters and Manners.* Ch. iv.

My love lies bleeding.

> CAMPBELL, *O'Connor's Child.* St. 5.

As meke as is a mayde.

> CHAUCER, *Canterbury Tales.* Pro., l. 69.

By virtue, not by men.
> EARL OF KERRY. His family motto.

Marriage is a science.
> BALZAC.

Silence gives consent.
> GOLDSMITH, *The Good-Natured Man.* ii, 1.

A wilderness of sweets.
> MILTON, *Paradise Lost.* Bk. IV, l. 294.

A lover is never wrong.
> BALZAC.

Love alone begets love.
> LA BRUYÈRE.

Love's great artillery.
> CRASHAW, *Prayer.* xviii.

Love is a pleasant woe.
> A. W., *Ode IX.* From Davison's Rhapsody.

Half-heart is no heart.
> ANON.

Two strings to his bow.
> BUTLER, *Hudibras.* Pt. III, canto i, l. 3.

By virtue and industry.
> EARL OF FIFE. His family motto.

Virtue never grows old.
> HERBERT, *Jacula Prudentum.*

By virtue, not by craft.
> VISCOUNT PERRY. His family motto.

To be loved, be lovable.
> OVID, *Ars Amatoria.* ii, l. 107.

Love those who love God.
> ANON.

Love makes labour light.
> ANON.

Love can vanquish Death.

> TENNYSON, *A Dream of Fair Women.*

Love is the life of man.

> SWEDENBORG, *Divine Love and Wisdom.*   Par. I.

Love 's not Time's fool.

> SHAKSPEARE, *Sonnet.*   cxvi.

Beauty doth varnish age.

> *Love's Labour 's Lost.*   iv, 3, 1. 244.

Beauty is but skin deep.

> ANON.

Beauty will buy no beef.

> Old Proverb.

Is she not passing fair?

> *Two Gentlemen of Verona.*   iv, 4.

Cupid is a blind gunner.

> FARQUHAR, *Love and a Bottle.*   i, 1.

My dear, my better half.

> SIDNEY, *Arcadia.*   Bk. III.

Woman is the lesser man.

> TENNYSON, *Locksley Hall.*   St. 76.

Women wear the breeches.

> BURTON, *Anat. of Melancholy.*   Democritus.

Romance is always young.

> WHITTIER, *Mary Garvin.*

The sum of earthly bliss.

> MILTON, *Paradise Lost.*   Bk. VIII, 1. 522.

Love hath a large mantle.

> ANON.

Love better is than Fame.

> TAYLOR, *Christmas Sonnets.*   Lyrics.   To J. L. G.

Love's pale sister, Pity.

> WILLIAM JONES, *Hymn to Darga.*

Lovers who dispute, adore.

> From the French.

Every lover is a soldier.

> OVID, *Amorum.* i, 9, 1.

All mankind love a lover.

> EMERSON, *Essays.* Of Love.

Benedick the married man.

> *Much Ado About Nothing.* i, 1.

Beware of two black eyes.

> ANON.

The fatal gift of beauty.

> BYRON, *Childe Harold.* Canto iv, st. 42.

Don't be a family magpie.

> ANON.

Virtue 's its own reward.

> VANBRUGH, *The Provoked Wife.* i, 1.

Virtue alone can ennoble.

> WALLSCOURT. His family motto.

Virtue is her own reward.

> PRIOR, *Ode in Imitation of Horace.* Bk. III, Ode 2.

Love is love for evermore.

> TENNYSON, *Locksley Hall.*

Love is an egotism of two.

> ANTOINE DE SALLE.

Love can supply all wants.

> FLETCHER, *The Sea Voyage.* ii, 1.

Love is a credulous thing.

> OVID, *Metamorphoses.* viii, 1. 826.

Love laughs at locksmiths.

> Old Proverb.

True love can fear no one.

> SENECA, *Medea,* xli, 6.

Woman is the heart of man.

LEROUX.

My wife shall not rule me.

MARTIAL, *Epigrammata*. viii, 12, 2.

Least said soonest mended.

Old Proverb.

Wretch'd, un-idea'd girls.

BOSWELL, *Life of Johnson*. 1752.

Love hath no need of words.

LYTTON, *Richelieu*. i, 2.

Love is the mother of love.

ANON.

Everybody in love is blind.

PROPERTIUS, *Elegiæ*. ii, 14, 18.

Marriage is a taming thing.

ELIOT, *Middlemarch*. Bk. VII, ch. 68.

Kisses honeyed by oblivion.

ELIOT, *Spanish Gypsy*. Book III.

Rank is a great beautifier.

LYTTON, *Lady of Lyons*. ii, 1.

The milk of human kindness.

Macbeth. i, 5.

Home is where the heart is.

PLINY.

Love is the sin of all men.

DU BOSC.

Love is superior to genius.

DE MUSSET.

Woman is a perfected devil.

HUGO.

Woman is the altar of love.

From the French.

Beauty, in woman, is power.

ROTROU.

All 's fair in love and war.

Old Proverb.

The pangs of despised love.

Hamlet. iii, 1.

Frailty, thy name is woman.

Hamlet. i, 2.

I dote on his very absence.

Merchant of Venice. i, 2.

Be a man before your mother.

ANON.

Love is wiser than ambition.

CORNWALL, *A Vision.*

Pity melts the mind to love.

DRYDEN, *Alexander's Feast.* v.

Cold love soon grows colder.

ANON.

The truth of truths is love.

BAILEY, *Festus.* Sc., Another and a Better World.

Fickle as a changeful dream.

SCOTT'S *Lady of the Lake.* Canto v, st. 30.

A world-without-end bargain.

Love's Labour's Lost. v, 2, l. 799.

Wise men pass a dressy lass.

ANON.

The very pink of perfection.

GOLDSMITH, *She Stoops to Conquer.* i, 1.

Familiarity breeds contempt.

SYRUS, *Maxims.* 640.

There shall be no love lost.

BEN JONSON, *Every Man Out of His Humour.*

ii, 1.

The age of chivalry is gone.

BURKE, *Reflections on Revolution in France.*

Doing nothing is doing evil.

ANON.

Speak low if you speak love.
Much Ado About Nothing. ii, 1, 1. 102.

Fantastic as a woman's mood.
SCOTT, *Lady of the Lake.* Canto v, st. 30.

Woman : man's first domicile.

DIDEROT.

Beauty draws more than oxen.
HERBERT, *Jacula Prudentum.*

Bless you, my fortunate lady !
All's Well that Ends Well. ii, 4.

Love is heaven ; hate is hell.

ANON.

Love's tongue is in the eyes.
FLETCHER, *Piscatorie Eclogues.* v, st. 13.

Virtue is a thousand shields.
EARL OF EFFINGHAM. His Family Motto.

What ills from beauty spring.
SAMUEL JOHNSON, *Vanity of Human Wishes.* 1. 321.

Trust not too much to beauty.
VIRGIL, *Eclogæ.* ii, 1. 17,

Handsome is as handsome does.
GOLDSMITH, *Vicar of Wakefield* ch. i.

In naked beauty more adorn'd.
MILTON, *Paradise Lost.* Bk. IV, 1. 713.

Marriages are made in heaven.
TENNYSON, *Aylmer's Field.* 1. 188.

Women's weapons, water-drops.
King Lear. ii, 4.

Widowed wife and wedded maid.
SCOTT, *The Betrothed.* Ch. ult.

I took it for a faery vision.
> MILTON, *Comus.* 1. 298.

I, too, have had my longings.
> STEDMAN, *Penelope.*

Kiss till the cows come home.
> BEAUMONT AND FLETCHER, *Scornful Lady.* ii. 2.

Love me little, love me long.
> MARLOWE, *Jew of Malta.* iv, 6.

To speak of love begets love.
> PASCAL.

Society is the book of women.
> ROUSSEAU.

Silence best speaks the mind.
> FLETCHER, *Piscatorie Eclogues.* v, st. 13.

The ideal wife never marries.
> ANON.

Half won, is match well made.
> *All's Well that Ends Well.* iv, 3.

That sovereign bliss, a wife.
> MALLETT, *Cupid and Hymen.*

Then shalt thou rule the rost.
> HEYWOOD, *Proverbs.* Bk. I, ch. v.

That talkative maiden, Rumour.
> ELIOT, *Felix Holt.*

Fine feathers make fine birds.
> Old Proverb.

Beauty wins, but bounty holds.
> ANON.

Love makes marriage merry age.
> ANON.

Marriage is a desperate thing.
> SELDEN, *Table Talk.* Marriage.

19

Women 's jars breed men 's wars.
> FULLER, *Holy and Profane States.*　Wise Statesman.

As the husband is the wife is.
> TENNYSON　*Locksley Hall.*

Beauty turns to ashes at last.
> ANON.

Her frailty doubles your love.
> IK MARVEL, *Reveries of a Bachelor.*　p. 41.

Love knows no mean or measure.
> FLETCHER, *Piscatorie Eclogues.*　iii, can. 22.

Love cannot feed on falsehood!
> LYTTON, *Richelieu.*　iii, 2.

Love 's sooner felt than seen.
> FLETCHER, *Piscatorie Eclogues.*　vi, st. 11.

These are Women, are they not?
> WYCHERLEY, *Love in a Wood.*　ii.

Slighted love is sair to bide.
> BURNS, *Duncan Gray.*

If you wish to be loved, love.
> SENECA, *Epistolæ ad Lucilium.*　ix.

What a woman wills, God wills.
> From the French.

The soul lives where it loves.
> ANON.

Love is the harvest of beauty.
> From the French.

That prime ill, a talking wife.
> PRIOR, *Alma.*　Canto ii, l. 364.

Words are the key to the heart.
> ANON.

Love cannot be cured by herbs.
> OVID, *Metamorphoses.*　i, l. 523.

The Devil and Love are but one.

VOLTAIRE.

Beware of men made of molasses.

ANON.

A woman was leader in the deed.

VIRGIL, *Æneid.* i, 364.

Happy love counts lost moments.

DIDEROT.

Though last, not least in love !

Julius Cæsar. iii, 1, 1. 189.

Sentiment is woman's conscience.

ANON.

God made the woman for the man.

TENNYSON, *Edwin Morris.*

When did women ever yet invent ?

TENNYSON, *The Princess.*

Beware of spooning and mooning.

ANON.

What 's done, cannot be undone.

Macbeth. v, 1.

It takes two to make a quarrel.

Old Saying.

I bow before thine altar, Love.

SMOLLETT, *Roderick Random.*

Thy love afar is spite at home.

EMERSON, *Self-Reliance.*

Don't snap ; you 're not a trap.

ANON.

Love cannot be mixed with fear.

SENECA, *Epistolæ ad Lucilium.* xlvii.

Words are women, deeds are men.

HERBERT, *Jacula Prudentum.*

Don't always harp on one string.

ANON.

Faint heart ne'er won fair lady.

    P. FLETCHER, *Brittain's Ida.*   Canto v, I, st. I.

Constant dropping wears a stone.

ANON.

Linked sweetness long drawn out.

    MILTON, *L'Allegro.*

I must be cruel only to be kind.

    Hamlet.   iii, 4.

Pity is sworn servant unto Love.

    DANIEL, *Queen's Arcadia.*   iii, I.

Flattery 's the nurse of crimes.

    GAY, *Fables.*   i.

There 's daggers in men's smiles.

    Macbeth.   ii, 3.

Virtue alone is happiness below.

    CRABBE, *The Borough.*   Letter xvi.

Marriage is either kill or cure.

ANON.

The eye is traitor to the heart.

    WYATT, *That the Eye Bewrayeth.*

Have a deaf ear for hasty words.

ANON.

You are not alone : *she* is there.

    IK MARVEL, *Reveries of a Bachelor.*   p. 33.

Two human loves make one divine.

    E. B. BROWNING, *Isobel's Child.*

Lips, however rosy, must be fed.

ANON.

Beware the fury of a patient man.

    DRYDEN, *Absalom and Achitophel.*   Pt. I, 1. 1005.

There 's no love lost between us.

> GOLDSMITH, *She Stoops to Conquer.* iv, 4.

Marriage is ever made by destiny.

> CHAPMAN, *All Fools.* v, 1.

A lovely lady garmented in light.

> SHELLEY, *The Witch of Atlas.* St. 5.

In maiden meditation, fancy free.

> *Midsummer Night's Dream.* ii, 2.

Stolen kisses are always sweeter.

> HUNT, *The Indicator.*

Love, and a Cough, cannot be hid.

> HERBERT, *Jacula Prudentum.*

Love and a red nose can't be hid.

> HOLCROFT, *Duplicity.* ii, 1.

Fills the air around with beauty.

> BYRON, *Childe Harold.* Canto iv, st. 49.

Love is the poetry of the senses.

> BALZAC.

Love begins too well to end well.

> DAUMAS.

Coquettes are the quacks of love.

> ROCHEFOUCAULD.

For lovers love the western star.

> SCOTT, *Lay of Last Minstrel.* Canto iii, st. 24.

A sight to dream of, not to tell !

> COLERIDGE, *Christabel.* Pt. I.

Modesty is the grace of the soul.

> DELILLE.

To speak of love is to make love.

> BALZAC.

Lovers ever run before the clock.

> *Merchant of Venice.* ii, 6.

Love is more than great richesse.
> LYDGATE, *The Story of Thebes.*   Pt. III.

Love illumes the realms of night!
> SCHILLER, *Triumph of Love.*   St. 21.

Pity, the tenderest part of love.
> YALDEN, *To Captain Chamberlain.*

To give her her Due she has Wit.
> CONGREVE, *Way of the World.*

Not to know love is not to live.
> GAY, *Plutus.*   Cupid and Time.   1. 135.

Better half-hanged than ill-wed.
> ANON.

I can enjoy her while she 's kind.
> DRYDEN, *Imitation of Horace.*   Book III, Ode 29, 1. 78.

Woman is the Sunday of man's life.
> MICHELET.

Be good and you will be lonesome.
> MARK TWAIN.

Constancy is the chimera of love.
> VAUVENARGUES.

Vanity ruins more women than love.
> DU DEFFAND.

The complement of love is passion.
> SAND.

He who loves little dares little.
> ANON.

Gold can do much, but beauty more.
> MASSINGER, *The Unnatural Combat.*   i, 1.

A cunning woman is a knavish fool.
> LYTTLETON, *Advice to a Lady.*

'T is better to buy love than law.
> ANON.

Happiness seems made to be shared.

CORNEILLE, *Notes par Rochefoucauld.*

Imparadis'd in one another's arms.

MILTON, *Paradise Lost.* Book IV, l. 50.

She is the goddess of my idolatry.

BURNEY, *Letter, to Miss S. Burney.* July 5, 1778.

Beauty is best when plainly drest.

ANON.

Too bright, too beautiful to last.

BRYANT, *The Rivulet.*

Fair and softly goes far in a day.

ANON.

Have not a mouth for every matter.

ANON.

The woman is so hard upon the man.

TENNYSON, *The Princess.*

A loveless life is a living death.

ANON.

I trust to virtue and not to arms.

DE WILTON.   His family motto.

All women are ambitious naturally.

MARLOWE, *Hero and Leander.*   Sestiad I.

Love stoops as fondly as he soars.

WORDSWORTH, *Poems of the Fancy.*   xviii.

Love is often a fruit of marriage.

MOLIÈRE, *Sganarelle.*   i, 1.

Dirty wives make drunken husbands.

ANON.

A handsome woman is soon dressed.

ANON.

A pretty woman is a welcome guest.

BYRON.

Women are coquettes by profession.

ROUSSEAU.

Wounds given to honour never heal.

CORNEILLE.

God created woman only to tame man.

VOLTAIRE.

Devotion is the last love of women.

SAINT-EVREMOND.

To love her was a liberal education.

STEELE, *Tatler*. No. 49.

Constraint is the mother of desires.

D'ARGENS.

Love is a tyrant that spares no one.

CORNEILLE.

The rarer daughter of a rare mother.

DOANE, *St. Agnes Addresses.*

Love and high rule allow no rivals.

FLETCHER, *Monsieur Thomas.* i, 1.

For virtue only finds eternal Fame.

PETRARCH, *Triumph of Fame.* Pt. I, 1. 183.

Marriage and hanging go by destiny.

MIDDLETON, *A Chaste Maid in Cheapside.* iii, 3.

Hanging and marriage go by destiny.

SMOLLETT, *The Reprisal.* ii, 15.

The man is what his wife makes him.

ANON.

There's two words to that bargain.

SWIFT, *Polite Conversation.* Dia. iii.

I do hate him, as I hate the devil.

BEN JONSON, *Every Man Out of His Humour.* i. 1.

Woman, thy vows are traced in sand.

BYRON, *Hours of Idleness.* To Woman.

Men have marble, women, waxen minds.
Rape of Lucrece. l. 178.

Each woman is a brief of womankind.
OVERBURY, *A Wife.* l. 1.

If your wife is short stoop to her.
ANON.

The God of Love is blinde as stone.
CHAUCER, *Romaunt of the Rose.* l. 3702.

To nurse a blind ideal like a girl.
TENNYSON, *The Princess.* iii.

Beauty is a fair but fading flower.
ANON.

Vows of love prove its inconstancy.
MARMONTEL.

For love reflects the thing beloved.
TENNYSON, *In Memoriam.* Pt. LII.

He was more than over shoes in love.
Two Gentlemen of Verona. i, 1, l. 23.

Motherless husband makes happy wife.
ANON.

I wonder what Mrs. Grundy would say?
MORTON, *Speed the Plough.* i. 1.

Quarrels of lovers renew their love.
TERENCE, *Andria.* iii, 3, l. 23.

A thing of beauty is a joy for ever.
KEATS, *Endymion.* l. 1.

Beauty doth blind all but the blind.
ANON.

Bridesmaids may soon be made brides.
ANON.

The spotless ether of a maiden life.
WORDSWORTH, *The Excursion.* Bk. VI.

The only reward of virtue is virtue.
> EMERSON, *Essays.* Friendship.

Assume a virtue, if you have it not.
> *Hamlet.* iii, 4, 1. 160.

A woman's honour rests on manly love.
> TEGNÉR, *Fridthjof's Saga.* Canto viii.

Have an open ear and a closed mouth.
> ANON.

Can man be free if woman be a slave?
> SHELLEY, *Revolt of Islam.* ii, 43.

Fine by defect, and delicately weak.
> POPE, *Moral Essays.* Ep. ii, 1. 43.

Shy she was, and I thought her cold.
> TENNYSON, *Edward Gray.*

Imitation is the sincerest flattery.
> COLTON, *Lacon.*

The sooty yoke of kitchen vassalage.
> TENNYSON, *Gareth and Lynette.*

One is always a woman's first lover.
> LACLOS.

Women are priestesses of the unknown.
> From the French.

Prudery is the hypocrisy of modesty.
> MASSIAS.

But shy withal as the young antelope.
> STODDARD, *The Lion's Cub.*

I wonder you will still be talking.
> *Much Ado About Nothing.*

A woman's nay doth stand for naught.
> *Passionate Pilgrim.* 1. 339.

With such a heart the mind fuses naturally.
> IK MARVEL, *Reveries of a Bachelor.* p. 83.

Of course she has good taste—for she accepts you.

> IK MARVEL, *Reveries of a Bachelor.* p. 137.

What is a man's heart given him for, if not to choose?

> IK MARVEL, *Reveries of a Bachelor.* p. 133.

Spoils all her scolding with a perfect shower of kisses.

> IK MARVEL, *Dream Life.* p. 41.

Toasts

With a woful ballad made to his mistress's eyebrow.
As You Like It.   ii, 7.

Toasts

ABSENT LORDS

Here 's to ye absent lords, may they
Long in a far countree stay,
Drinking at other ladies' boards,
The health of other absent lords.

Old Song.

ACQUAINTANCES

May the hinges of friendship never grow rusty.

ACTOR'S SPOOK

Here 's that a spook may us affright,
Wherever we may roam ;
For if the " ghost walks " not all right,
We actors must walk home.

ANON.

ADAM'S CRYSTAL ALE

Here 's to Old Adam's crystal ale,
Clear, sparkling and divine,
Fair H2O, long may you flow !
We drink your health (in wine).

OLIVER HERFORD.

A GLASS IS GOOD

A glass is good, and a lass is good,
And a pipe to smoke in cold weather ;
The world is good, and the people are good
And we 're all good fellows together.

JOHN O'KEEFE, Sprigs of Laurel.   ii, 1.

ALL CONDITIONS

A garland for the hero's crest,
And twined by her whom he loves best ;
To every lovely lady bright,
What can I wish but faithful knight ?
To every faithful lover, too,
What can I wish but lady true ?
And knowledge to the studious sage ;
And pillow soft to head of age.

SIR WALTER SCOTT.

ALL THE TAILS

Here 's a health to Detail, Retail, and Curtail —
Indeed, all the Tails but Tell-Tales.

Old Saying.

ALL YOUR BEAUTIES

If all your beauties, one by one,
I pledge, dear, I am thinking
Before the tale were well begun
I had been dead of drinking.

OLIVER HERFORD.

AMERICAN ARMY

May it ever be very small in peace, but grow to mighty
dimensions and mightier achievements in war.

AMERICAN EAGLE

The liberty bird that permits no liberties.

AMERICAN NAVY

May it always be as anxious to preserve peace as to
uphold the honour of the flag in war.

AMERICA'S DAUGHTERS

To America's daughters — Let all fill their glasses,
Whose beauty and virtue the whole world surpasses ;
May blessings attend them, go wherever they will,
And foul fall the man e'er offers them ill.

A MIGHTY PAIN

A mighty pain to love it is,
And 't is a pain that pain to miss ;
But, of all pains, the greatest pain
Is to love, but love in vain.
ABRAHAM COWLEY, *Anacreontiques.* vii. Gold.

A PRESSING LOVER

A pressing lover seldom wants success,
Whilst the respectful, like the Greek, sits down
And wastes a ten years' siege before one town.
NICHOLAS ROWE, *To the Inconstant.* Epi., 1. 18.

A PRETTY LASS

A cheerful glass, a pretty lass,
A friend sincere and true ;
Blooming health, good store of wealth,
Attend on me and you.

ANON.

AS BAD AS I AM

Here 's to you, as good as you are,
And here 's to me, as bad as I am ;
But as good as you are, and as bad as I am,
I 'm as good as you are, as bad as I am.

Old Scotch Toast.

AWAY WITH GLOOM

Then fill the bowl — away with gloom !
Our joys shall always last ;
For hope will brighten days to come,
And memory gild the past.

THOMAS MOORE.

BANISH THAT FEAR

Banish that fear ; my flame can never waste,
For love sincere refines upon the taste.

COLLEY CIBBER, *The Double Gallant.* v, I.

BETTER THE QUICKER

If you 'd dip in such joys, come—the better, the quicker,
But remember the fee — for it suits not my ends
To let you make havoc, scot free, with my liquor,
As though I were one of your heavy-pursed friends.

HORACE, *To Virgil.* Bk. IV, Ode 12.

BLUSH, HAPPY MAIDEN

Blush, happy maiden, when you feel
The lips which press love's glowing seal ;
But as the slow years darklier roll,
Grow wiser, the experienced soul
Will own as dearer far than they
The lips which kiss the tears away.

ELIZABETH AKERS ALLEN, *Kisses.*

BORE

May he give us a few brilliant flashes of silence.

BRISK WINE AND LOVELY WOMEN

Brisk wine and lovely women are
The source of all our joys ;
A bumper softens every care
And beauty never cloys.
Then let us drink, and let us love,
While yet our hearts are gay ;
Women and wine we all approve,
As blessing night and day.

BUBBLE WINKED

The bubble winked at me and said,
" You 'll miss me brother when you 're dead."
OLIVER HERFORD.

BUT I CAN DRINK

I cannot eat but little meat,
My stomach is not good ;
But sure I think that I can drink
With him that wears a hood.
BISHOP STILL, *Gammer Gurton's Needle.* Act ii.

BYRON'S TOAST

Fill the goblet again ; for I never before
Felt the glow which now gladdens my heart to its core.
Let us drink ; who would not? since through life's varied
round
In the goblet alone no deception is found.

CADDIE'S WISH

'Ere 's to the 'ealth o' your royal 'ighness ; hand may
the skin o' ha gooseberry be big henough for han hum-
brella to cover hup hall your henemies.
In *Erminie.*

CANNOT LIVE WITHOUT THEM

As for the women, though we scorn and flout 'em,
We may live with, but cannot live without 'em.
                    F. REYNOLDS, *The Will.* i, i.

CHAIN OF SYMPATHY

Thus circling the cup, hand in hand, ere we drink,
    Let sympathy pledge us, through pleasure, through
        pain,
That, fast as a feeling but touches one link,
    Her magic shall send it direct through the chain.
                    THOMAS MOORE.

CHAPERONES

Here's to the chaperone,
    May she learn from Cupid
Just enough blindness
    To be sweetly stupid.
                    ANON.

CHARITY

A link from the chain of gold that angels forge.

CHEMIST OF LOVE

The chemist of love
    Will this perishing mould,
Were it made out of mire,
    Transmute into gold.
                    MOHAMMED HAFIZ, *Divan.*

CLINK YOUR GLASSES

Clink, clink your glasses and drink !
Why should we trouble borrow !
Care not for sorrow,
A fig for the morrow !
To-night let's be merry and drink !

ANON.

COLD BOTTLE AND ANOTHER ONE

Here 's to a long life and a merry one,
A quick death and a happy one,
A good girl and a pretty one,
A cold bottle and another one.

Clover Club.

COLUMBIA, THE PRIDE

Here 's a health to Columbia, the pride of the earth,
The stars and the stripes—drink the land of our birth !
Toast the army and navy who fought for our cause,
Who conquered and won us our freedom and laws.

COME, FILL THE BOWL

Come, fill the bowl, each jolly soul,
Let Bacchus guide our revels ;
Join cup to lip, with hip, hip, hip,
And bury the blue devils.

COME LIVE WITH ME.

Come live with me, and be my love,
And we will all the pleasures prove,
That valleys, groves, or hills, or fields,
Or woods and steepy mountains, yield.

CHRISTOPHER MARLOWE, *Passionate Shepherd
to his Love.* St. I.

CONTENTMENT

May we never murmur without a cause, and never have
cause to murmur.

COULD WE FORBEAR DISPUTE

Could we forbear dispute, and practise love,
We should agree as angels do above.
EDMUND WALLER, *Divine Poems.* Divine Love.
Canto. iii, l. 25.

DASHING COQUETTE

Health to the bold, dashing coquette
Who careth not for me ;
Whose heart, untouched by love as yet,
Is wild and fancy free.
Toasts of love to the timid dove
Are always going 'round ;
Let mine be heard to the untamed bird,
And make your glasses sound !
ANON.

DEAR OLD TIMES

I drink it as the Fates ordain it,
Come, fill it, and have done with rhymes ;
Fill up the lonely glass, and drain it
In memory of dear old times.
WM. MAKEPEACE THACKERAY.

DOUBLE HEALTH TO THEE

My boat is on the shore,
And my bark is on the sea ;
But, before I go, Tom Moore,
Here 's a double health to thee.
LORD BYRON, *To Thomas Moore.*

DOWN AMONG THE DEAD MEN

And he that will this health deny,
Down among the dead men let him lie.
JOHN DYER, published in reign of George I.

DRINK DEEP

A little learning is a dangerous thing ;
Drink deep, or taste not the Pierian spring ;
There shallow draughts intoxicate the brain,
And drinking largely sobers us again.
ALEXANDER POPE.

DRINK DIVINE

The thirst that from the soul doth rise
Doth ask a drink divine ;
But might I of Jove's nectar sup,
I would not change from thine.
BEN JONSON.

DRINK WHILE YOU CAN

Drink to-day and drown all sorrow ;
You shall perhaps not do 't to-morrow ;
Best while you have it, use your breath,
There 's no drinking after death.
BEAUMONT AND FLETCHER, *The Blood Brother.* ii, 2.

DRINK WITH SINCERITY

Here 's long life and prosperity,
To all of your posterity,
And those that don't drink with sincerity
May they be damned to eternity.
ANON.

DRINKS LIKE A FISH

A fig then for Burgundy, Claret or Mountain,
A few scanty glasses must limit your wish ;
But he's the true toper that goes to the fountain,
The drinker that verily "drinks like a fish!"
THOMAS HOOD.

ECONOMY

The daughter of Prudence, the sister of Temperance, and
the parent of Independence.

EMBLEM OF ETERNITY

Love is the emblem of eternity : it confounds all notion
of time : effaces all memory of a beginning, all fear
of an end.
MADAME DE STAËL, *Corinne.* Bk. VIII, ch. 2.

ETERNAL HEALTH GOES ROUND

Nothing in Nature's sober found,
But an eternal "health" goes round,
Fill up the bowl, then, fill it high—
Fill all the glasses there ; for why
Should every creature drink but I ;
Why, man of morals, tell me why?
ABRAHAM COWLEY.

EVER WELCOME

Come in the evening, or come in the morning—
Come when you 're looked for, or come without warning ;
A thousand welcomes you 'll find here before you,
And the oftener you come here the more I 'll adore you !
Old Irish Toast.

FAIRNESS

Charity without ostentation and religion without bigotry.

FAREWELL OF DRINKING

We saw how the sun looked sinking,
  The waters beneath him how bright,
And now let our farewell of drinking
  Resemble that farewell of light.
You saw how he finished by darting
  His beam o 'er a deep billow's brim—
So fill up, let 's shine at our parting,
  In full, liquid glory like him.
And oh, may our life's happy measure
  Of moments like this be made up ;
'Twas born on the bosom of pleasure,
  It dies 'mid the tears of the cup.

                              THOMAS MOORE.

FICKLENESS

May we never have friends who, like shadows, follow us
in sunshine only to desert us in a cloudy day.

FILL THE BUMPER FAIR

Fill the bumper fair !
  Every drop we sprinkle
O 'er the brow of care
  Smoothes away a wrinkle.
Wit's electric flame
  Ne'er so swiftly passes
As when through the frame
  It shoots from brimming glasses.

                              THOMAS MOORE.

FILL THE WINE CUP HIGH

O, fill the wine cup high !
The sparkling liquor pour,
For we will care and grief defy,
They ne 'er shall plague us more ;
And ere the snowy foam
From off the wine departs,
The precious draught shall find a home,
A dwelling in our hearts.

ROBERT F. WILLIAMS.

FILL UP THE GOBLET

Fill up the goblet and reach me some.
Drinking makes wise, but dry fasting makes glum!

WM. R. ALGER, *Oriental Poetry*. Wine Song.

FIRST PLEDGE OUR QUEEN

First pledge our Queen this solemn night,
Then drink to England, every guest ;
That man 's the best Cosmopolite
Who loves his native country best.

SIR A. TENNYSON, *Hands All Round*.

FIVE REASONS FOR DRINKING

If on my theme I rightly think,
There are five reasons why men drink :
Good wine, a friend. because I 'm dry,
Or lest I should be by and by,
Or any other reason why.

JOHN SIRMOND.

FORGET TROUBLE

Fill up the bowl, upon my soul,
　Your trouble you 'll forget, sir,
If it takes more, fill twenty score,
　Till you have drowned regret sir.
ALFRED BRENN.

FRIENDS AND WIVES

A health to our sweethearts,
　Our friends and our wives,
And may fortune smile on them
　The rest of their lives.

FRIENDSHIP

May differences of opinion only cement it.

FUTURE

May the best day we have seen be worse than the worst
that is to come.

GIRL I LOVE

Here 's to the girl that I love,
　And here 's to the girl who loves me,
And here 's to all those that love her whom I love
And all those that love her who loves me.
ANON.

GIVE ME A KISS

Give me a kisse, and to that kisse a score ;
Then to that twenty, adde a hundred more ;
A thousand to that hundred ; so kiss on,
To make that thousand up a million ;
Treble that million, and when that is done,
Let 's kisse afresh, as when we first begun.
ROBERT HERRICK, *Hesperides*.　To Anthea.

GIVE ME KISSES

Give me kisses! Nay, 't is true
I am just as rich as you ;
And for every kiss I owe,
I can pay you back, you know.
        Kiss me, then
        Every moment—and again.
            JOHN GODFREY SAXE, *To Lesbia.*

GOOD TIMES

May the pleasures of youth never bring us pain in old
age.

HAPPINESS WITH WOMEN

Here 's to woman, whose heart and whose soul
  Are the light and the life of each spell we pursue ;
Whether sunn'd at the tropics or chilled at the pole,
  If women be there, there is happiness, too.
            ANON.

HARVESTS

May sunshine of plenty dispel the clouds of care.

HERE 'S TO HELL

Here 's to Hell, toss it off in a quaff, lads,
Drink the health of the Devil, and laugh, lads,
Pledge the tale of the Wheat and the Chaff, lads ;
  Here 's to Hell.
            EUGENE R. WHITE.

HERE 'S TO OUR FATHERLAND

The sparkling juice now pour,
  With fond and liberal hand ;
O, raise the laughing rim once more,
  Here 's to our Fatherland !
            ROBERT F. WILLIAMS.

HERE 'S TO THE HEART

Here 's to the heart
  Though another 's it be ;
Here 's to the cheeks,
  Though they bloom not for me.

HERE WITH MY BEER

Here
With my beer
I sit,
While golden moments flit :
Alas !
They pass
Unheeded by :
And as they fly,
I,
Being dry,
Sit, idly sipping here
My beer.

GEORGE ARNOLD, Beer.

HE WOOLD LOVE

Much ado there was, God wot ;
He woold love, and she woold not,
She sayd, "Never man was trewe " ;
He sayes, " None was false to you."

NICHOLAS BRETON, Phillida and Corydon.

HOLD THEE TO MY HEART

Thus let me hold thee to my heart,
  And every care resign :
And we shall never, never part,
  My life—my all that 's mine !

OLIVER GOLDSMITH, The Hermit. St. 39.

HOME

A world of strife shut out, and a world of love shut in.

HOPE

May the sunshine of hope dispel calamity's clouds.

HOST WHO CARVED THE ROAST

Here 's a toast to the host who carved the roast ;
And a toast to the hostess—may none ever "roast" us.

ANON.

HOW THEY TAKE IT

Some take their gold in minted mold,
And some in harps hereafter,
But give me mine in tresses fine,
And keep the change in laughter.

OLIVER HERFORD.

HUMANITY

May we never feel want nor want feeling.

I AM YOUNG

I am young—so is she—and how fair !
Then love shall my moments employ ;
I am caught by her berry-brown hair,
And the rose on her cheek is my joy !

ROBERT BLOOMFIELD, *Hazelwood Hall.*   i, 1.

I FILL THIS CUP

I fill this cup, to one made up
Of loveliness alone,
A woman, of her gentle sex
The seeming paragon.
Her health ! and would on earth there stood
Some more of such a frame,
That life might be all poetry,
And weariness a name.

EDWARD CATE PINCKNEY.

IF LOVE WERE YOUNG

If all the world and love were young,
And truth in every shepherd's tongue,
These pretty pleasures might me move
To live with thee, and be thy love.
    Sir Walter Raleigh, *Nymph's Reply*
              to Passionate Shepherd.

IF YOU BECOME A NUN

If you become a Nun, dear,
   The bishop Love will be ;
The Cupids every one, dear,
   Will chant—" We trust in thee ! "
          Leigh Hunt, *The Nun.*

I LOVE BUT THEE

I love thee, I love but thee,
With a love that shall not die
   Till the sun grows cold,
   And the stars are old,
And the leaves of the Judgment Book unfold !
       Bayard Taylor, *Bedouin Song.*

IN HER FIRST PASSION

In her first passion woman loves her lover ;
In all the others, all she loves is love.
    Lord Byron, *Don Juan.* Canto iii, st. 3.

IN-LAWS

Here 's to bride and mother-in-law,
Here 's to groom and father-in-law,
Here 's to sister and brother-in-law,
Here 's to friends and friends-in-law.
May none of them need an attorney-at-law.
                Anon.

INDISCRETIONS

They are heavy drafts upon Old Age, payable with compound interest about thirty years from date.

IRISHMAN'S TOAST

Here's to the land of the shamrock so green,
Here's to each lad and his darling colleen,
Here's to the ones we love dearest and most,
And may God save old Ireland!—that's an Irishman's
toast.

ANON.

I THROW A KISS

I throw a kiss across the sea,
I drink the winds as drinking wine,
And dream they all are blown from thee,
I catch the whisper'd kiss of thine.

JOAQUIN MILLER, *England*. 1871. Introduction.

IT LEAVES NO STING BEHIND

Friend of my soul! this goblet sip —
'T will chase the pensive tear;
'T is not so sweet as woman's lip,
But, oh 't is more sincere.
Like her delusive beam,
'T will steal away the mind,
But unlike affection's dream,
It leaves no sting behind.

THOMAS MOORE.

JOLLY OLD BOUNCER

To Death, the jolly old bouncer, now
Our glasses let's be clinking,
If he had n't put others out, I trow,
To-night we'd not be drinking.

OLIVER HERFORD.

KEEPS LOVERS GUESSING

Here 's lovers two to the maiden true,
And four to the maid caressing,
But the wayward girl with the lips that curl
Keeps twenty lovers guessing.

ANON.

KISSES

Kisses tender, kisses cold,
Kisses timid, kisses bold,
Kisses joyful, kisses sad,
Pass the bowl or I 'll go mad.

OLIVER HERFORD.

LASS WITH BLACK EYES

Here 's a health to the lass with the merry black eyes.
Here 's a health to the lad with the blue ones.

WILLIAM WINTER, *Blue and Black*.

LAUGH, AND BE FAT

Laugh, and be fat, sir, your penance is known.
They that love mirth, let them heartily drink,
'T is the only receipt to make sorrow sink.

BEN JONSON, *Entertainments*. The Penates.

LAUGH AT ALL THINGS

Laugh at all things,
Great and small things,
  Sick or well, at sea or shore ;
  While we 're quaffing,
  Let 's have laughing —
Who the devil cares for more ?

LORD BYRON.

LAUGH AT YOUR FRIENDS

Laugh at your friends, and if your friends are sore
So much the better, you may laugh the more.
ALEXANDER POPE, *Epilogue to Satire.*
Dia. i, 1. 55.

LEAVE A KISS IN THE CUP

Drink to me only with thine eyes,
And I will pledge with mine ;
Or leave a kiss but in the cup,
And I 'll not look for wine.
The thirst that from the soul doth rise,
Doth ask a drink divine,
But might I of Jove's nectar sip,
I would not change from thine.
BEN JONSON, *The Forest.*   To Celia.

LEAVE DULL EARTH BEHIND

Then wreathe the bowl !
With flowers of soul,
The brightest wit can find us ;
We 'll take a flight
Towards heaven to-night
And leave dull earth behind us !
THOMAS MOORE.

LET MY LIVER HEAT WITH WINE

Let me play the fool ;
With mirth and laughter let old wrinkles come ;
And let my liver rather heat with wine,
Than my heart cool with mortifying groans.
SHAKESPEARE.

LITTLE FISHES

O little fishes of the sea,
  Had I the power divine,
I 'd turn ye into silver cups
  And your sea to purple wine.

ANON.

LITTLE HOUSE AND FREEDOM

A little health, a little wealth,
  A little house and freedom,
With some few friends for certain ends,
  But little cause to need 'em.

ANON.

LIVE IN CLOVER

While we live, let 's live in clover,
But when we 're dead, we 're dead all over.

ANON.

LONG LIFE AND TREASURE

To the old, long life and treasure;
To the young, all health and pleasure;
  To the fair, their face,
  With eternal grace;
And the rest, to be loved at leisure!
  BEN JONSON, *Metamorphosed Gypsies.*

LOVE CANNOT DIE

They sin who tell us Love can die;
With life all other passions fly,
And others are but vanity.
  ROBERT SOUTHEY, *Curse of Kehama.*
    Mount Meru. St. 10.

LOVE HATH MY HEART

My true love hath my heart, and I have his,
By just exchange, one for the other given ;
I hold his dear, and mine he cannot miss,
There never was a better bargain driven.
SIR PHILIP SIDNEY, *My True Love Hath My Heart.*

LOVE IS BLIND

I have heard of reasons manifold
Why Love must needs be blind,
But this is the best of all, I hold—
His eyes are in his mind.
S. T. COLERIDGE, *To a Lady.* St. ii.

LOVE IS LIGHT FROM HEAVEN

Yes, Love indeed is light from heaven ;
A spark of that immortal fire
With angels shared, by Allah given,
To lift from earth our low desire.
LORD BYRON, *The Giaour.* l. 1131.

LOVE KNOWS NO LAW

Oh, rank is good, and gold is fair,
And high and low mate ill ;
But love has never known a law
Beyond its own sweet will.
JOHN G. WHITTIER, *Amy Wentworth.* St. 18.

LOVES ONLY ONE

Here 's to one and only one,
And that is she,
Who loves but one and only one,
And that is me.
ANON.

LOVE US WELL

Here 's to those who love us well;
Those who don't may go to H——.

ANON.

MADE FRESH AND FAIR

The thirsty Earth soaks up the rain,
And drinks and gapes for drink again;
The plants suck in the earth, and are
With constant drinking fresh and fair.

ABRAHAM COWLEY, *Anacreon II.* Drinking.

MAIDEN'S EYES

Here 's to the girl with eyes of blue,
  Whose heart is kind and love is true;
Here 's to the girl with eyes of brown,
  Whose spirit proud you cannot down;
Here 's to the girl with eyes of gray,
  Whose sunny smile drives care away;
Whate'er the hue of their eyes may be,
  I 'll drink to the girls this toast with thee!

ANON.

MAIDS OF ALL AGES

Here 's to the maiden of bashful fifteen;
Here 's to the widow of fifty;
Here 's to the flaunty, extravagant queen,
And here 's to the housewife that 's thrifty.
Let the toast pass;
Drink to the lass;
I 'll warrant she 'll prove an excuse for the glass.

RICHARD BRINSLEY SHERIDAN,
School for Scandal. iii, 3.

MAN IN FASHION

Would you be a man in fashion?
Would you lead a life divine?
Take a little Dram of Passion
In a lusty dose of wine.

ANON.

MAN MADE WINE

God made Man frail as a bubble;
God made Love, Love made Trouble.
God made the Vine; was it a sin
That Man made Wine to drown Trouble in?

ANON.

MANNERS

Give us good form, but not formality.

MARRIAGE

The happy estate which resembles a pair of shears: so joined that they cannot be separated; often moving in opposite directions, yet always punishing anyone who comes between.

MAY GOOD HUMOUR PRESIDE

May the juice of the grape enliven each soul,
And good humour preside at the head of each bowl.

MEMORY

May it always be used as a storehouse and never as a lumber-room.

MINISTERS OF LOVE

All thoughts, all passions, all delights,
    Whatever stirs this mortal frame,
All are but ministers of Love,
    And feed his sacred flame.

S. T. COLERIDGE, Love. St. 1.

MORE SINCERE

Here 's to good old whiskey,
    So amber and so clear ;
'T is not so sweet as woman's lips,
    But a d—— sight more sincere.

ANON.

MY BOUNTY IS BOUNDLESS

My bounty is as boundless as the sea,
My love as deep ; the more I give to thee
The more I have, for both are infinite.

Romeo and Juliet.   ii, 2, 1. 133.

MY DEARIE

While waters wimple to the sea ;
    While day blinks in the lift sae hie ;
Till clay-cauld death shall blin' me e'e,
    Ye shall be my dearie.

ROBERT BURNS.

MY LUVE 'S LIKE A ROSE

Oh my luve is like a red, red rose,
    That 's newly sprung in June ;
Oh my luve is like the melodie
    That 's sweetly played in tune.

ROBERT BURNS, A Red, Red Rose.

MYSTERIOUS LOVE

Mysterious love, uncertain treasure,
Hast thou more of pain or pleasure?
JOSEPH ADDISON, *Rosamond.*   iii, 2.

NATURE FILLS THE CUP

'T is Nature's self the cup that fills,
In spite of folly's frown,
And Nature from her vine-clad hills,
That rains her life-blood down.
OLIVER WENDELL HOLMES.

NECTAR ON A LIP

I ne'er could any lustre see
In eyes that would not look on me;
I ne'er saw nectar on a lip
But where my own did hope to sip.
RICHARD BRINSLEY SHERIDAN.

NEGRO'S WISH

Little ter-day an' little ter-morrer,
Out o' meal an' boun' ter borrer;
Hoe cake an' dab o' dough,
Dash her down an' say no mo'.
Peace at home an' pleasure abroad,
Please your neighbour an' sarve th' Lord.
God bless you!
ANON.

NOBILITY

He who thinks most good and speaks least ill of his
neighbours.

NOT TO KNOW LOVE

Love, then, hath every bliss in store ;
'T is friendship, and 't is something more.
Each other every wish they give ;
Not to know love is not to live.
    JOHN GAY, *Plutus*. Cupid and Time. 1. 135.

NOW IS THE TIME

Let us have wine and women, mirth and laughter,
Sermons and soda-water the day after.
    LORD BYRON.

OLD FAMILIAR JUICE

" Well," murmured one, "let whoso make or buy,
My clay with long oblivion is one dry,
But fill me with the old familiar juice,
Methinks I might recover by and by."
    OMAR KHAYYÁM.

ONE KIND KISS

One kind kiss before we part,
Drop a tear and bid adieu ;
Though we sever, my fond heart
Till we meet shall pant for you.
    ROBERT DODSLEY, *Colin's Kisses*. Parting Kiss.

ONE LONG KISS

Once he drew
With one long kiss my whole soul thro'
My lips, as sunlight drinketh dew.
    SIR A. TENNYSON, *Fatima*. St. 3.

OPINIONS

May they never float in the sea of ignorance.

OTHER MEETINGS

Oh, here 's to other meetings,
    And merry greetings then,
And here 's to those we 've drunk with,
    But never can again.

MAJOR.

OUR COUNTRY

Our Country—May she always be in the right—
But our country, right or wrong.

STEPHEN DECATUR.

OUR SWEETHEARTS

Here 's to our sweethearts and wives :
May our wives always remain our sweethearts,
And our sweethearts some day become wives.

ANON.

PLENTY

May we always be under the orders of General Peace,
General Plenty, and General Prosperity.

PRECIOUS LIPS

Precious fingers, precious toes,
Precious eyes and precious nose,
Precious chin and precious lip,
Precious fool that lets 'em slip.

ANON.

PROSPERITY

May your shadow never grow less.

QUENCH YOUR LOVE'S HOT FIRE

I do not seek to quench your love's hot fire,
But qualify the fire's extreme rage,
Lest it should burn above the bounds of reason.
Two Gentlemen of Verona. ii, 7, l. 21.

READY CURE

Don't die of love ; in heaven above
Or hell they 'll not endure you ;
Why look so glum when Doctor Rum
Is waiting for to cure you?
OLIVER HERFORD.

RESPECT

May we have keen wit, but never make a sword of our
tongues to wound the reputation of others.

RIDDLE

Here is a riddle most abstruse :
Canst read the answer right?
Why is it that my tongue grows loose
Only when I grow tight ?
ANON.

RIP VAN WINKLE

Here 's to your good health, and your family's good
health, and may you all live long and prosper.
Used by JOSEPH JEFFERSON.

SEASON FOR MARRIAGE

Misses, the tale that I relate
This lesson seems to carry,—
Choose not alone a proper mate,
But proper time to marry.
WILLIAM COWPER, *Pairing Time.*

SEND THEE GOOD ALE

Back and side go bare, go bare,
  Both foot and hand go cold ;
But, belly, God send thee good ale enough,
  Whether it be new or old.
      BISHOP STILL, *Gammer Gurton's Needle.*

SHE WAS FAIR

Oh ! she was good as she was fair.
  None — none on earth above her !
As pure in thought as angels are,
  To know her was to love her.
      SAMUEL ROGERS, *Jacqueline.* Pt. I, l. 86.

SING MY TRUE LOVE

I 'll bid the hyacinth to blow,
  I 'll teach my grotto green to be ;
And sing my true love, all below
  The holly bower and myrtle tree.
      THOMAS CAMPBELL, *Caroline.* Pt. I.

SMELL OF WINE

Let those who drink not, but austerely dine,
Dry up in law ; the Muses smell of wine.
      HORACE.

SOLDIERS OF AMERICA

  The soldiers of America,
  Their arms our defence,
  Our arms their reward :
  Fall in, men, fall in !

      ANON.

SO LIVE

On parent knees, a naked new-born child
Weeping thou sat'st while all around thee smiled ;
So live, that, sinking in thy last sleep,
Calm thou mayst smile, while all around thee weep.

SIR WM. JONES, From the Persian.

SOME HAE MEAT

Some hae meat that canna eat ;
   And some wad eat that want it ;
But we hae meat, and we can eat,
   Sae let the Lord be thankit.

BURNS, Grace before Meat.

SO SANG OLD CRATINUS

Nought wise a water-drinker's brain can spin ;
   So sang old Cratinus in his jollity,
Redolent daily, not of one good skin,
   But a whole barrel of the choicest vintage.

The Flask of Cratinus.

SPARKLES BRIGHTLY

Say, why did Time
His glass sublime
   Fill up with sands, unsightly,
When wine he knew
Runs brisker through
   And sparkles far more brightly ?

THOMAS MOORE.

SPARKLING AND BRIGHT

Sparkling and bright in the liquid light,
  Does the wine our goblets gleam in ;
With hue as red as the rosy bed
  Which a bee would choose to dream in.
Then fill to-night, with hearts as light,
  To loves as gay and fleeting
As bubbles that swim on the beaker's rim,
  And break on the lips while meeting.
                    CHARLES FENNO HOFFMAN.

STAND TO YOUR GLASSES

Ho ! stand to your glasses steady !
  'T is all we have left to prize.
A cup to the dead already,—
  Hurrah for the next that dies !
BARTHOLOMEW DOWLING, *Revelry in India.*

SUCCESS

May we court and win all the daughters of Fortune
except the eldest — Miss Fortune.

SUNNY SIDE OF LIFE

As half in shade and half in sun
  This world along its path advances,
May that side the sun 's upon
  Be all that e'er shall meet thy glances !
                    THOMAS MOORE.

SWEAR, STEAL, AND LIE

Here 's that we may swear, steal, and lie :
When we swear may it be by the hand of justice ;
When we steal may it be away from bad company ;
When we lie may it be in the arms of the one we love
best.

ANON.

TELL ME, WHAT 'S LOVE

"Tell me, what 's Love," said Youth, one day
    To drooping Age, who crost his way.
"It is a sunny hour of play ;
    For which repentance dear doth pay ;
    Repentance ! Repentance !
    And this is Love, as wise men say."

THOMAS MOORE, Youth and Age.

THAT HEALTH SHALL BE THINE

While there 's life on the lip, while there 's warmth in
the wine,
One deep health I 'll pledge, and that health shall be
thine.

OWEN MEREDITH.

THAT WE MAY CLINK

The old word " swink,"
Means work, I think,
It rhymes exceeding well with " chink " ;
Then here 's to " swink "
That we may clink
The wherewithal a while to drink.

ALFRED BRENN.

THAT WE MAY LIVE

Here 's that we may live to eat the hen,
That scratches on our grave.

ANON.

THEE AND THINE

Here 's a health to me and mine,
Not forgetting thee and thine ;
And when thee and thine
Come to see me and mine,
May me and mine make thee and thine
As welcome as thee and thine
Have ever made me and mine.

ANON.

THESE HOURS REDEEM

Oh Love! young Love! bound in thy rosy band,
Let sage or cynic prattle as he will,
These hours, and only these, redeem Life's years of ill.

LORD BYRON, *Childe Harold.* Canto ii, st. 81.

THIS BOTTLE 'S THE SUN

This bottle 's the sun of our table,
His beams are rosy wine ;
We, planets that are not able
Without his help to shine.

R. B. SHERIDAN, *The Duenna.* iii, 5.

THOSE I LOVE

Here 's a health for those I love,
And a curse for those I hate !
For, despite my God above,
The two will I separate !

ANON.

THOSE THAT ARE SINGLE

May those that are single get wives to their mind,
And those that are married true happiness find.

ANON.

THOSE WHO HATE

Here 's a sigh to those who love me,
And a smile to those who hate ;
And whatever sky 's above me,
Here 's a heart for every fate.

LORD BYRON.

THREE RULING POWERS

Here 's to the press, the pulpit, and the petticoat,
The three ruling powers of the day ;
The first spreads knowledge,
The second spreads morals,
And the third spreads considerably.

ANON.

TIME IS SHORT

Time is short, life is short.
Life is sweet, love is sweet, use to-day while you may ;
Love is sweet, and to-morrow may fail ;
Love is sweet, use to-day.

CHRISTINA G. ROSSETTI, *The Prince's Progress.*
St. 7.

'T IS TO THEE

Were 't the last drop in the well,
As I gasp'd upon the brink,
Ere my fainting spirit fell,
'T is to thee that I would drink.

LORD BYRON, *To Thomas Moore.* St. 4.

TOAST ALL THE LADIES

For let her be clumsy, or let her be slim,
  Young or ancient, I care not a feather ;
So fill up a bumper, nay, fill to the brim,
  Let us toast all the ladies together !

ANON.

TO-DAY IS TO-DAY

Yesterday 's yesterday while to-day 's here,
  To-day 's to-day till to-morrow appear,
To-morrow 's to-morrow until to-day 's past,
  And kisses are kisses as long as they last.

ANON.

TOO BOLD A USE

For highest cordials all their virtues lose,
  By a too frequent and too bold a use ;
And what would cheer the spirits in distress
Ruins our health when taken to excess.

JOHN POMFRET, The Choice. 1. 139.

TO SEE HER WAS TO LOVE HER

But to see her was to love her,
Love but her, and love forever.

ROBERT BURNS, Song, Ae Fond Kiss.

UNITED

Distinct as the billows, yet one as the sea.

JAMES MONTGOMERY.

VALOUR

May no war require it, but may it be always ready for
every foe.

VIRTUE

May we have the wit to discover what is true and the fortitude to practise what is good.

WAIT ON EACH

The cups that cheer, but not inebriate, wait on each.

WILLIAM COWPER.

WAY TO LIVE

Care to our coffin adds a nail, no doubt,
And every grin, so merry, draws one out.

JOHN WOLCOTT.

WEDDING

May the single all be married and all the married be happy.

WHAT HARM IN DRINKING?

What harm in drinking can there be?
Since punch and life so well agree?

THOMAS BLACKLOCK, *An Epigram on Punch.* 1. 15.

WHAT IS LOVE?

Ask not of me, love, what is love?
Ask what is good of God above;
Ask of the great sun what is light;
Ask what is darkness of the night;
Ask sin of what may be forgiven;
Ask what is happiness of heaven;
Ask what is folly of the crowd;
Ask what is fashion of the shroud;
Ask what is sweetness of thy kiss;
Ask of thyself what beauty is.

PHILIP J. BAILEY, *Festus.*

WHAT 'S OUR BAGGAGE?

What 's our baggage? Only vows,
Happiness, and all our care,
And the flower that sweetly shews
Nestling lightly in your hair.
VICTOR HUGO, *Eviradnus.*

WHAT THIS RIBAND BOUND

A narrow compass, and yet there
Dwelt all that 's good, and all that 's fair ;
Give me but what this riband bound,
Take all the rest the sun goes round.
EDMUND WALLER.

WHEN AGE CHILLS THE BLOOD

When age chills the blood, when our pleasures are past—
For years fleet away with the wings of the dove—
The dearest remembrance will still be the last,
Our sweetest memorial the first kiss of love.
LORD BYRON, *First Kiss of Love.* St. 7.

WHEN DARING IN DRESS

Divine in hookas, glorious in a pipe,
When tipped with amber, mellow, rich, and ripe ;
Like other charmers, wooing the caress,
More dazzling when daring in full dress ;
Yet thy true lovers more admire by far
Thy naked beauties—Give me a cigar !
LORD BYRON.

WHEN RAINING KISSES

Here's to a girl who 's bound to win
Her share at least of blisses,
Who knows enough not to go in
When it is raining kisses.

ANON.

WHERE LOVE IS GREAT

Where love is great, the little doubts are fear ;
When little fears grow great, great love grows there.
SHAKESPEARE, *Hamlet.* iii, 2, 1. 181.

WHILE YOU MAY

Gather kittens while you may,
Time brings only sorrow,
And the kittens of to-day
Will be old cats to-morrow.
From *The Bashful Earthquake.*

WHIRL-A-GIG WORLD

May this be our maxim whene'er we are twirled
A fig for the cares of this whirl-a-gig world
ANON.

WHY SHOULD WE KILL LOVE ?

Why should we kill the best of passions, love ?
It aids the hero, bids ambition rise
To nobler heights, inspires immortal deeds,
Even softens brutes, and adds a grace to virtue.
JAMES THOMSON, *Sophonisba.* v, 2.

WHY SO PALE?

Why so pale and wan, fond lover,
 Prithee, why so pale?
Will, when looking well can't move her,
 Looking ill prevail?
 Prithee, why so pale?
        SIR JOHN SUCKLING, *Song*. St. 1.

WILL NOT ASK HER NAME

Drink ye to her that each loves best,
 And if you nurse a flame
That's told but to her mutual breast,
 We will not ask her name.
            THOMAS CAMPBELL.

WINE AND LIBERTY

Come, fill the glass and drain the bowl;
 May Love and Bacchus still agree;
And every American warm his soul
 With Cupid, Wine, and Liberty.

WINE IS GOOD

 Wine is good,
  Love is good,
And all is good if understood;
  The sin is not in doing,
  But in overdoing;
How much of mine has gone that way?
Alas! How much more that may?

WINE WELL USED

Come, come, good wine is a good familiar creature, if it
 be well used; exclaim no more against it.
            Othello.

WINE, WOMAN, AND SONG

He who loves not wine, woman, or song
Remains a fool his whole life long.

LUTHER (Attributed to).   Probably by J. H. Voss.

WIN THE WOMAN

How should great Jove himself do else than miss
To win the woman he forgets to kiss.

COVENTRY PATMORE, *De Natura Deorum.*

WIVES

Come ! a health ! and it 's not to be slighted with sips,
  A cold pulse, or a spirit supine—
All the blood in my heart seems to rush to my lips
  To commingle its flow with the wine.
Then with wine, as is due, let the honours be paid,
  Whilst I give my hand, heart, and head ;
" Here 's to her, the fond mother, dear partner, kind maid,
  Who first taught me to love, woo, and wed ! "

THOMAS HOOD.

WOMAN

The fairest work of the great Author ; the edition is large,
  and no man should be without a copy.

YOU KNOW NOT WHY

Drink, for you know not
Whence you came, nor why ;
Drink, for you know not why
You go, nor whence.

OMAR KHAYYÁM.

Menu Verses

Read o 'er this ;
And after, this ; and then to breakfast, with
What appetite you have.
SHAKESPEARE, *Henry VIII.*   iii, 2.

Menu Verses

ACCEPTANCE

Barkis is willin'.

> DICKENS, *David Copperfield.* Ch. 5.

I will show myself highly fed.

> *All's Well that Ends Well.* ii, 2.

Catch occasion by the foretop.

> UNKNOWN, *Lingua.* v, 2.

I'll go with thee, cheek by jowl.

> *Midsummer Night's Dream.* iii, 2.

My teeth are on an edge till I do eat.

> CARTWRIGHT, *The Ordinary.* ii, 1. 50.

Obliged by hunger and request of friends.

> POPE, *Pro. to Satires.*

He did receive his letters and is coming.

> *Julius Cæsar.* iii, 1.

Defer no time, delays have dangerous ends.

> *King Henry VI.* Pt. I, iii, 2.

I think, or hope at least, the coast is clear.

> DRYDEN, *Pro. Cleomenes.*

We may live with, but cannot live without 'em.

> F. REYNOLDS, *The Will.* i, 1.

Custom, then, is the great guide of human life.

> HUME, *Concerning Human Understanding.*
> Pt. I, sec. v.

When was the hour I ever contradicted your desire?

> *King Henry VIII.* ii, 4.

I feel my strength increase with every thought on 't.

> CARTWRIGHT, *The Ordinary,* ii, 1.

Cloy the hungry edge of appetite by bare imagination of
a feast.

> *King Richard II.* i, 3.

Are these things then necessities? Then let us meet
them like necessities.

> *King Henry IV.* Pt. II, iii, 1.

ANNIVERSARIES

We have high doings to-day.
>   COLLEY CIBBER, *Love Makes a Man.* ii.

The gods to-day stand friendly.
>   *Julius Cæsar.* v, 1.

The better the day the better the deed.
>   MIDDLETON, *The Phœnix.* iii, 1.

A thing of custom ;— 't is no other.
>   *Macbeth.* iii, 4.

Now 's the day, and now 's the hour.
>   BURNS, *Bannockburn.*

More such days as these to us befall !
>   *King Henry VI.* Pt. II, v, 3.

These reasons made his mouth to water.
>   BUTLER, *Hudibras.* i, 3.

What ado here is to bring you together !
>   *Merry Wives of Windsor.* iv, 5.

This day is ours as many more shall be.
>   *King Henry VI.* Pt. II, i, 5.

This night I hold an old accustomed feast.
>   *Romeo and Juliet.* i, 2.

To solemnise this day the glorious sun stays in his course.
>   *King John.* iii, 1.

The day for whose returns, and many, all these pray, and
so do I.
>   BEN JONSON, *Underwoods.*

You shall have no cause to curse the fair proceedings of
this day.
>   *King John.* iii, 1.

O, hour of all hours, the most bless'd upon earth, the
blessed hour of our dinners !
>   LYTTON, *Lucile.* Pt. I, canto ii, st. 32.

BERRIES

Your homes amidst green leaves.
> CORNWALL, *Invocation to Birds.*

In the hedge the frosted berries grow.
> SARAH WHITMAN, *Day of Indian Summer.*

Large, luscious berries of sanguine dye.
> MULOCK, *Mulberry Tree.*

Union in partition ; two lovely berries moulded on one stem.
> *Midsummer Night's Dream.* iii, 2, 1. 208.

And sweete as is the brembul flour that bereth the rede hepe.
> CHAUCER, *Tale of Sir Thopas.* 1. 35.

Thy fruit full well the schoolboy knows, wild bramble of the brake.
> EBENEZER ELLIOTT, *To the Bramble Flower.*

Doubtless God could have made a better berry, but doubtless God never did.
> WALTON, *The Complete Angler.* Pt. I, ch. 5.

The strawberry grows underneath the nettle, and wholesome berries thrive and ripen best neighbour'd by fruit of baser quality.
> *King Henry V.* i, 1, 1. 60.

The strawberry-field its sweets shall yield
While the western winds are breathing.
> STEDMAN, *Alice of Monmouth.*

Bend to the crimson fruit, whose stain
Is glowing on lips and fingers.
> STEDMAN, *Alice of Monmouth.*

The dark, green curtains gemmed with dew ;
But each blushful berry, peering through.
> STEDMAN, *Alice of Monmouth.*

BEVERAGES

Nothing but claret wine.

> *King Henry VI.* Pt. II, iv, 6.

Give me my tankard, then.

> BEN JONSON, *Every Man in His Humour.*

Sparkling in a golden cup.

> *King Henry VI.* Pt. III, ii, 5.

Doubtless Burgundy will yield him help.

> *King Henry VI.* Pt. III, iv, 6.

He drains his draughts of Rhenish down.

> *Hamlet.* I, 4.

And brought of mighty ale a large quart.

> CHAUCER, *Miller's Tale.*

Your honour's claret is good enough for me.

> SWIFT, *Polite Conversations.* II.

Dry as the remainder biscuit after a voyage.

> *As You Like It.* ii, 7.

Sweet is old wine in bottles, ale in barrels.

> BYRON, *Sweet Things.* St. 5.

I do now remember the poor creature, small beer.

> *King Henry IV.* Pt. II, ii, 2.

And we meet with champagne and a chicken at last.

> LADY MONTAGU, *The Lover.*

Loves a cup of hot wine with not a drop of allaying Tiber in 't.

> *Coriolanus.* ii, 1.

Have you sent to the apothecary for a sufficient quantity of cream of tartar to make lemonade ?

> COLMAN (the Elder), *Man and Wife.* iii.

Claret is the liquor for boys ; port for old men ; but he who aspires to be a hero must drink brandy.

> BOSWELL, *Life of Johnson.*

BIRDS

The birds were warm.
> TENNYSON, *Aylmer's Field.*

The royal game of goose.
> GOLDSMITH, *Deserted Village.* 1. 231.

Now is the woodcock near the gin.
> *Twelfth Night.* ii, 5.

Stuffed with all honourable virtues.
> *Much Ado About Nothing.* i, 1.

Made ducks and drakes with shillings.
> CHAPMAN, *Eastward Ho.* i, 1.

Her elbow pinioned close upon her hips.
> COWPER, *Truth.*

Am I your bird? I mean to shift my bush!
> *Taming of the Shrew.* v, 2.

Here he comes, swelling like a turkey-cock.
> *King Henry V.* v, 1.

A bird in the hand is worth two in the bush.
> CERVANTES, *Don Quixote.* Pt. I, ch. iv.

Ah, nutbrown partridge! Ah, brilliant pheasants!
> BYRON, *Don Juan.* Canto xiii, st. 75.

Learn from the birds what food the thickets yield.
> POPE, *Essay on Man.* Ep. iii, 1. 173.

Here's a pigeon so finely roasted, it cries, Come, eat
me!
> SWIFT, *Polite Conversations.* ii.

Fear to kill a woodcock, lest thou dispossess the soul of
thy grandam.
> *Twelfth Night.* iv, 2.

Thou wast never with me for anything when thou wast
not there for the goose.
> *Romeo and Juliet.* ii, 4.

BREAD—ROLLS

A baker's dozen.
> RABELAIS, *Works.*　Bk. V, ch. xxii.

Bread is the staff of life.
> SWIFT, *Tale of a Tub.*

I speak this in hunger for bread.
> *Coriolanus.*　i, 1.

Better halfe a loafe than no bread.
> CAMDEN, *Proverbs.*　p. 293.

I am not in the roll of common men.
> *King Henry IV.*　Pt. I, iii, 1.

I won't quarrel with my bread and butter.
> SWIFT, *Polite Conversations.*　Christmas.

Dry as the remainder Biscuit after a voyage.
> *As You Like It.*　ii, 7.

Makes up his feast, with a crust of brown bread.
> From *Antidote against Melancholy.*　Old Eng. Song.

Gets him to rest, cramm'd with distressful bread.
> *King Henry V.*　iv, 1, l. 286.

A loaf of bread, the Walrus said, is what we chiefly need.
> CARROLL, *Through the Looking-Glass.*

Give me again my hollow Tree, a crust of bread and Liberty.
> POPE, *Horace.*　Last line, Bk. II.

Honest bread is very well—it's the butter that makes the temptation.
> JERROLD, *The Catspaw.*

Here is bread, which strengthens man's heart, and therefore is called the staff of life.
> MATTHEW HENRY, *Commentaries.*

He that keeps nor crust nor crumb,
Weary of all, shall want some.
> *King Lear.*　i, 4, l. 216.

CAKES

A piece of simple goodness.

> JERROLD, *Postman's Budget.*

Linked sweetness long drawn out.

> MILTON, *L'Allegro.* 1. 136.

With spots quadrangular of diamond form.

> COWPER, *The Task.* iv.

A cake that seemed mosaic-work in spices.

> ALDRICH, *The Lunch.*

Couldst thou both eat thy cake and have it?

> HERBERT, *The Church.* The Size.

Chewing the food of sweet and bitter fancy.

> *As You Like It.* iv, 3.

My cake is dough ; but I 'll in among the rest.

> *Taming of the Shrew.* v, i.

Sweets with sweets war not, joy delights in joy.

> *Sonnet viii.*

In all the wedding-cake, hope is the sweetest of the plums.

> JERROLD, *Jerrold's Wit.* The Catspaw.

Fresh as the roseate morn displays, and seeming sweet and fair.

> TAGGART, *Ode to the Poppy.* St. 5.

Everye white will have its blacke, and everye sweet its soure.

> PERCY, *Reliques.* Sir Curline.

Dost thou think because thou art virtuous there shall be no more cakes and ale?

> *Twelfth Night.* ii, 3.

The taste of sweetness, whereof a little more than a little, is much too much.

> *King Henry IV.* Pt. I, iii, 2

CANDY

Sweets to the sweet.

> *Hamlet.* v, I, l. 266.

A box where sweets compacted lie.

> HERBERT, *The Church.* Vertue. St. 3.

Sweet'ner of life, and solder of society.

> BLAIR, *The Grave.* l. 87.

Thrills with the sweetness you shall take.

> HARRIET SPOFFORD, *O Soft Spring.* Airs! St. 4.

Sweet as the dew shut in a lily's golden core.

> MARGARET PRESTON, *Agnes.*

Things sweet to taste prove in digestion sour.

> *King Richard II.* i, 3, l. 237.

A seeming length, proportioned to their sweetness.

> CAMPBELL. Suggested by New Year.

I am glad that my Adonis has a sweete tooth in his head.

> LILY, *Euphues and his England.*

But there 's nothing half so sweet in life as love's young
dream.

> MOORE, *Love's Young Dream.* St. I.

One poor pennyworth of sugar-candy to make thee long-
winded.

> *King Henry IV.* Pt. I, iii, 3.

A perpetual feast of nectar'd sweets where no crude surfeit reigns.

> MILTON, *Mask of Comus.* l. 476.

Whose are the sweets that never pall,
Delicious, pure, and crowning all?

> COLES, *The Microcosm.*

Their wives have sense like them : they see and smell,
And have their palates both for sweet and sour.

> *Othello.* iv, 3, l. 94.

CIGARS

I 'll fume with them !

Taming of the Shrew.   ii, 5.

Shall burn thee up and thou shalt turn to ashes.

King John.   iii, 1.

Tobacco, an outlandish weed,
Doth in the land strange wonders breed.

FAIRHOLT, *J. Payne Collier's MS.*

Thou through a mist dost show us,
That our best friends do not know us.

LAMB, *A Farewell to Tobacco.*

The man who smokes, thinks like a sage and acts like a
Samaritan !

LYTTON, *Night and Morning.*   Book I, ch. 6.

For life is Love and Love is death,
It was my hap, a well-a-day !
To burn my little hour away.

H. A. PAGE, *Vers de Société.*

He who doth not smoke hath either known no great
griefs or refuseth himself the softest consolation,
next to that which comes from Heaven.

LYTTON, *What Will He Do with It ?*

Some sigh for this and that ;
My wishes don't go far ;
The world may wag at will,
So I have my cigar.

HOOD, *The Cigar.*

Woman in this scale, the weed in that, Jupiter,
Hang out thy balance and weigh them both ;
And if thou give the preference to woman,
All I can say is, the next time Juno ruffles
Thee, O, Jupiter, try the weed.

LYTTON, *What Will He Do with It ?*

COCKTAIL—CORDIAL

A modern ecstacy.

Macbeth. iv, 3.

Divine, nectareous juice.

Odyssey. IX. Pope's trans.

My nearest and dearest enemy.

MIDDLETON, *Anything for Quiet Life.* v, 1.

It must be done like lightning.

BEN JONSON, *Every Man in his Humour.* iv, 5.

Which draught to me were cordial.

Winter's Tale. i, 2.

A thing of custom ;—'t is no other.

Macbeth. iii, 4.

His orient liquor in a crystal glass.

MILTON, *Comus.*

'T is nothing when you are used to it.

SWIFT, *Polite Conversations.* iii.

He that sips often at last drinks it up.

COWPER, *Progress of Error.*

Seasoned life of man preserved and stored up.

MILTON, *Areopagitica.*

We 'll teach you to drink deep ere you depart.

Hamlet. i, 2.

He calls for something bitter, something sour.

POPE, *Imitation of Horace.* ii, 2.

He does it with a better grace but I do it more natural.

Twelfth Night. ii, 3.

This is nectar, the very nepenthe the gods were drunk with.

RANDOLPH, *Aristippus.*

This cordial julep here, that flames and dances in his crystal bounds.

MILTON, *Comus.*

COFFEE

Water with berries in 't.
> *The Tempest.* i, 2.

A little pot and soon hot.
> *Taming of the Shrew.* iv, 1.

Could fill its little cup twice over.
> WILDE, *The Burden of Stys.*

Will pass away as the taste for coffee.
> MME. DE SÉVIGNÉ (attributed to).

Or o'er cold coffee trifle with a spoon.
> POPE, *To Miss Blount.*

'T is strong, and it does indifferent well.
> *Twelfth Night.* i, 3.

The berries crackle and the mill turns round.
> POPE, *Rape of the Lock.* iii.

For lo ! the board with cups and spoons is crowned.
> POPE, *Rape of the Lock.* iii.

Thou art all the comfort the gods will diet me with.
> *Cymbeline.* iii, 4.

Freely welcome to my cup, could 'st thou sip and sip
it up.
> OLDYS, *On a Fly Drinking.*

Oft times many things fall out between the cup and the
lip.
> ALBERT GREENE, *Perimedes.* 1588.

Coffee, which makes the politician wise,
And see through all things with his half-shut eyes.
> POPE, *Rape of the Lock.* iii.

And while the bubbling and loud hissing urn
Throws up a steamy column, and the cups,
That cheer but not inebriate, wait on each,
So let us welcome peaceful evening in.
> COWPER, *Winter Evening.* Bk. IV, 1. 34.

COMMITTEES

The labour is not small.

TENNYSON, *Stanzas.*

The labour we delight in.

Macbeth. ii, 3, l. 55.

On hospitable thoughts intent.

MILTON, *Paradise Lost.* Bk. V, l. 331.

Taste the joy that springs from labour.

LONGFELLOW, *Masque of Pandora.* Pt. VI.

I have ta'en a due and wary note upon 't.

Macbeth. iv, 1.

Report me and my cause aright to the unsatisfied.

Hamlet. v, 2.

Join we together for the public good in what we can.

King Henry VI. Pt. II, i, 1.

Find those persons out whose names are written there.

Romeo and Juliet. i, 2.

I 'll tell you them all by their names as they pass by.

Troilus and Cressida. i, 2.

Never idle a moment, but thrifty and thoughtful of others.

LONGFELLOW, *Miles Standish.* Pt. VIII, l. 46.

I am by my place to know how to please the palates of
the guests.

BEN JONSON, *Neptune's Triumph.*

But now my task is smoothly done,
I can fly, or I can run.

MILTON, *Comus.* l. 1012.

News is your food, and you enough provide,
Both for yourselves and all the world beside.

DRYDEN, Pro. to, *Lee's Cæsar Borgia.*

I charge thee invite them all : let in the tide
Of knaves once more ; my cook and I 'll provide.

Timon of Athens. iii, 4, l. 118.

COVER—BACK

Enough is good as a feast.
> FIELDING, *Covent Garden Tragedy.*

All is well that ends well.
> HEYWOOD, *Proverbs.* i, 10.

Blest hour ! it was a luxury to be.
> COLERIDGE, *Reflections.*

I had an extraordinary good dinner.
> PEPYS, *Diary.* March 23, 1660.

And all went merry as a marriage-bell.
> BYRON, *Childe Harold.* Canto iii, st. 21.

I have more care to stay than will to go.
> *Romeo and Juliet.* iii, 5.

So comes a reckoning when the banquet 's o'er.
> GAY, *The What Do You Call It.*

And then to breakfast with what appetite you have.
> *Henry VIII.* iii, 2, 1. 201.

Now good digestion wait on appetite, and health on both.
> *Macbeth.* iii, 6.

O, leave the gay and festive scenes, the halls of dazzling light.
> VANDYKE, *Light Guitar.*

When a man fell into his anecdotage, it was a sign for him to retire.
> DISRAELI, *Lothair.*

Who rises from a feast with that keen appetite that he sits down ?
> *Merchant of Venice.* ii, 6.

Serenely full, the epicure would say,
Fate cannot harm me,—I have dined to-day.
> SYDNEY SMITH, *Recipe for Salad.*

COVER—FRONT

A dinner lubricates business.

STOWELL, *Boswell's Johnson.*

Read these instructive leaves.

POPE, *Epistle to Jervas.*

I do perceive here a divine duty.

Othello. i, 3.

Sport that wrinkled Care derides.

MILTON, *L' Allegro*, 1. 31.

The chiming clocks to dinner call.

POPE, *Essay on Morals.* iv.

A kind of excellent dumb discourse.

The Tempest. iii, 3.

To live and die in scenes like this.

MOORE, *As Slow Our Ship.*

Why muse you, sir? 't is dinner time.

Two Gentlemen of Verona. ii, 1.

Therefore put you in your best array !

As You Like It. v, 2.

Take the goods the gods provide thee.

DRYDEN, *Alexander's Feast.*

The devil is in you if you cannot dine !

POPE, *Imitation of Horace.* ii, 2.

'T is now upon the point of dinner time.

BEAUMONT AND FLETCHER, *Woman Hater.* iii, 3.

Here is everything advantageous to life.

The Tempest. ii, 1.

This night I hold an old accustom'd feast.

Romeo and Juliet. i, 2.

Magnificent spectacle of human happiness.

SIDNEY SMITH, *America.* " Edinburgh
Review," July, 1824.

CRACKERS AND CHEESE

And smelt so ? pah !

Hamlet. v, 1.

Not a mouse shall disturb this.

Midsummer Night's Dream. v, 1.

At which my nose is in great indignation.

The Tempest. iv, 1.

Art thou come ? Why my cheese, my digestion !

Troilus and Cressida. ii, 3.

Bachelor's fare ; bread and cheese and kisses.

SWIFT, *Polite Conversations.* i.

Digestive cheese and fruit there sure will be.

BEN JONSON, *Epigrams.* ci.

I having been acquainted with the smell before!

Two Gentlemen of Verona. iv, 4.

And prove that she 's not made of green cheese.

BUTLER, *Hudibras.* Pt. II, canto iii.

You must eat no cheese . . . it breeds melancholy.

BEN JONSON, *The Alchemist.* iii.

I had rather live with cheese and garlic in a wind-mill.

King Henry IV. Pt. I, iii, 1, 1. 159.

Pray, does anybody here hate cheese ? I would be glad of a bit.

SWIFT, *Polite Conversations.* ii.

I will make an end of my dinner, there 's pippins and cheese to come.

Merry Wives of Windsor. i, 2.

While you have been arranging to make your will, have I sent you cheese cakes.

MARTIAL, *Epigrams.* Bk. V, No. 39.

And entered, far from mouse, or cat, or man,
A thick-walled cheese, the best of Parmesan.

PIGNOTTI, *Mouse Turned Hermit.*

DECLINATION

Vow me no vows.
> BEAUMONT AND FLETCHER, *Wit without Money.*
> iv, 4.

For men must work.
> KINGSLEY, *The Three Fishers.*

Do not put me to 't.
> *Othello.* ii, 1.

There 's no place like Home.
> PAYNE, *Home, Sweet Home.*

Of them, but not among them.
> ANON.

Press not a falling man too far.
> *King Henry VIII.* iii, 2.

For every "why" he had a " wherefore."
> BUTLER, *Hudibras.* Bk. I, canto i, l. 131.

Every pleasure hath a payne, they say.
> CHAPMAN, *Blind Beggar of Alexandria.*

Distance sometimes endears friendship.
> HOWELL, *Familiar Letters.* Bk. I, sec. i, let. 6.

I wish you all the joy that you can wish.
> *Merchant of Venice.* iii, 2, l. 192.

Don't say nuthin' that you can be held *tu.*
> LOWELL, *Biglow Papers.* ii, 5.

But let not therefore my good friend be grieved !
> *Julius Cæsar.* i, 2.

Solitude is as needful to the imagination as society is
wholesome for the character.
> LOWELL, *Among my Books.* Dryden.

We do that in our zeal,
Our calmer moments are afraid to answer.
> SCOTT, *Woodstock.* Ch. 17.

DRINKING

This do I drink to thee.
Romeo and Juliet. iv, 3.

Drink deep or taste not.
POPE, *Essay on Criticism.*

Eat and drink as friends.
Taming of the Shrew. i, 2.

Drink with me, and drink as I.
OLDYS, *On a Fly Drinking.*

They never taste who always drink.
PRIOR, Upon "Scaligerani."

The more you drink, the more you crave.
POPE, *Satires.* vi.

Judicious drank, and greatly daring din'd.
POPE, *Dunciad.* iv, l. 318.

I hope we shall drink down all unkindness.
Merry Wives of Windsor. i, 1. 203.

I prithee, take the cork out of thy mouth, that I may
drink.
As You Like It. iii, 2.

Well, he was an ingenious man that first found out eating and drinking.
SWIFT, *Polite Conversations.* ii.

Now and then you men of wit
Will condescend to take a bit.
SWIFT, *Cadenus and Vanessa.*

With you I will drink to the solemn past,
Though the cup that I drain shall be my last.
WINTER, *Orgia.* Song, "Ruined Man."

I have very poor and unhappy brains for drinking; I
could wish courtesy would invent some other custom
of entertainment.
Othello. ii, 3.

EGGS

Almost as like as eggs.

Winter's Tale. i, 2.

And kill him in the shell.

Julius Cæsar. ii, 1, 1. 32.

Going as if he trod upon eggs.

Burton, *Anatomy of Melancholy*,
Pt. III, sec. ii, memb. 3.

You would eat chickens i' the shell.

Troilus and Cressida. i, 2, 1. 147.

Take a dejeune of muskadel and eggs.

Ben Jonson, *The New Inn.* iii, 1.

Those bright blue eggs together laid.

Wordsworth, *Sparrow's Nest.*

But the more the eggs the worse the hatch.

Hood, *Miss Kilmansegg.* Her Courtship. St. 7.

The vulgar boil, the learned roast, an egg.

Pope, *Satires.* Horace. Bk. II, Ep. ii, 1. 85.

Laid, without knowing it, the egg of democracy.

Lowell, *Among my Books.* New England.

A short-legged hen, if we can get her, full of eggs.

Ben Jonson, *Epigram.* ci.

Thy head is as full of quarrels as an egg is full of meat.

Romeo and Juliet. iii, 1, 1. 23.

We have learned to bottle our parents twain in the yelk
of an addle.

Kipling, *Conundrum of Workshop.*

People may have too much of a good thing :
Full as an egg of wisdom thus I sing.

Wolcot, *Gentleman and his Wife.*

And ye who on the flat sands hoard your eggs
For suns to ripen, come !

Cornwall, *Invocation to Birds.*

ENTRÉES

A morsel for a monarch.
Antony and Cleopatra. i, 5.

A dish fit for the gods.
Julius Cæsar. ii, 1.

The glory of the kitchen.
BEN JONSON, *Staple of News.*

There 's no meat like 'em.
Timon of Athens. i, 2.

Infinite riches in a little room.
MARLOWE, *Jew of Malta.* i.

A dish that I do love to feed upon.
Taming of the Shrew. iv, 3.

Can one desire too much of a good thing.
CERVANTES, *Don Quixote.* Pt. I, Bk. I, ch. 6.

I smell it ; upon my life, it will do well.
King Henry IV. Pt. I, i, 3.

O, dainty and delicious ! Food for the gods !
CROFFUT, *Clam Soup.*

He 's keeping a corner for something that 's nice.
GOLDSMITH.

Our intent was at this time to move inward delight.
BEAUMONT AND FLETCHER, *Kt. of Burning Pestle.*

My soul tasted that heavenly food, which gives new
appetite.
DANTE, *Purgatorio.* xxxi, 1. 128.

Give us the luxuries of life, and we will dispense with
the necessaries.
MOTLEY.

The discovery of a new dish does more for the happiness
of man than the discovery of a new star.
BRILLAT-SAVARIN.

FAREWELL

We only part to meet again.

GAY, *Black-eyed Susan.*

Let us leave here, gentlemen.

Cymbeline. i, 4.

All farewells should be sudden.

BYRON, *Sardanapalus.* v, i.

Dearest friends, alas! must part.

GAY, *Hare and Many Friends.*

Gude nicht, and joy be wi' you a'.

LADY NAIRNE, *Gude Nicht.*

'T is grievous parting with good company.

ELIOT, *Spanish Gypsy.* ii.

And often took leave ; but was loth to part.

PRIOR, *Thief and Cordelier.*

The goodness of the night upon you, friends !

Othello. i, 2.

Fare thee well ; the elements be kind to thee.

Antony and Cleopatra. iii, 2.

But fate ordains that dearest friends must part.

YOUNG, *Love of Fame.* Satire ii, 1. 232.

Welcome ever smiles, and farewell goes out sighing.

Troilus and Cressida. iii, 3.

Here 's my hand, and mine, with my heart in 't : and now farewell.

The Tempest. iii, 1.

To all, to each, a fair good-night,
And pleasing dreams, and slumbers bright.

SCOTT, *Marmion.* L'Envoy.

Let us take a ceremonious leave
And loving farewell of our friends.

King Richard II. i, 3.

FISH

There will be a fish.   OVID, *Ars Amatoria.* iii.

The fish was taken but this night.
> BEAUMONT AND FLETCHER, *Woman Hater.* i, 2.

But who is this, what thing of sea or land?
> MILTON, *Samson Agonistes.*

From the rude sea's enraged and foamy mouth.
> *Twelfth Night.* v, 1.

Swift trouts diversified with crimson stains.
> POPE, *Windsor Forest.*

Neither fish, nor flesh, nor good red-herring.
> HEYWOOD'S *Proverbs.*

Some choice sous'd fish brought couchant in a dish.
> CARTWRIGHT, *The Ordinary.* ii, 2.

I shall no more to sea, to sea ; here shall I die ashore !
> *The Tempest.* ii, 2.

See how eagerly the lobsters and the turtles all advance.
> CARROLL, *Alice in Wonderland.*

This trout looks lovely, it was twenty-two inches when it was taken.
> WALTON, *Complete Angler.*

This dish of meat is too good for any but anglers or very honest men.
> WALTON, *Complete Angler.* Pt. I, ch. 8.

When if or chance or hunger's powerful sway
Directs the roving trout this fatal way.
> GAY, *Rural Sports.* Canto i, l. 150.

3rd Fish : " Master, I marvel how the fishes live in the sea."

1st Fish : " Why, as men do a-land ; the great ones eat up the little ones."
> *Pericles.* ii, 1, l. 29.

FRUIT

The pine's tasteful apple.

> J. PHILIPS, *Cider.*

In the name of the Prophet—figs!

> HORACE SMITH, *Johnson's Ghost.*

Its fruit in clusters drooping down.

> OSGOOD, *The Cocoanut Tree.*

Like Autumn fruit that mellow'd long.

> DRYDEN, *Œdipus.* iv, 1.

Grape that dims the purple tyrants wear.

> HORACE, *Country Life.*

Fill all fruit with ripeness to the core.

> KEATS, *To Autumn.*

Blooming ambrosial fruit of vegetable gold.

> MILTON, *Paradise Lost.* Bk. IV, l. 139.

Sing now the lusty song of fruits and flowers.

> BLAKE, *To Autumn.* St. 1.

At once with glowing fruit and flowers crowned.

> LOWELL, *The Sirens.* l. 94.

My news shall be the fruit to that great feast.

> *Hamlet.* ii, 2.

Give cherries at time of year or apricots; and say they were sent you out of the country.

> BEN JONSON, *Silent Woman.* iv, 1.

Peaches, apricots, and malecotoons, with other choicer plumbs, will serve for large-sized bullets.

> CARTWRIGHT, *The Ordinary.* ii, 1.

Hunger and thirst at once powerful persuaders, quicken'd at the scent of that alluring fruit, urged me so keen.

> MILTON, *Paradise Lost.* Bk. IX, l. 584.

GAME

The game is up.

> *Cymbeline.* iii, 3, 1. 108.

Cut and come again.

> CRABBE, *Tales.* vii, 1. 26.

Frieth in her own grease.

> HEYWOOD, *Proverbs.* Pt. I, ch. xi.

I thank you for my venison.

> *Merry Wives of Windsor.* i, 1.

The bore will use us kindly

> *King Richard III.* iii, 2.

I saw him now going the way of all flesh.

> WEBSTER, *Westward Hoe.* ii, 2.

Why dost thou whet thy knife so earnestly?

> *Merchant of Venice.* iv, 1.

A very gentle beast and of good conscience.

> *Midsummer Night's Dream.* v, 1.

But if you have a stomach, to 't i' God's name.

> *Taming of the Shrew.* i, 2.

Balm'd and entreasured with full bags of spice.

> *Pericles.* iii, 2.

You 're not always sure of your game when you 've
treed it.

> LOWELL, *Fable for Critics.*

'T is not right to think that only toothsome which can
bite.

> EDWARD HIDE, *To T. Randolph.*

Let 's carve him as a dish fit for the gods, not hew him
as a carcass.

> *Julius Cæsar.* ii, 1.

If you could be drawn to affect beef, venison, or fowl, it
would be far better.

> BEAUMONT AND FLETCHER, *Woman Hater.* iii, 3.

GUEST OF HONOUR

Glory 's a great thing.

BYRON, *Don Juan.* viii.

Here 's our chief guest.

Macbeth. iii, 1.

You have heard of my poor services.

Winter's Tale. iv, 4.

A man he was to all the country dear.

GOLDSMITH, *Deserted Village.* 1, 141.

Most illustrious six or seven times honoured.

Troilus and Cressida. iii, 3.

Your high self, the gracious mark o' the land.

Winter's Tale. iv, 4.

Look in our eyes ! Your welcome waits you there.

HOLMES, *To the President.*

As a wit, if not first, in the very first line.

GOLDSMITH, *Retaliation.* 1, 96.

Your name is great in mouths ·of wisest censure.

Othello. ii, 3.

The gentleman is learned and a most rare speaker.

King Henry VIII. i, 2.

If Knowledge be the mark, to know thee shall suffice.

Passionate Pilgrim. v.

Here is a man—but 't is before his face ; I will be silent !

Troilus and Cressida. ii, 3.

Right welcome, sir !
Ere we depart we 'll share a bounteous time.

Timon of Athens. i, 1.

You are wisely silent
In your own worth, and therefore 't were a sin
For others to be so.

RANDOLPH, *Muses' Looking-Glass.*

ICES

Our mouths be cold.

The Tempest. i, 1.

As cold as cucumbers.

BEAUMONT AND FLETCHER, *Cupid's Revenge.* i, 1.

Swooning in sweetness.

THOS. READ, *New Pastoral.* Bk. vii, 1. 51.

A mockery king of snow.

King Richard II. iv, 1.

A little snow, tumbled about.

King John. iii, 4, 1. 176.

The cold that moderates heat.

CERVANTES, *Don Quixote.* Pt. II, 65.

Then farewell heat and welcome frost.

Merchant of Venice. ii, 7.

A cool mouth, and warm feet, live long.

HERBERT, *Jacula Prudentum.*

My very lips might freeze to my teeth.

Taming of the Shrew. iv, 1, 1. 5.

So coldly sweet, so deadly fair, we start.

BYRON, *The Giaour.* 1. 90.

Who 's that calls so loudly?   A piece of ice.

Taming of the Shrew. iv, 1.

He rolls it under his tongue as a sweet morsel.

HENRY, *Commentaries.*

He sips the single drop of sweetness closely pressed.

BOTTA, *Lesson of the Bee.*

Seeing only what is fair, sipping only what is sweet.

EMERSON, *The Humble-Bee.*

All that 's sweet was made but to be lost when sweetest.

MOORE, *All that 's bright must fade.*

Retain their sweetness after they have lost their beauty.

HANNAH MORE. *On Dissipation.*

INVITATIONS

I will have no excuse.

Pericles. ii, 3.

What think you, sirs, of killing Time?

COWPER, *Beau's Reply.*

Go to a gossips' feast and go with me.

Comedy of Errors. v, 1.

Who scorns it stays deservedly at home.

COWPER, *The Task.* i.

Invite the friend that loves thee to a feast.

HESIOD.

Where is the man that can live without dining?

LYTTON, *Lucile.* i, 2.

Will you go with me? We 'll mend our dinner here.

Comedy of Errors. iv, 3, l. 60.

Come, be every one officious to make this banquet.

Titus Andronicus. v, 2.

Put on manly readiness and meet i' the hall together.

Macbeth. ii, 3.

There 's other of our friends will greet us here anon.

Measure for Measure. iv, 5.

At dinner time, I pray you, have in mind where we
must meet.

Merchant of Venice. i, 1, l. 70.

Put on your boldest suit of mirth, for we have friends
that purpose merriment.

Merchant of Venice. ii, 2.

Live while you live, the epicure would say,
And seize the pleasures of the present day.

DODDRIDGE, *Epigram.*

We 'll bring your friends and ours to this large dinner :
It works the better eaten before witness.

CARTWRIGHT, *The Ordinary.* ii, 1.

JELLY

As firm as faith.
Merry Wives of Windsor. iv, 4.

I like their delicacy.
SAMUEL JOHNSON, *Seward's Johnsoniana.* 617.

Feel, masters, how I shake!
King Henry IV. Pt. II, ii, 4.

Every part about me quivers.
Romeo and Juliet. ii, 4.

Yet have I something in me dangerous.
Hamlet. v, 1.

Thou wouldst tremble to receive thyself.
Pericles. i, 2.

Flames and dances in his crystal bounds.
MILTON, *Comus.*

With the desserts of poetry they feed him.
COWLEY, *To Royal Society.*

Thrills with the sweetness you shall take.
SPOFFORD, *O Soft Spring Airs!* St. 4.

The daintiest last to make the end most sweet.
King Richard II. i, 3.

My sense with their deliciousness was spell 'd.
KEATS, *To a Friend Who Sent Roses.*

The hand that hath made you fair hath made you good.
Measure for Measure. iii, 1.

A reflection, made from the false glories of the gay
reflected bow, is a more solid thing than thou.
COWLEY, *Life and Fame.*

Though deep, yet clear; though gentle, yet not dull;
Strong without rage; without o'erflowing, full.
DENHAM, *Cooper's Hill.*

LIBATIONS

The gadding vine.

          MILTON, *Lycidas.* 1. 40.

Off with his head.

          King Richard III. iii, 4.

And who gave thee that jolly red nose?

          RAVENSCROFT, *Deuteromela.*

Shallow draughts intoxicate the brain.

          POPE, *Essay on Criticism.*

To-day it is our pleasure to be drunk.

          FIELDING, *Tom Thumb the Great.*

He that is tight is as great as a king.

          "The Old Squire."

And carouse together like friends long lost.

          Antony and Cleopatra. iv, 12.

Whose liquid murmur heard new thirst excites.

          MILTON, *Paradise Lost.* vii.

Then hasten to be drunk, the business of the day.

          DRYDEN, *Cymon and Iphigenia.*

And damn'd be him that first cries " Hold, enough ! "

          Macbeth. v, 8.

Thy spirit which keeps thee is noble, courageous, high,
    unmatchable.

          Antony and Cleopatra. ii, 3.

When flowing cups pass swiftly round with no allaying
    Thames.

          LOVELACE, *To Attica from Prison.*

          Minister'st a potion unto me
That thou wouldst tremble to receive thyself?

          Pericles. i, 2.

Our cheerful guests carouse the sparkling tears
Of the rich grapes, whilst music charms the ears.

          DENHAM.

MEATS

It is meat and drink to me.
> *As You Like It.* v, 1.

But to rule the rost is the matter.
> MIDDLETON, *Blurt, Master Constable.* iii, 3.

The nature of the spirit asketh meat.
> CARTWRIGHT, *The Ordinary.* iii, 5.

A breast of mutton stuffed with pudding.
> CARTWRIGHT, *The Ordinary.* ii, 1.

God sends meat and the Devil sends cooks.
> JOHN TAYLOR. 1630.

Bid them cover the table, serve in the meat.
> *Merchant of Venice.* iii, 5.

What say you to a piece of beef and mustard ?
> *Taming of the Shrew.* iv, 3, l. 23.

Don't talk all the talk, nor eat all the meat.
> Proverb.

What 's one man's poison, signor, is another's meat.
> BEAUMONT AND FLETCHER, *Love's Cure.* iii.

O, my sweet beef, I must still be good angel to thee.
> *King Henry IV.* Pt. I, iii, 3.

We 'll have a dozen of bones well charged with marrow.
> CARTWRIGHT, *The Ordinary.* ii. 1.

If you give me any conserves give me conserves of beef.
> *Taming of the Shrew.* Induction.

A joint of mutton and any pretty little tiny kickshaws.
> *King Henry IV.* Pt. II, v, 1.

I am a great eater of beef, and I believe that does harm
to my wit.
> *Twelfth Night.* i, 3.

I protest I do honour a chine of beef, I do reverence a
loin of veal.
> BEAUMONT AND FLETCHER, *Woman Hater.* iii, 3.

MISCELLANEOUS

I eat and eat, I swear.

King Henry V. v, 1.

I am resolved to grow fat.

DRYDEN, *Maiden Queen.* iii, 1.

Living from hand to mouth.

DU BARTAS, *Divine Weekes.* Pt. IV.

Hire me twenty cunning cooks.

Romeo and Juliet. iv, 2, l. 2.

Keep what the gods provide you.

PLAUTUS, *Rudens.* iv, 8.

Would the cook were of my mind!

Much Ado About Nothing. i, 3, l. 74.

Hunger is sharper than a sword.

BEAUMONT AND FLETCHER, *Honest Man's Fortune.*

He was a man of an unbounded stomach.

King Henry VIII. iv, 2.

Unquiet meals make ill digestions.

Comedy of Errors. v, 1, l. 75.

Hungry as the sea, and can digest as much.

Twelfth Night. ii, 4.

Since Eve ate apples, much depends on dinner.

BYRON, *Don Juan.* Canto xiii, st. 99.

The belly is the commanding part of the body.

HOMER.

Room! Make way! Hunger commands; my valour must obey.

BEAUMONT AND FLETCHER, *Woman Hater.*

We may live without friends; we may live without books;
But civilised man cannot live without cooks.

MEREDITH, *Lucile.* Pt. I, canto ii, st. 24.

MUSIC

Music's golden tongue.
> KEATS, *Eve of St. Agnes.*

Now then for soft music.
> SHERIDAN, *The Critic.* ii, 2.

Ye soft pipes, play low.
> KEATS, *Ode on Grecian Urn.*

Music make their welcome!
> *Timon of Athens.* i, 2.

But now, I 'm all for music.
> BEN JONSON, *Volpone.* iii, 2.

O Music! sphere-descended maid.
> COLLINS, *The Passions.*

If music be the food of love, play on.
> *Twelfth Night.* i, 1.

It will discourse most eloquent music.
> *Hamlet.* iii, 2.

I 'll charm the air to give a sound.
> *Macbeth.* iv, 1.

Sentimentally I am disposed to harmony.
> LAMB, *Chapter on Ears.*

What harmony is this? My good friends, hark!
> *The Tempest.* iii, 3.

Music is well said to be the speech of angels.
> CARLYLE, *Essays.* The Opera.

Music her soft, assuasive voice applies.
> POPE, *St. Cecilia's Day.*

Eftsoones they heard a most melodious sound.
> SPENSER, *Faerie Queene.* Bk. II, canto xii, st. 70.

Whilst I sit meditating on that celestial harmony.
> *King Henry VIII.* iv, 2.

NUTS

Across the walnuts and the wine.
> TENNYSON, *Miller's Daughter.*

And with his nuts larded many swine.
> SPENSER, *Shepheard's Callender.* Februarie.

Sweet is the nut, but bitter is his pill.
> SPENSER, *Amoretti.* Sonnet **xxvi.**

When the brain gets as dry as an empty nut.
> DOBSON, *Ballad of Prose and Rhyme.*

The heavy fruit of the tall black-walnut tree.
> BRYANT. Third of November, 1861.

Take the nuts from the fire with the dog's foot.
> HERBERT, *Jacula Prudentum.*

Nuts are given to us, but we must crack them ourselves.
> Proverb.

As brown in hue as hazel-nuts and sweeter than the kernels.
> *Taming of the Shrew.* ii, 1.

The partridge whirs, and the frosted burs are dropping for you and me.
> STEDMAN, *Autumn Song.*

And close at hand the basket stood
With nuts from brown October's wood.
> WHITTIER, *Snow-bound.*

Enticing walnuts, I have known ye well
In youth, when pickles were a passing pain.
> TAYLOR, *Echo Club.*

And a large chestnut, the delicious meat
Which Jove himself, were he a mouse, would eat.
> COWLEY, *Country Mouse.*

Thou wilt quarrel with a man for cracking nuts, having no other reason but because thou hast hazel eyes.
> *Romeo and Juliet.* iii, 1, 1. 18.

OYSTERS

This treasure of an oyster.
>*Antony and Cleopatra.* i. 5.

An oyster may be crossed in love.
>SHERIDAN, *The Critic.* iii, 1.

Sometimes with oysters we combine.
>GAY, *Fables.* No. 39.

My way is to begin with the beginning.
>BYRON, *Don Juan.* i, 7.

Shall be steeped in his own salt tear.
>TENNYSON, *War-Song.*

Canst tell how an oyster makes his shell?
>*King Lear.* i, 5.

He was a bold man that first eat an oyster.
>SWIFT, *Polite Conversations.* 1.

'T was a fat oyster—live in peace—Adieu.
>POPE. Verbatim from Boileau.

I 'll be with you in the squeezing of a lemon.
>GOLDSMITH, *She Stoops to Conquer.* i.

The world 's mine oyster, which I with sword will open.
>*Merry Wives of Windsor.* ii, 2.

Now if you 're ready, Oysters, dear, we can begin to feed!
>CARROLL, *Alice in Looking-Glass.*

Ladies and Gentlemen, will you eat any oysters before dinner?
>SWIFT, *Polite Conversations.* ii.

The oyster-women lock'd their fish up, and trudged away to cry.
>BUTLER, *Hudibras.* Pt. I, canto ii.

It is unseasonable and unwholesome in all months that have not an R in their names to eat an oyster.
>BUTLER, *Dyet's Dry Dinner.* 1599.

PASTRY

Trifles light as air.

Othello. iii, 3.

Simplicity talks of pies !

WILLIS, *Love in a Cottage.* St. 3.

We live merely on the crust.

FROUDE, *Lucian.*

A puff by her husband much praised.

Epitaph on a Yorkshire Cook.

In hopes that her crust may be raised.

Epitaph on a Yorkshire Cook.

Cookery is become an art, a noble science.

BURTON, *Anatomy of Melancholy.*

Pt. I, sec. ii, memb. 2.

Go help your mother to make the gooseberry pye.

GOLDSMITH, *Vicar of Wakefield.* Ch. vii.

What neat repast shall feast us, light and choice.

MILTON, *To Mr. Lawrence.*

Gives to airy nothing a local habitation and a name.

Midsummer Night's Dream. v, 1.

What calls back the past like the rich pumpkin pie ?

WHITTIER, *The Pumpkin.*

Swears he is not dead yet, but translated in some immortal crust.

BEN JONSON, *Staple of News.* iii, 1.

Well versed in the arts of pies, custards, and tarts,
And the lucrative trade of the oven.

Epitaph on a Yorkshire Cook.

An endless host
Of syllabubs and jellies and mince pies
And other such ladylike luxuries.

SHELLEY, *Letter to Maria Gisborne.*

PUDDING

How we apples swim.

SWIFT, *Brother Protestants.*

You are come in Pudding-time.

SWIFT, *Polite Conversations.* ii.

I hunger for less costly delicacies.

MARTIAL, *Epigrams.* Bk. VII, ep. 27.

And solid pudding against empty praise.

POPE, *The Dunciad.* Bk. I, 1. 54.

Pudding that might have pleased a Dean.

POPE, *Imitation of Horace.* ii.

The proof of the pudding is in the eating.

CERVANTES, *Don Quixote.* Ch. xxiv.

Strange I should never of a dumpling dream !

WOLCOTT, *Apple Dumplings and a King.*

And lo ! two puddings smok'd upon the board.

POPE, *Moral Essays.* Ep. iii, 1. 461.

The poor man will praise it so hath he good cause.

Old Eng. Song, *Antidote against Melancholy.* 1661.

That last piece of pudding at Mr. Gillman's did the business.

LAMB, *Autobiographical Recollections.*

It almost makes me wish, I vow,
To have two stomachs, like a cow !

HOOD, *The Turtles.*

" Very astonishing indeed ! strange thing ! "
Turning the Dumpling round, rejoined the King.

WOLCOTT, *Apple Dumplings and a King.*

I sing the sweets I know, the charms I feel,
My morning incense, and my evening meal,
The sweets of Hasty-Pudding.

BARLOW, *The Hasty Pudding.* Canto i.

PUNCH

Potations pottle-deep.

Othello.　ii, 3.

What man dare, I dare !

Macbeth.　iii, 4.

A thing devised by the enemy.

King Richard III.　v, 3.

It goes much against my stomach.

As You Like It.　iii, 2.

My firm nerves shall never tremble.

Macbeth.　iii, 4.

Yet have I something in me dangerous.

Hamlet.　v, 1.

And who gave thee that jolly red nose ?

RAVENSCROFT, *Deuteromela.*

My bane and antidote are both before me.

ADDISON, *Cato.*　v, 1.

Born but to banquet and to drain the bowl.

POPE, *Odyssey.*　x.

The more thou stir it the worse it will be.

CERVANTES, *Don Quixote.*　Pt. I, Book III, ch. 8.

And purer spirits swell the sprightly flood.

POPE, *Windsor Forest.*

There is something in this more than natural.

Hamlet.　ii, 2.

Though this be madness, yet there is method in 't.

Hamlet.　ii. 2.

Now let thy friendly hand put strength enough to 't.

King Lear.　iv, 6.

In vain I trusted that the flowing bowl
Would banish sorrow, and enlarge the soul.

PRIOR, *Solomon.*　ii.

RELEVÉS

Do you like the taste?

King Henry VI. Pt. I, iii, 2.

Push on—keep moving.

MORTON, *Cure for Heartache.* iii, 1.

To return to our wethers.

RABELAIS, *Works.* Bk. I, ch. 1.

To feed again, though full.

Cymbeline. ii, 4.

There, though last, not least.

SPENSER, *Colin Clout.* l. 444.

My appetite comes to me while eating.

MONTAIGNE, *Of Vanity.* Bk. III, ch. 9.

A cheerful look makes a dish a feast.

HERBERT, *Jacula Prudentum.*

And they say they 're half fish, half flesh.

Pericles. ii, 1.

All things come round to him who will but wait.

LONGFELLOW, *Student's Tale.*

Things which in hungry mortals' eyes find favour.

BYRON, *Don Juan.* Canto v, st. 47.

If it will feed nothing else, it will feed my revenge.

Merchant of Venice. iii, 1.

He that can live upon love deserves to die in a ditch.

CONGREVE. Sayings.

What 's there? Things for the cook, sir : but I know
not what.

Romeo and Juliet. iv, 4, l. 14.

The table is the only place where we do not get weary
the first hour.

BRILLAT-SAVARIN.

SALAD

Mine eyes smell onions, I shall weep anon.
> *All's Well that Ends Well.* v, 3.

A cheap and wholesome salad from the brook.
> COWPER, *The Task.* vi.

My salad days, when I was green in judgment.
> *Antony and Cleopatra.* i, 5.

I warrant there 's vinegar and pepper in 't.
> *Antony and Cleopatra.* i, 5.

And with forced fingers rude shatter your leaves.
> MILTON, *Lycidas.*

I will have the beards of barbels served instead of salads.
> BEN JONSON. *The Alchemist.* ii.

Three several salads have I sacrificed, bedew'd with
precious oil and vinegar.
> BEAUMONT AND FLETCHER, *Woman Hater.* i, 3.

Well read, deeply learned, and thoroughly grounded in
the hidden knowledge of all salad and all potherbs
whatsoever.
> BEAUMONT AND FLETCHER, *Woman Hater.* i, 3.

Let onion atoms lurk within the bowl
And, half suspected, animate the whole.
> SYDNEY SMITH, *Recipe for Salad.*

Yet shall you have, to rectify your palate,
An olive, capers, or some better salad.
> BEN JONSON, *Epigram ci.*

Back to the world he 'd turn his fleeting soul,
And plunge his fingers in the salad bowl.
> SYDNEY SMITH, *Recipe for Salad.*

The glory of the kitchen ! that holds cookery
A trade from Adam, quotes his broths and salads.
> BEN JONSON, *Staple of News.* iii, 1.

SAUCE

A crier of green sauce.

> RABELAIS, *Works.* Bk. II, ch. 31.

Hunger is the best sauce.

> ANON.

The mustard is too hot a little.

> *Taming of the Shrew.* iv, 3.

With all appliances and means to boot.

> *King Henry IV.* Pt. II, iii, 1.

But sundrie sauces are more dangerous.

> PLINY, *Natural History.* Bk. XI, ch. 53.

'T is the sour sauce to the sweet meat.

> DRYDEN, *To Etheredge.*

Change is the sauce that sharpens appetite.

> DEKKER AND FORD, *Sun's Darling.* ii, 1.

A most sharp sauce.—And is it not well served ?

> *Romeo and Juliet.* ii, 4.

Epicurean cooks sharpen with cloyless sauce his appetite.

> *Antony and Cleopatra.* ii, 1.

Instead of tears let them pour capon-sauce upon my hearse.

> BEAUMONT AND FLETCHER, *Woman Hater.* i, 3.

The sauce to meat is ceremony ; meeting were bare without it.

> *Macbeth.* iii, 4.

How many things by season season'd are, to their right praise and true perfection !

> *Merchant of Venice.* v, 1.

An exquisite and poignant sauce, for which I 'll say unto my cook, "There 's gold, go forth and be a knight."

> BEN JONSON, *The Alchemist.* ii.

SONGS

I thank you for your voices.

Coriolanus. ii, 3.

Such a choice collection of songs !

FOOTE, *The Cozeners.*

All that we ask is but a patient ear.

POPE, *Satires.* iii.

Sing,—though I shall never hear thee.

WOLFE. *Song.*

We did keep time, sir, in our catches.

Twelfth Night. ii, 3.

Filled the air with barbarous dissonance.

MILTON, *Comus.* 1. 550.

My lungs began to crow like chanticleer.

As You Like It. ii, 7.

Good savage gentlemen, your own kind spare.

DRYDEN, *Epi. to Secret Love.*

What harmony is this? My good friends, hark.

The Tempest. iii, 3.

Chromatic tortures soon shall drive them hence.

POPE, *The Dunciad.* iv.

In what key shall a man take you to go in the song ?

Much Ado About Nothing. i, 1.

For my voice, I have lost it with halloing and singing of anthems.

King Henry IV. Pt. II, i, 2.

Shall we rouse the night-owl in a catch that will draw three souls out of one weaver ?

Twelfth Night. ii, 3.

They do no more adhere and keep place together, than the Hundredth Psalm to the tune of Green Sleeves.

Merry Wives of Windsor. ii, 1.

SOUP

Taste of it first.
King Richard II. v, 5.

With open mouths swallowing.
King John. iv, 2.

Dip a spoonful out.
G. W. DOANE, *On Homeopathy.*

A genial savour of certain stews.
BYRON, *Don Juan.* Canto v, st. 47.

Spare your breath to cool your porridge.
CERVANTES, *Don Quixote.* Pt. II, ch. 5.

Expect spoon-meat ; or bespeak a long spoon.
Comedy of Errors. iv, 3, l. 61.

His mouth was oozing, and he worked his jaw.
HOOD, *The Turtles.*

Therefore it behooveth hir a ful long spoon.
CHAUCER, *Squire's Tale.* l. 15,378.

I will eat these broths with spoons of amber.
BEN JONSON, *The Alchemist.*

It is not strength, but art, obtains the prize.
POPE, *Iliad XXIII.* 383.

He must have a long spoon that must eat with the devil.
Comedy of Errors. iv, 3, l. 64.

To blow and swallow at the same moment is n't easy to
be done.
PLAUTUS, *Mostellaria.* iii, 2.

You must stay the cooling too, or you may chance to
burn your lips.
Troilus and Cressida. i, 1, l. 15.

Famish'd people must be slowly nurst,
And fed by spoonfuls, else they always burst.
BYRON, *Don Juan.* Canto ii, st. 158.

SPEAKERS

It was my hint to speak.

Othello.   i, 3.

Let 's talk, my friends.

POPE, *Satires.*

Let it serve for table-talk.

Merchant of Venice.   iii, 5.

Now turn to different sports.

POPE, *The Dunciad.*   ii.

Much may be said on both sides.

FIELDING, *Covent Garden Tragedy.*

Thence to the famous orators repair.

MILTON, *Paradise Regained.*   iv, 267.

The windy satisfaction of the tongue.

POPE, *Odyssey.*   iv.

With thee conversing I forget all time.

MILTON, *Paradise Lost.*   iv.

And when I ope my lips let no dog bark !

Merchant of Venice.   i, 1.

There 's a skirmish of wit between them.

Much Ado About Nothing.   i, 1.

I pray you jest, sir, as you sit at dinner.

Comedy of Errors.   i, 2.

All my skill shall beg but honest laughter.

RANDOLPH, *Aristippus.*

Then he will talk—good gods ! how he will talk.

LEE, *Alexander the Great.*

But hark ! The chamber where the good man meets his
fate.

YOUNG, *Night Thoughts.*   ii.

TOASTMASTER

Let us do or die.
> BURNS, *Bannockburn.*

Laugh and be fat.
> J. TAYLOR, *Title of a Tract.* 1615.

Masters, spread yourselves.
> *Midsummer Night's Dream.* i, 2.

It is my authority to command.
> *Winter's Tale.* i, 2.

The dignity and height of honour.
> *King Richard III.* iv, 4.

Now am I seated as my soul delights.
> *King Henry VI.* Pt. III, v, 7.

And skill in thee now grew authority.
> BEN JONSON, *Underwoods.*

Where inward dignity joins outward state.
> YOUNG, *Love of Fame.*

My heart is thirsty for that noble pledge.
> *Julius Cæsar.* iv, 3.

And bears his blushing honours thick upon him.
> *King Henry VIII.* iii, 2.

Where Macgregor sits, there is the head of the table.
> Quoted by EMERSON (MACDONALD) in *Am'n Scholar.*

Let me sit where I will, that is the upper end to thee.
> CERVANTES, *Don Quixote.* Pt. II, Bk. II, ch. 14.

We'll have a speech straight: come, give us a taste of your quality.
> *Hamlet.* ii, 2.

I am not only witty in myself, but the cause that wit is in other men.
> *King Henry IV.* Pt. II, i, 2.

TOBACCO

Divine Tobacco.

SPENSER, *Faerie Queene.* Bk. III, c, 5.

Divine in hookas, glorious in pipe.

BYRON, *The Island.*

To study how to drink and take tobacco.

RANDOLPH, *Muses' Looking-Glass.*

God bless you, does your pipe taste sweetly?

PFEFFEL, *Tobacco Pipe.*

The spirit of wine and tobacco walks in your brain.

DEKKER, *Gull's Hornbook.*

For thy sake, tobacco, I would do anything but die.

LAMB, *A Farewell to Tobacco.*

Ods me I marle what pleasure or felicity they have in
taking their roguish tobacco.

BEN JONSON, *Every Man in His Humour.* iii, 2.

The pipe with solemn interposing puff,
Makes half a sentence at a time enough.

COWPER, *Conversation.*

Sublime tobacco! which from east to west,
Cheers the tar's labour or the Turkman's rest.

BYRON, *The Island.* Canto ii.

Yes, social friend, I love thee well,
  In learned doctors' spite ;
Thy clouds all other clouds dispel
  And lap me in delight.

SPRAGUE, *To My Cigar.*

Pernicious weed, whose scent the fair annoys,
Unfriendly to society's chief joys,
Thy worst effect is banishing for hours
The sex whose presence civilises ours.

COWPER, *Conversation.*

VEGETABLES

Let the sky rain potatoes.
> *Merry Wives of Windsor.* v, 5.

Heap high the golden corn !
> WHITTIER, *Corn-Song.*

The mushrooms show his wit.
> POPE. *To——.*

How green you are and fresh !
> *King John.* iii, 4.

A most fresh and delicate creature.
> *Othello.* ii, 3.

The first-born infants of the Spring.
> *Love's Labour 's Lost.* i, 1.

Out of the bowels of the harmless earth.
> *King Henry IV.* Pt. I, i, 3.

Cowcumbers are cold to the third degree.
> SWIFT, *Polite Conversations.* ii.

Thou hast described a hot friend cooling.
> *Julius Cæsar.* iv, 2.

Herbs that have on them cold dew o' the night.
> *Cymbeline.* iv, 2.

Those roots that shall first spring and be most delicate.
> *King Henry V.* ii, 4.

Although his anatomical construction
Bears vegetables in a grumbling way.
> BYRON, *Don Juan.* Canto ii, st. 67.

Oh herbaceous treat !
'T would tempt the dying anchorite to eat.
> SYDNEY SMITH, *Recipe for Salad.*

O, mickle is the powerful grace that lies
In herbs, plants, stones, and their true qualities.
> *Romeo and Juliet.* ii, 3.

WATERS

And drink of Adam's ale.

> PRIOR, *Wandering Pilgrim.*

Water is the mother of the vine.

> MACKAY, *Dionysia.*

I deal with water and not with wine.

> BEN JONSON, *Every Man in His Humour.*

This business will never hold water.

> COLLEY CIBBER, *She Would.*

Some food we had and some fresh water.

> *The Tempest.* i, 2.

Can you eat roots, and drink cold water?

> *Timon of Athens.* v, 1.

I find the settled thirst still gnawing.

> PHILIPS, *Splendid Shilling.*

Bring sweet water from affection's spring.

> MRS. HEMANS, *Woman and Fame.*

'T is a little thing to give a cup of water.

> TALFOURD, *Sonnet iii.*

Men really know not what good water 's worth.

> BYRON, *Don Juan.* Canto ii, st. 84.

Nought wise a water-drinker's brain can spin.

> *The Flask of Cratinus.*

A cup of cold Adam from the next purling stream.

> TOM BROWN, *Works.* Vol. iv, Pt. II.

Though we eat little flesh and drink no wine, yet let 's
be merry.

> SHELLEY, *Letter to M. G.*

Here 's that which is too weak to be a sinner,—honest
water which ne'er left man i' the mire.

> *Timon of Athens.* i 2.

WELCOME

Welcome friend.
> CRASHAW, *Wishes to Supposed Mistress.*

Welcome ; fall to.
> *As You Like It.* ii, 7.

Most dearly welcome!
> *Winter's Tale.* v, 1.

Welcome, my friends all !
> *The Tempest.* v, i.

You are passing welcome.
> *Taming of the Shrew.* ii, 1.

You 're welcome, my fair guests.
> *King Henry VIII.* i, 4.

He 's safe for these three hours.
> *The Tempest.* iii, 1.

My Lord, will you walk ? dinner is ready.
> *Much Ado About Nothing.* ii, 3.

Sit down and feed and welcome to our table.
> *As You Like It.* ii, 7, 1. 106.

Bid your friends welcome, show a merry cheer.
> *Merchant of Venice.* iii, 2.

Once more I shower a welcome on ye, welcome all.
> *King Henry VIII.* i, 4.

Bear welcome in your eye, your hand, your tongue.
> *Macbeth.* i, 5.

Small cheer and great welcome make a merry feast.
> *Comedy of Errors.* iii, 1.

Welcome ever smiles, and farewell goes out sighing.
> *Troilus and Cressida.* iii, 3.

The appurtenance of welcome is fashion and ceremony.
> *Hamlet.* ii, 2.

WINE

The real Simon Pure.

> CENTLIVRE, *Bold Stroke for Wife.* v.

Good wine needs no bush.

> *As You Like It.* Epilogue.

Across the walnuts and the wine.

> TENNYSON, *Miller's Daughter.*

And much of mirth and moderate wine.

> COWLEY, *Liberty.*

He calls for wine : "a health" quoth he.

> *Taming of the Shrew.* iii, 2.

The choice and master spirits of this age.

> *Julius Cæsar.* iii, 1.

From wine what sudden friendship springs ?

> GAY, *Fables.* Pt. II, 6.

Flow, wine ! smile, woman ! and the universe is con-
soled !

> BÉRANGER.

Put this in any liquid thing you will, and drink it off.

> *Romeo and Juliet.* v, 1.

For it stirs the blood in an old man's heart, and makes
his pulses fly.

> WILLIS, *Saturday Afternoon.*

Come, come, good wine is a good familiar creature, if it
be well used ; exclaim no more against it.

> *Othello*, ii, 3, 1. 313.

Let those who drink not, but austerely dine,
Dry up in law : the Muses smell of wine.

> HORACE.

And wine can of their wits the wise beguile,
Make the sage frolic, and the serious smile.

> HORACE, *Odyssey.* Bk. XIV, 1. 520.

Popular Terms Explained

Call things by their right names. . . . Glass of brandy and water. That is the current, but not the appropriate name ; ask for a glass of liquid fire and distilled damnation.—ROBERT HALL.

Popular Terms Explained

ABSINTHE.—A highly aromatic liqueur, opaline-green in colour, and bitter to the taste. It is made by steeping such herbs as Artemisia Absinthium, A. Autellina, A. Spicata, in alcohol or strong spirit. It acts as a tonic, but excessive use creates a morbid condition.

APOTHECARY'S MEASURE :

60 minims (drops)	1 dram
8 drams (teasp.)	1 ounce
16 ounces	1 pint
2 pints	1 quart
4 quarts	1 gallon
31½ gallons	1 barrel
2 bbls. (63 gals.)	1 hogsh'd
2 hogsh'ds	1 pipe
2 pipes	1 tun

BARBECUE.—Originally, the meaning was to cure by smoking or drying on a barbecue ; to dress and roast whole as an ox or a hog, by splitting it to the backbone, and roasting it on a gridiron ; so that now the word signifies something in the nature of a crude sort of banquet or picnic in the woods at which such festivities are enjoyed, usually during campaigns of political nature.

BARREL.—A wine-barrel contains 31½ wine-gallons ; the London ale-barrel contains 32 beer gallons ; the London beer-barrel contains 36 beer gallons. The contents are equivalent to 126 quarts ; 252 pints ; 504 breakfast-cups or tumblers ; 1,008 gills or teacups ; 2,016 wineglasses ; 4,032 ounces ; 8,064 tablespoons ; 16,128 dessertspoons ; 32,256 drams or teaspoons ; 64,512 drops or minims. Two barrels make one hogshead ; 4 make one pipe ; 8 make one tun.

BEAKER.—An earthen wine-vessel of Eastern origin, but more commonly a glass of the sort used by chemists for making solutions, of thin glass, flat bottom and perpendicular sides, with a lip for pouring, and having a capacity varying from one to 30 fluid ounces.

BENEDICTINE.—A cordial or liqueur, resembling chartreuse. It is distilled at Fecamp in Normandy ; originally prepared by the Benedictine monks, but since the French Revolution it has been produced by a secular company. It is sweet to the taste, sugary and oily, and but small quantity is sipped at a time. It is furnished to the trade in America in squatty bottles, the cork secured by a strip of lead, a red seal upon a circular indenture in the glass, and bearing the intelligence upon several labels : "Imported from Fecamp, France. D. O. M. +Le Directeur. Veritable liqueur Benedictine."

BITTERS.—An infusion from roots of herbs or bark, having a harsh taste, as of wormwood, and used in concocting cocktails and a few other drinks.

BREAKFAST-CUP.—The contents are equivalent to 2 teacups or gills ; 4 wineglasses ; 8 ounces ; 16 tablespoons ; 32 dessertspoons ; 64 teaspoons or drams ; 3,840 minims or drops. There are 2 breakfast-cups in a pint ; 4 in a quart ; 16 in a gallon ; 504 in a barrel ; 1,008 in a hogshead.

BUMPER.—A glass filled to the brim, especially when drunk as a toast.

CANDELABRA.—This word is the plural of candelabrum, a kind of stand used by the Romans for holding candles in groups, and copied for modern use upon the table at which one dines ; usually having a central shaft from which branches extend, holding candles.

CARAFE.—A glass water-bottle, as a decanter, in which water is sometimes frozen before serving, thus keeping the water iced while being used, and increasing the amount of liquid by melting.

CASE.—A dozen bottles of wine, placed for shipment in long, low, willow wicker-basket, or a box with compartments sufficient to prevent breaking.

CASSEROLE.—A small dish, usually of porcelain, with handle, and holding from five to twenty ounces, used to prepare a stew. Also, the term applied to a food cup formed of rice, mashed potatoes, and the like, to contain highly flavoured food.

CHAFING-DISH.—A metal dish fitted above a lamp, and having a cover, for cooking fancy dishes, such as lobsters, welsh-rarebit, and the like.

CHARTREUSE.—A highly esteemed tonic cordial, obtained by the distillation of various aromatic plants, especially nettles, growing on the Alps. It derives its name from the celebrated monastery of the Grande Chartreuse in France, where it is made.

COCKTAIL.—An American drink, strong, stimulating, and is one of the best appetizers. It always employs crushed or scraped ice, usually to the extent of half a glassful ; the liquid is stirred with a spoon, and the melting ice forms part of the drink. They generally have as a basis brandy, gin, or whiskey, and vermouth is a common addition. In a dry cocktail there is little sweetening.

COMPOTE.—Fruit that has been stewed or preserved in syrup.

COMPOTIER.—A china, metal, or glass dish used upon the dining-table to hold preserved fruit, bon-bons, or other trifles of a dessert. One or several generally occupy places throughout the repast. It varies from a dish or platter in being usually raised upon a high base or stem.

CONFETTI.—Bon-bons; also pellets composed of lime in imitation of a bon-bon; which persons use in the streets and theatres of Italian cities at carnival time in sportful pelting one another. The plural of confetto.

CORDIAL.—A medicine or draught which increases the action of the heart and stimulates circulation; a sweet and aromatic liquor, originally made in foreign monastic establishments, whence they derive their name, such as Benedictine, Chartreuse, Certosa, and Curaçoa.

CRUET.—A vial or small glass bottle, especially one for holding vinegar, oil, etc.; also used in church service for holding the wine and the water for the Eucharist.

CURAÇAO.—A cordial made of sweetened spirit and flavoured with the peel of the bitter orange, named from the island of Curaçao, north of Venezuela. Also written Curaçoa.

DECANTER.—A vessel used for receiving decanted liquors; especially, a glass bottle, more or less ornamental, into which wine is poured, for use upon the table.

DEMIJOHN.—A large glass vessel or bottle with bulging body and small neck, usually cased in wickerwork but sometimes in a wooden box, with a notch in the top extending over the neck of the vessel, for convenience in pouring; called from a town in northern Persia, Damagan, once famous for its glass-works. The forced resemblance to John is in accordance with colloquial use of proper names as names for vessels, such as jack, jill, etc.

DESSERTSPOON.—The contents are equivalent to 2 teaspoons or drams; 120 minims or drops. There are 2 dessertspoons in a tablespoon; 4 in an ounce; 8 in a wineglass; 16 in a teacup or gill; 32 in a breakfast-cup or tumbler; 64 in a pint; 128 in a quart; 512 in a gallon; 16,128 in a barrel; 32,256 in a hogshead.

DOILY.—A small, ornamental napkin, often embroidered or fringed, frequently of delicate lace or open work, placed between finger-bowl and dessert-plate; named after Mr. Doily (or Doyley), who is described "as a very respectable warehouseman, whose family had resided in the great old house next to Hodsoll's, the banker's, from the time of Queen Anne." (*Notes and Queries.*)

DRAM.—The contents are equivalent to 60 drops or minims. There are 2 drams in a dessertspoon; 4 in a tablespoon; 8 in an ounce; 16 in a wineglass; 32 in a teacup or gill; 64 in a tumbler or breakfast-cup; 128 in a pint; 256 in a quart; 1,024 in a gallon; 32,256 in a barrel; 64,512 in a hogshead. Its equivalent weight is 59.9618 grams, 2 dwts., 8.96 grains. A dram is equal to a teaspoon.

DROP.—There are 60 drops in a teaspoon or dram; 120 in a dessertspoon; 240 in a tablespoon; 480 in an ounce; 960 in a wineglass; 1,920 in a teacup or gill; 3,840 in a breakfast-cup or tumbler; 7,680 in a pint; 15,360 in a quart; 61,440 in a gallon; 2,935,360 in a barrel; 3,870,720 in a hogshead. Its equivalent weight is .9493 grams. A drop is equal to a minim.

ENTRÉE.—A made dish served between courses.

FLAGON.—A vessel for holding liquids, especially for table use, and common in feudal times; having a spout, a handle, and generally a cover.

26

GALLON.—The contents are equivalent to 4 quarts ; 8 pints ; 16 breakfast-cups or tumblers ; 32 gills or teacups ; 64 wineglasses ; 128 ounces ; 256 tablespoons ; 512 dessert-spoons ; 1,024 drams or teaspoons ; 1,440 minims or drops. There are 63 gallons in a hogshead ; 31½ gallons in a barrel. It contains 231 cubic inches ; equivalent to 58,372.2 Troy grams ; or 10 lbs., 1 oz., 10 dwts., 8.88 grs., which may be expressed as 8.332698 lbs. avoirdupois.

GILL.—A measure for wine, being one-fourth of a pint in the United States and British systems. In the former country, the gill contains 7.2175 cubic inches. A gill is equivalent to a teacup, and it contains 1,920 minims or drops ; 32 teaspoons or drams ; 16 dessertspoons ; 8 table-spoons ; 4 ounces ; 2 wineglasses ; requiring 2 in a break-fast-cup ; 2 in a tumbler ; 4 in a pint ; 32 in a gallon ; 1,008 in a barrel ; 2,016 in a hogshead.

HAMPER.—A wicker-work basket or receptacle of con-siderable size, used as a packing-case to hold a number of bottles.

HOGSHEAD.—The contents are equivalent to 2 barrels ; 63 gallons ; 252 quarts ; 504 pints ; 1,008 breakfast-cups or tumblers ; 2,016 teacups or gills ; 4,032 wineglasses ; 8,004 ounces ; 16,128 tablespoons ; 32,256 dessertspoons ; 64,-512 teaspoons or drams ; 3,870,720 drops or minims. There are 2 hogsheads in a pipe and 4 hogsheads in a tun.

JIGGER.—The contents are equivalent to 2 ounces ; 4 tablespoons ; 8 dessertspoons ; 16 teaspoons or drams ; 960 minims or drops. There are 2 jiggers in a teacup or gill ; 4 in a breakfast-cup or tumbler ; 8 in a pint ; 16 in a quart ; 64 in a gallon ; 2,016 in a barrel ; 4,032 in a hogshead. It is equivalent to a wineglass in capacity.

LIQUEUR.—An alcoholic drink, usually sweet and of high flavour and perfume ; a cordial.

MEASURE OF LIQUIDS :

60 drops (minims)	1 teaspoon, or dram
2 teaspoons (drams)	1 dessertspoon
2 dessertspoons	1 tablespoon
2 tablespoons	1 ounce
2 ounces	1 wineglass
2 wineglasses	1 teacup, or gill
2 teacups (gills)	1 breakfast-cup, tumbler
2 breakfast-cups (tumb.)	1 pint
2 pints	1 quart
4 quarts	1 gallon
31½ gallons	1 barrel
2 bbls. (63 gals.)	1 hogshead
2 hogsheads	1 pipe
2 pipes	1 tun

MINIM.—There are 60 minims in a dram or teaspoon ; 120 in a dessertspoon ; 240 in a tablespoon ; 480 in an ounce ; 960 in a wineglass ; 1,920 in a teacup or gill ; 3,840 in a breakfast-cup or tumbler ; 7,680 in a pint ; 15,-360 in a quart ; 61,440 in a gallon ; 2,935,360 in a barrel ; 3,870,720 in a hogshead. Its equivalent weight is .9493 grams. A minim is equal to a drop.

MIXING-GLASS.—It usually holds 12 ounces, which is equal to 6 jiggers, or about 24 tablespoonfuls, and allows room for shaking of liquids.

OUNCE.—The contents are equivalent to 2 tablespoons ; 4 dessertspoons ; 8 teaspoons or drams ; 480 minims or drops. There are 2 ounces in a wineglass ; 4 in a tea-cup or gill ; 8 in a breakfast-cup or tumbler ; 16 in a pint ; 32 in a quart ; 128 in a gallon ; 4,032 in a barrel ; 8,064 in a hogshead. Its equivalent weight is .0625 of a pound ; 455.6944 grams, 18 dwts., 23.69 grains ; 1.041587 ounces avoirdupois.

PINT.—The contents are equivalent to 2 breakfast-cups or tumblers; 4 teacups or gills; 8 wineglasses; 16 ounces; 32 tablespoons; 64 dessertspoons; 128 teaspoons or drams; 7,680 minims or drops. There are 2 pints in a quart; 8 in a gallon; 252 in a barrel; 504 in a hogshead. A pint contains 28.875 cubic inches; 7291.1107 grs.; equivalent to 1 lb., 3 oz., 9.11 grs. Expressed in avoirdupois it equals 1.041587 lbs. Being nearly equivalent to a pound in weight, it is an old popular saying that a pint's a pound the world over.

PIPE.—A wine measure, the contents of which are equivalent to 2 hogsheads; 4 barrels; 126 gallons; 504 quarts; 1,008 pints. There are 2 pipes in a tun.

PONY.—A glass holding about a mouthful of spirits, as brandy, or a glass that will contain about a gill of beer.

PUNCH.—A drink made with wine or spirits, and either water or a substitute, as a decoction of tea, and flavoured with lemon juice and sugar, served cold.

PUNCHEON.—A wine measure equal to 2 tierces, or 84 gallons, or 336 quarts, or 672 pints.

QUART.—The contents are equivalent to 2 pints; 4 breakfast-cups or tumblers; 8 teacups or gills; 16 wineglasses; 32 ounces; 64 tablespoons; 128 dessertspoons; 256 teaspoons or drams; 15,360 minims or drops. There are 4 quarts in a gallon; 126 in a barrel; 252 in a hogshead. It contains 57.75 cubic inches. A quart of distilled water at 39.83 F. would weigh 14,593 Troy grains. It has an equivalent weight of 2.083175 lbs. avoirdupois.

SHERBET.—A cooling drink of the East, made of fruit juices, diluted with water and variously sweetened and flavoured; as a water-ice.

STEIN.—A drinking vessel of earthen-ware, generally used in Germany for serving beer, and often decorated in colours and with mottoes.

TABLESPOON.—The contents are equivalent to 2 dessert-spoons; 4 teaspoons or drams; 240 minims or drops. There are 2 tablespoons in an ounce; 4 in a wineglass; 8 in a teacupful or gill; 16 in a breakfast-cup or tumbler; 32 in a pint; 64 in a quart; 256 in a gallon; 8,064 in a barrel; 16,128 in a hogshead.

TEACUP.—The contents are equivalent to 2 wine-glasses; 4 ounces; 8 tablespoons; 16 dessertspoons; 32 teaspoons or drams; 1,920 minims or drops. There are 2 teacups in a breakfast-cup or tumbler; 4 in a pint; 8 in a quart; 32 in a gallon; 1,008 in a barrel; 2,016 in a hogshead. A teacup contains the same amount as a gill.

TEASPOON.—The contents are equivalent to 60 minims or drops. There are 2 teaspoons in a dessertspoon; 4 in a tablespoon; 8 in an ounce; 16 in a wineglass; 32 in a teacup or gill; 64 in a tumbler or breakfast-cup; 128 in a pint; 256 in a quart; 1,024 in a gallon; 32,256 in a barrel; 64,512 in a hogshead. Its equivalent weight is 59.9618 grams, 2 dwts., 8.96 grains. A teaspoon is equal to a dram.

TEETOTALER.—One who more or less formally pledges or binds himself to entire abstinence from intoxicating liquors, unless used medicinally.

TIERCE.—A wine measure containing 42 gallons, or 168 quarts, or 336 pints.

TOAST.—To drink a toast is to wish success or prosperity when a health is drunk; also, to designate as the person or subject to whom or to which other persons are requested to drink.

TOAST-MASTER.—One who presides at a festive occasion, a wedding breakfast, a banquet, and the like, calling upon those present to respond to toasts.

TOBY.—A small jug usually in the form of a stout old man with a three-cornered hat, the angles of which form spouts for pouring out the liquor contained therein; frequently used as a mug.

TODDY.—A sweetened, spirituous drink, as of whiskey and water, with sugar, sometimes warmed.

TOKAY.—A wine made at Tokay, or Tokaj, a small town, Zemplen county, in the north-east of Hungary; light in colour, as of bright amber or topaz; decidedly sweet.

TUMBLERFUL.—The contents are equivalent to 2 teacups or gills; 4 wineglasses; 8 ounces; 16 tablespoons; 32 dessertspoons; 64 teaspoons or drams; 3,840 minims or drops. There are 2 tumblers in a pint; 4 in a quart; 16 in a gallon; 504 in a barrel; 1,008 in a hogshead.

TUN.—A cask for wine whose contents are equivalent to 2 pipes; 4 hogsheads; 8 barrels; 252 gallons; 1,008 quarts; 2,016 pints.

VERMOUTH.—A sort of mild cordial consisting of white wine flavoured with wormwood and other ingredients, prepared in France and Italy, that from Turin being most esteemed.

WINEGLASS.—The contents are equivalent to 2 ounces; 4 tablespoons; 8 dessertspoons; 16 teaspoons or drams; 960 minims or drops. There are 2 wineglasses in a teacup or gill; 4 in a breakfast-cup or tumbler; 8 in a pint; 16 in a quart; 64 in a gallon; 2,016 in a barrel; 4,032 in a hogshead.

Proper Wines for Certain Courses

Claret is the liquor for boys ; port for men ; but he who aspires to be a hero must drink brandy.

SAMUEL JOHNSON, *Boswell's Life*.

Proper Wines for Certain Courses

Clams, raw	. .	Sherry or sauterne
Duck	. . .	Chambertin
Entrée	. . .	Sherry
Fillet of beef, mushrooms		Champagne
Fruits	. . .	Pousse-café, cordials
Ice-cream .	. .	Champagne
Lamb	. . .	Pommery Sec
Lobster cutlets, croquets		Claret
Lobster, Newburgh .		Chablis
Nuts	. . .	Liqueurs, coffee
Oysters, raw	. .	Sauterne, sherry
Partridge .	. .	Pommery and Greno Sec
Pig, roast	. .	Floriac
Relêves .	. .	Rauenthaler-Berg, Rhine wines
Salmon .	. .	Sauterne
Soup	. . .	Amontillado, sherry
Squab	. . .	Moet & Chandon champagne
Sweetbreads	. .	Chateau Latour
Terrapin .	. .	Pemartin, Chateau Latour
Trout	. . .	Rhine wines
Turkey .	. .	Champagne
Turkey (Thanksgiving)		Cider
Turtle .	. .	Claret
Venison .	. .	Oporto, Malmsey
Welsh Rarebit .	.	Ale, lager

Calendar of Vintages

I love everything that 's old : old friends, old times, old
manners, old books, old wine.

GOLDSMITH, *She Stoops to Conquer.* i, 6.

Calendar of Uintages

Year	Port	Champagne	Burgundy	Claret	Hock and Moselle
1842	ex	......	......	......	......
1847	su	......	......	......	......
1851	ex	......	......	......	......
1852	gd	......	......	......	......
1853	ex	......	......	......	......
1854	fi	......	......	......	......
1855	pr	......	......	......	......
1856	pr	......	......	......	......
1857	pr	......	......	......	......
1858	gd	......	......	......	......
1859	av	......	......	......	......
1860	gd	......	......	......	......
1861	fa	......	......	......	......
1862	gd	......	......	......	......
1863	ex	......	......	......	......
1864	pr	......	......	......	......
1865	fa	su	......	......	......
1866	pr	......	......	......	......
1867	gd	......	......	......	......
1868	ex	ex	.....	......	......
1869	pr	......	......	......	......
1870	ex	......	......	......	......
1871	pr	......	......	......	......
1872	fi	......	......	......	......
1873	fi	......	......	......	......
1874	pr	su	gd	gd	oo
1875	fi	oo	fa	su	oo
1876	pr	oo	av	pr	oo
1877	pr	oo	gd	ex	oo
1878	ex	ex	gd	fi	oo
1879	pr	oo	pr	pr	oo
1880	pr	su	fa	fa	gd

Year	Port	Champagne	Burgundy	Claret	Hock and Moselle
1881	gd	oo	gd	gd	pr
1882	pr	oo	pr	pr	pr
1883	pr	oo	gd	pr	gd
1884	gd	ex	pr	pr	gd
1885	su	gd	fi	pr	fa
1886	pr	oo	gd	pr	fi
1887	fi	fi	gd	gd	pr
1888	pr	oo	ex	fi	pr
1889	fa	ex	fi	gd	fi
1890	fi	oo	fi	gd	pr
1891	av	oo	gd	fa	pr
1892	gd	fi	fi	av	gd
1893	pr	su	ex	su	ex
1894	pr	oo	gd	pr	pr
1895	pr	fa	fi	fa	su
1896	pm	oo	av	fi	pr
1897	oo	oo	pr	pr	fa
1898	oo	oo	oo	oo	pr

This calendar is based on the universal opinion of connoisseurs, and shows in which years the vintages of certain wines were better than the average. In the years not mentioned the vintages were mediocre. If particularly bad, attention is called to the fact by the rating "poor."

N.B.—su, superb. ex, excellent. fi, fine. gd, good. fa, fair. pm, promising. av, average. pr, poor. oo, mediocre.

Popular Beverages

Serenely full, the epicure would say,
Fate cannot harm me, I have dined to-day.
    SYDNEY SMITH, *Recipe for Salad.*

Popular Beverages

COBBLER

The liquor decided upon should be poured over and allowed to run through cracked ice. Put in a suitable amount of sugar and shake. Drop on top any proper fruit. It should be served with straws.

COLLINS

Slice a lemon into the mixture in which is cracked ice, and cover with fine sugar ; then pour in a jigger of gin ; shake and strain into a glass containing soda.

EGG-NOG

Beat an egg with a teaspoonful of sugar ; pour into this a jigger of whiskey, or brandy if preferred, while stirring ; shake with milk, and add a few drops of lemon.

FIZZES

A Gin Fizz consists of juice from half of a lemon squeezed on cracked ice, a jigger of gin, and one teaspoonful of powdered sugar, shaken, then strained into a thin glass upon which is forced aerated water.

A Golden Fizz is made by adding the yolk of an egg before shaking a Gin Fizz.

A Silver Fizz substitutes the white of an egg for the yolk, before shaking.

A Royal Fizz includes both yolk and the white, shaken with the Gin Fizz.

27

FLIP

Shake well a jigger of sherry and an egg, with a small amount of sugar and cracked ice.

HOT SCOTCH

Use one jigger of either brandy, rum, or rye whiskey ; add the juice of a lemon ; sugar to suit the taste, and fill with hot water.

LEMON SHERBET

Allow one quart of water, with one pint of sugar therein, boil for twenty minutes ; pour in one teaspoon of granulated gelatine that has been soaked in two tablespoonfuls of cold water. When this is cold strain, and add one cup of lemon juice. Freeze in a freezer.

MINT JULEP

Secure some mint from the grocery and, after freshening it, cover it with fine sugar ; bruise it, and pour a small amount of boiling water over it. Let it stand a short time, whereupon strain into a glass prepared with cracked ice. Some leaves of the mint may be dropped in. Brandy should then be poured in and the whole allowed to stand unshaken.

ORANGE SHERBET

Boil one quart of water, with one pint of sugar therein, for twenty minutes ; add one teaspoonful of granulated gelatine that has been soaked in two tablespoonfuls of cold water. Strain when cold ; pour in one pint of orange juice and the juice of one lemon for strengthening. Freeze in a freezer.

POUSSE-CAFÉ

This drink displays liqueurs arranged by colours in a tall, slim glass. The pouring must be done slowly and with extreme care. To show five colours pour in first some grenadine, then, in the order named, maraschino, curaçao, green chartreuse, and last of all brandy.

PUNCH

Most punches use a combination of strong liquors and wines, such as gin and champagne. Lemon is indispensable, and they are usually well sweetened with sugar. The ingredients should be mixed thoroughly by stirring or shaking. Apollinaris or plain soda forms a major portion of some of them. They should be served cold, with ice floating in the bowl, and using straws if the liquid is not served in a bowl, when it requires small glass cups. Champagne punch contains one quart of champagne, juice of one lemon, two tablespoonfuls of sugar, quart of soda, slices of pineapple or strawberries, and ice. Another variety consists of one quart of dry champagne, a pint or quart of soda (to weaken), a jigger of brandy, a pony of orange curaçao, juice of two lemons, a pony of Medford rum, a tablespoonful of sugar, and a cup of strong tea.

RICKIES

A fresh lime should be slashed in many places and then crushed into a glass holding ice. Pour in a jigger of brandy, gin, or whiskey, and complete by introducing carbonic water.

SHANDYGAFF

A bottle of cold ginger ale and a jigger of whiskey shaken, or ice may be placed in the mixture before shaking. It is an excellent out-door drink on a warm day and has no ill effects.

SHERRY MOUSSE

Add to one quart of good cream one cupful of powdered sugar and four tablespoonfuls of sherry ; beat with
a mechanical whip-churn, removing the froth as it comes
up ; drain through a sieve, and place the froth in the
freezer.   When frozen allow it to stand quietly for three
hours.

SNOWBALL

Thoroughly shake a pony of brandy, an egg, some sugar, and cracked ice ; then add cold ginger ale.

STRAWBERRY SHERBET

Boil for ten minutes one quart of water with one pint
of sugar, add one teaspoonful of granulated gelatine that
has been soaked in three tablespoonfuls of cold water ;
strain through cheese-cloth ; when cold, pour in one pint
of strawberry-juice (the berries having been mashed and
the juice pressed through a coarse cloth) and add the
juice of two lemons ; then freeze.

Cocktails

Which draught to me were cordial.

SHAKESPEARE, *Winter's Tale.* i, 2.

Cocktails

APPLE BRANDY

Fill a mixing-glass half full of crushed ice, and apply two dashes of bitters ; then employ a jigger of apple brandy, and after straining, squeeze in a few drops of lemon, or allow a piece of the peel to float.

BRANDY

This cocktail contains a jigger of brandy, part of a lemon, and a dash or two of bitters.

BRANT

Having filled the mixing-glass with crushed ice, employ a third of a jigger of white crême de menthe and two-thirds of a jigger of brandy ; then give two dashes of bitters ; mix and strain, then add a lemon peel.

CHAMPAGNE

Saturate a lump of loaf-sugar with bitters, throw in a lemon peel, and fill up with cold champagne.

CIDER

Saturate a lump of loaf-sugar with bitters, add a lemon peel, and complete with cold cider.

CLAM

Use half a dozen of the smallest clams and their liquor ; some pepper and salt ; then squeeze in a lemon and put in a few drops of tobasco sauce.

DAISY

It consists of a gin fizz with a dash of raspberry syrup, or use the juice of any fruit.

GEORGE WASHINGTON

Use a pint of champagne and a quarter of grape-fruit, a dash of orange bitters, and a little sugar.

GREATER NEW YORK

This consists of half a jigger each of Plymouth and sloe gin, with a dash or two of orange bitters.

HARVARD

This consists of a jigger of vermouth, another of brandy, a few dashes of bitters, and seltzer.

IRISH

Employ half a jigger of Italian vermouth and an equal portion of whiskey, several dashes of phosphate, and the same of orange bitters.

JAMAICA RUM

Use a jigger of Jamaica rum and add a dash or two of orange bitters.

MANHATTAN

Use half a jigger of vermouth, as much of whiskey, a few dashes of bitters, and a lemon peel.

MARTINI

Take half a jigger of tom gin, as much of Italian vermouth, several dashes of orange bitters, and a lemon peel.

METROPOLE

Into a mixing-glass half filled with scraped ice, shake two dashes of gum-syrup, two of Peychaud bitters and one of orange bitters ; add as much of French vermouth; shake, strain, and add a clip of a lemon.

NEW YORK

Into half a mixing-glass of scraped ice put half a jigger of whiskey and as much of Italian vermouth ; give a couple of dashes of bitters, and add one-half teaspoonful of sherry, then straining, drop in a lemon cutting.

OYSTER

A good appetizer, especially for the weak stomach on land or sea, is made of several dashes of lemon juice, to which is added only a dash of tobasco sauce and a tea-spoonful of vinegar. Complete it by as much tomato catsup as of tobasco, the liquor of and half a dozen small oysters, with pepper and salt to suit.

RACQUET CLUB

This one was originated, like most of the others, in New York, and is not unlike the Vermouth cocktail ; in fact, one uses half a jigger of French vermouth, half a jigger of Plymouth gin, and three dashes of orange bitters.

RIDING CLUB

This is a bracing beverage, and owes its tonic force to a spoonful of acid phosphate (Horsford's), a couple of dashes of gum syrup, and a jigger of calisaya.

ROB ROY

A little stronger than the vermouth is this one, which is made warmer by half a jigger of Scotch whiskey and the same amount of the vermouth (Italian), with lemon peel and two dashes of bitters.

STAR

This sparkling drink is composed of three dashes of Peychaud or Boker's bitters, half a jigger of apple brandy, half a jigger of Italian vermouth, and a piece of lemon peel.

TURF

This is simply made by using a dash of Angostura bitters, a jigger of tom gin, and a piece of lemon peel.

VERMOUTH

This cocktail is liked by not a few and generally secures constant advocates. It is concocted from a dash or two of either Boker's or Peychaud bitters, one jigger of French or Italian vermouth, which is the base, and a piece of lemon peel.

WHISKEY

This is a stronger drink than the Vermouth cocktail and is made by taking one jigger of whiskey, two dashes of Peychaud bitters, and a piece of lemon peel.

YALE

This bracing cocktail consists of three dashes of orange bitters, one jigger of tom gin, a piece of lemon peel, and a squirt of seltzer.

Sample Menu

This folio of four pages, happy work
Which not e'en critics criticise.

WM. COWPER, The Task.   IV.

*Fell asleep after dinner, and did not hear
the conversation of the gods.*

HENRY D. THOREAU.

" This day is ours as many more shall be."
" King Henry VI."

Twenty-Fifth Annual Banquet

of the

Academy Alumni Association

" Read these instructive leaves."
POPE

Held at the Golden Eagle Inn

Wednesday
December 31
MDCCCXCVIII

" Now 's the day, and now 's the hour."
ROBERT BURNS

" The day
For whose returns, and many, all these pray ;
And so do I."
BEN JONSON

Welcome

" This night I hold an old accustom'd feast,
Whereto I have invited many a guest,
Such as I love : and you among the store.
One more, most welcome, makes my number more."

" Romeo and Juliet "

The Menu

"Now good digestion wait on appetite
And health on both."   "Macbeth"

MUSIC
"Music make their welcome !"
     "Timon of Athens"

OYSTERS
"Now if you're ready, Oysters, dear,
We can begin to feed !"
     LEWIS CARROLL

Oysters : Half-Shell

POTAGE
"To blow and swallow at the same moment is n't easy to be done."
     PLAUTUS

Terrapin Soup, à la Reine

POISSON
"From the rude sea's enraged and foamy mouth."
     "Twelfth Night"

Kennebec Salmon, Anchovy Sauce
Potatoes Hollandaise

RELEVÉS
"Things which in hungry mortals' eyes find favour."
     "Don Juan"

Filet de Bœuf, aux Champignons
Potato Croquettes

ENTRÉES
"Can one desire too much of a good thing ?"
     CERVANTES

Chicken Croquettes, Green Peas
Lobster Chops, à la Diable
Celery   Asparagus

PUNCH

"There is something in this more than natural."

"Hamlet"

Punch, à la Romaine

SERVICE FROID

"My appetite comes to me while eating."

MONTAIGNE

Galatine of Boned Turkey, à la Française

Patés de Foies Gras, aux Truffes

Chicken Salad, Mayonnaise

Langue de Bœuf, à la Gelée

Pickled Oysters   English Sandwiches

GAME

"Let's carve him as a dish fit for the gods, not hew him as a carcass."

"Julius Cæsar"

Roast Partridges, larded, Cream Sauce

"I thank you for my venison."

"Merry Wives"

Quartiers de Venaison, Gelée groseille

WINE

"Come, come, good wine is a good familiar creature, if it be well used; exclaim no more against it."   "Othello"

Champagne   Sherry

GROSS PIÈCES DE PATISSERIE

"What neat repast shall feast us, light and choice."

MILTON

Charlotte de Russe, à la Moderne

Nougat Pyramids, à la Militaire

Grand Méringue, à la Crême

ENTREMETS FROIDS

"Then farewell heat and welcome frost."

"Merchant of Venice"

Macédoine de Fruits Gelées

Neapolitan Cream

JELLY

"Every part about me quivers."

"Romeo **and** Juliet"

Wine Jelly   Rum Jelly

Éclairs au Chocolat   Glaces aux Fruits

GATEAUX ASSORTES

"Do you look for ales and cakes here, you rude rascals ?"

"King Henry VIII."

CAFÉ

"For lo ! the board with cups and spoons is crowned."

"Rape of the Lock"

CRACKERS   CHEESE

"Pray, does anybody here hate cheese ?   I would be glad of a bit."

SWIFT

CIGARS

"O thou weed who art so lovely fair and smell'st so sweet."

"Othello"

Finis

*"And damned be he that first cries
'Hold, enough !'"*   "Macbeth"

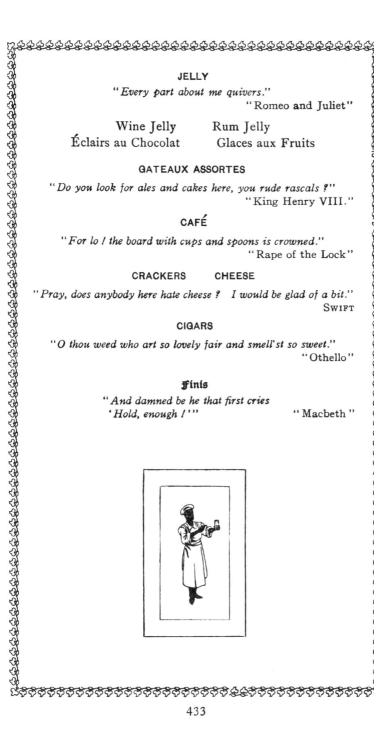

Toasts

"Thence to the famous orators repair."
"Paradise Regained"

___

Toastmaster, Marcus T. Aristotle

"My heart is thirsty for that noble pledge."
"Julius Cæsar"

___

MUSIC
"Eftsoones they heard a most melodious sound."
"Faerie Queene"

"The President of the United States," Hon. Theodore Depew

"Your high self, the gracious mark o' the land."
"Winter's Tale"

MUSIC
"Sentimentally I am disposed to harmony."
CHARLES LAMB

"The State" . . . . . . Gov. David B. Adams

"What constitutes a state ?
. . . .
Men who their duties know,
But know their rights, and knowing, dare maintain."
SIR WM. JONES

MUSIC
"What harmony is this ? My good friends, hark."
"The Tempest"

"Our Noble City of New York" . Mayor Thomas B. Thacher

" Breathes there the man with soul so dead,
Who never to himself hath said,
This is my own, my native land ! "
"Lay of Last Minstrel"

MUSIC
" *Give me some music; music, moody food*
Of us that trade in love."
"Antony and Cleopatra"

" **Our Dear Friends — The Guests** " . . . Amicus Brown

" *Right welcome, sir !*
Ere we depart we'll share a bounteous time."
"Timon of Athens"

" **The Ladies** " . . . . Adonis Abélard

" *The sex whose presence civilises ours.*"
WILLIAM COWPER

MUSIC
" *If music be the food of love, play on.*"
"Twelfth Night"

" **The Founders — Our Past** " . . . . Hon. Senex Gray

" *Time whereof the memory of man runneth not to the contrary.*"
SIR WM. BLACKSTONE

" **The Outlook — Our Future** " . . . . Juvenal Optimis

" *For the future is of more consequence than the past.*"
BISHOP WM. C. DOANE

MUSIC
" *It will discourse most eloquent music.*"
"Hamlet"

" **Our Monitors — The Clergy** " . . . Rev. Ira D. Jones

" *Wait till you hear me from the pulpit, there you cannot answer me.*"
BISHOP GILBERT HAVEN

" **Our Preservers — The Doctors** " . Herbert S. Huxley, M.D.

" *The doctors are our friends;*
Let's please them well."
BEAUMONT AND FLETCHER

"Our Reliance — The Lawyers" . Judge Wm. Day Choate

> *" Do as adversaries do in law,*
> *Strive mightily, but eat and drink as friends."*
> "Taming of the Shrew"

MUSIC
"But now, I 'm all for music."
BEN JONSON

"Our Comrades in Arms" . . Gen. Tecumseh Sheridan

> *" True courage, well directed, can neither be overpaid*
> *nor overpraised."*
> C. C. COLTON

"Progress in Science" . . . . . Nicola T. Edison

> *" Science is a first-rate piece of furniture for a man's upper*
> *chamber, if he has common-sense on the ground-floor."*
> O. W. HOLMES

"The Press" . . . . Walter S. Cooper

> *"Here shall the Press the People's right maintain,*
> *Unawed by influence, and unbribed by gain."*
> JOSEPH STORY

MUSIC
"Music her soft, assuasive voice applies."
POPE

"The Artists" . . . . . . T. Moran Le Farge

> *" Life without industry is guilt. Industry without art is*
> *brutality."*
> ELBERT HUBBARD

"The Stage" . . . . Edwin B. Jefferson

> *"For his acts so much applauded."*
> "King Henry VI."

"Our Athletic Friends" . . . . Hercules J. Sandow

> *"Allow me such exercises as may become a gentleman."*
> "As You Like It"

436

"The Absent" . . . . Fidelis Standish

"*Should auld acquaintance be forgot,
And never brought to mind ?*"
ROBERT BURNS

MUSIC
"*Here will we sit, and let the sounds of music
Creep in our ears.*"
"Merchant of Venice"

LIBATION
"*From wine what sudden friendship springs.*"
JOHN GAY

SONGS
"*Shall we rouse the night-owl in a catch that will draw
three souls out of one weaver ?*"
"Twelfth Night"

Volunteer Toasts

"*I would be loath to cast away my speech; for besides that it
is excellently well-penn'd, I have taken great pains to con it.*"
"Twelfth Night"

LIBATION
"*And carouse together like friends long lost.*"
"Antony and Cleopatra"

MUSIC
"*Music arose with its voluptuous swell,*

. . . .

And all went merry as a marriage bell."
LORD BYRON

Farewell
"*Fare thee well; the elements be kind to thee.*"
"Antony and Cleopatra"

Committees

"On hospitable thoughts intent."
"Paradise Lost"

Invitation

" I charge thee invite them all: let in the tide
Of knaves once more; my cook and I 'll provide."
"Timon of Athens"

ARTHUR T. ELIOT   CHARLES W. HADLEY
ADAM V. V. RAYMOND

Banquet

"I am by my place to know how to please the palates of the guests."
BEN JONSON

PIERRE DEJEUNER   HENRI DEVORER
FELIX FESTIN

Finance

"I have ta'en a due and way note upon 't."
" Macbeth "

P. BARING BROWN   ANDREW C. MORGAN
RUFUS ROTHSCHILD

Menu and Toasts

" The labour is not small."
TENNYSON

JOHN BACON   FRANCIS DRYDEN
ABRAHAM POPE

438

Music

" But now my task is smoothly done,
I can fly, or I can run."

MILTON.

RICHARD SULLIVAN   ARTHUR WAGNER

P. SOUSA MENDELSSOHN

Decorations

" The labour we delight in."
"Macbeth"

FRANCIS D. SARGENT   JOHN E. MILLAIS

MAX AUDUBON

Printing and Press

" News is your food, and you enough provide,
Both for yourselves and all the world beside."

DRYDEN

JAS. GORDON HOE   ROBERT BENNETT

BLACKCOURT REID

439

Officers

"For some must follow, and some command."
LONGFELLOW

President

"Most illustrious six or seven times honoured."
"Troilus and Cressida"

JOHN HALIFAX

Vice=Presidents

"They also serve who only stand and wait."
MILTON

HENRY ESMOND   DANIEL DERONDA

Secretary

"Nor set down aught in malice."
"Othello"

DAVID COPPERFIELD

Treasurer

"Goodness is the only investment that never fails."
THOREAU

ADAM BEDE

Index

I can tell thee where that saying was born.
Twelfth Night. i, 5, 1. 9.

Knowledge is of two kinds. We know a subject ourselves, or we know where we can find information upon it.

Boswell's Life of Johnson, 1775.

Classical quotation is the parole of literary men all over the world.

Boswell's Life of Johnson, 1781.

Index

Index of Authors

One writer, for instance, excels at a plan or a title-page, another works away the body of the book, and a third is a dab at an index.

GOLDSMITH, *The Bee.* No. 1, Oct. 6, 1759.

Index of Authors

A

Addison, Joseph
Æschylus *
Akenside, Mark
Alcott, Amos Bronson
Alcuin, Flaccus Albinus
Aldrich, Thomas Bailey
Alfieri, Vittorio
Alford, (Dean) Henry
Alger, William Rounseville
Allen, (Mrs.) Elizabeth Akers
Allston, Washington
Ames, Fisher
Ampère, Jean Jacques
Andersen, Hans Christian
Antiphanes *
Aquinas, Thomas
Arbiter, Petronius
Aristotle *
Armstrong, John
Arnold, (Sir) Edwin
Arnold, George
Aubert, Jean Louis

B

Bacon, Francis
Bailey, Philip James

* Complete name.

455

* Complete name.

* Complete name.

* Complete name.

* Complete name.

Lytton, (Earl) Edward Robert, [known as Owen Meredith]

M

Macaulay, (Lord) Thomas Babington
Macdonald, George
Mackay, Charles
Mackintosh, (Sir) James
Macklin, Charles
Maffei, Raffaelo [Raphael]
Malesherbes, Chrétien Guillaume de Lamoignon de
Malherbe, François de
Mallett, David
Mann, Horace
Marcy, William Learned
Marlowe, (Sir) Christopher
Marmion, Shackerly or Shakerly [also Shakerley]
Marmontel, Jean François
Marston, John
Martial, Marcus Valerius
Marvel, Ik [pseud. of Donald Grant Mitchell]
Marvell, Andrew
Massillon, Jean Baptiste
Massinger, Philip
Maturin, Charles Robert
McKinley, William
Mellin, Grenville
Mercier, Alfred
Méré*
Meredith, Owen [pseud. of Earl Edward Robert Lytton]
Méry, Joseph
Metastasio, Pietro Bonaventura
Michelet, Jules
Mickle, William Julius
Middleton, Thomas

*Complete name.

* Complete name.

Osgood, Frances Sargent
Ossoli, (Marchioness) Sarah Margaret [*née* Fuller]
Otway, Thomas
Overbury, (Sir) Thomas
Ovid, Publius Ovidius Naso

P

Page, H. A. [pseud. of Alexander Hay Japp]
Paine, Thomas
Paley, William
Palissot, Charles de Montenoy
Parker, Theodore
Parnell, Thomas
Pascal, Blaise
Patmore, Coventry
Pyne, J. Howard
Peele, George
Penn, William
Pepys, Samuel
Percy, (Bishop) Thomas
Perry, (Commodore) Oliver Hazard
Petit-Senn, J.
Petrarch, Francesco
Pfeffel, Gottlieb Konrad
Phædrus*
Phelps, Elizabeth Stuart
Philips, Ambrose
Philips, John
Phillips, Wendell
Piatt, Donn
Pignotti, Lorenzo
Pilpay*
Pinckney, Charles Cotesworth
Pinckney, Edward Cate
Pindar, Peter [pseud. of John Wolcott]

* Complete name.

* Complete name.

* Complete name.

* Complete name.

* Complete name.

* Complete name.